**Studies on the
South African
Media**

The Press
in South Africa

Edited by
Keyan Tomaselli
Ruth Tomaselli
& Johan Muller

James Currey. London
St Martins. New York
Anthrops. Bellville, Cape

First published in South Africa by
Richard Lyon and Company
Distributed by Anthropos, Bellville, Cape

Published in the USA and Canada by
St Martin's Press Inc
175 Fifth Avenue
New York 10010

and the rest of the world by
James Currey Ltd
54b Thornhill Square, Islington
London N1 1BE

First published in 1987

This edition 1989

ISBN 0-620-10575-5 (Anthropos)

ISBN 0-85255-310-2 (James Currey)

© 1987 Keyan Tomaselli, Ruth Tomaselli and Johan Muller

All rights reserved. No portion of this book may be reproduced without the express written consent of the publishers.

Other titles in this series:

Broadcasting in South Africa
The Alternative Press in South Africa

Printed by The Natal Witness Printing and Publishing Company (Pty) Ltd, Pietermaritzburg, Natal.

Contents

Preface 1
Ruth Tomaselli, Keyan Tomaselli and Johan Muller

1. A Conceptual Framework for Media Analysis 5
Ruth Tomaselli, Keyan Tomaselli and Johan Muller
Thinking about Ideology; Beyond the Dominant Ideology; Ideology and Social Classes; How Ideological Discourse Works; Culture and Adaptive Responses; Hegemony — The Negotiation of Consent; Voicing Class Aspirations; The Struggle for the Sign; Ideology, Culture and Hegemony — Towards a Resolution

2. The Construction of News in the South African Media 22
Keyan Tomaselli, Ruth Tomaselli and Johan Muller
Journalists and Ideological Discourse; Selection and Organisation of News; The Contradictions of 'Press Freedom'; Conclusion — Maintaining Hegemony

3. The Political Economy of the South African Press 39
Ruth Tomaselli and Keyan Tomaselli
Class Alliances in South Africa; Urban Permanence and Co-option; Strategies to Divide the Working Class; The 'Black' Press — Ideological Ambivalence; From Mission Press to Corporate Ownership; The Limits of Black Editorial Control; The English-Language Press — Limited Opposition to Apartheid; Rural Images — Disease, Drought and Disaster; Labour Reporting — Using the Gaps; State Intervention and Harassment; Extras — 'Black' News in 'White' Newspapers; The Press War — Aunty Argus' 'Orrible Appetite; "Sundays are no Longer SAAN Days"; Centralisation and Control; Diversification into broadcasting and information; The Demise of the *Rand Daily Mail* — A Lesson for the Marketplace?; Politics and the Afrikaans Press; The Legislation of Coercion and Consent; Restrictions of Readership and Revenue; Conclusion

4. Press Houses at War: A Brief History of Nasionale Pers and Perskor 118
Johan Muller
North Versus South — 1915-1981; In the Wake of the Rebellion — 1915-1934; The Ruptures of Fusion — 1934-1939; Towards the Capitalist Republic — 1939-1947; A Giant Awakes; In Search of the 'Real' National Party; The Fight for the Heartland — 1982-1983; The Demise of 'Rueful Candour'; Slowly Towards the (Far) North; Resumé — A Question of Class

5. Cacophony of Consent: The Press in the Struggle for Educational Reform   141
Johan Muller

The State, Afrikaner Nationalism and 'Crisis'; 'Crisis' of Capital Accumulation, 1960s-1970s; Shifting Patterns of Alliance and the Structure of Afrikaner Society; The Travails of 'Volkseenheid', 1948-1980; Forms of Consent to Reform in South Africa; Afrikaner Identity and Ideological Discourse; Making the Volkskongres Mean; 'Us' and 'Them' — Media Management of Identity; The Cacophony of Consent

6. Ideology on the Beat: Labour and the English-Language Press   174
Simon Burton

Unpacking the Issues; Contemporary Labour History; The Discourse of Labour Reporting; Exploring the Reporter; Who Makes the News?; The Press, the State and the Reporter in South Africa; Conclusion

7. On the Social Construction of Urban Problems: The Press and Black Housing, 1925-1979   200
Jeffery McCarthy and Michelle Friedman

Housing and Ideology in Capitalist Societies; The South African Case; Black Housing and the Media in South Africa; *The Star* and South Africa's 'Urban Issues', 1927-1979; The *Financial Mail*, the *Weekend World* and the Black Housing Issue, 1970-1979; Conclusion and Postscript

Selected Bibliography   244
Ideology, Culture and Hegemony; Media Theory; The South African Political Economy; Media Studies in South Africa

Preface

Addressing the Nation is the series title for three books on the South African media. The series brings together a variety of related disciplines and a fairly wide spectrum of authors. We have tried to integrate the various contributions through a measure of team editing and the circulation of chapters during the drafting stages. Most chapters combine a general theoretical approach with historical and case study material.

Studying the media can be a peculiarly difficult task in a country like South Africa. Unlike scholars in America or Britain, who seem to gain at least a modicum of access to the institutions they are studying, would-be students of South African conditions often find that lines of communication and previously accessible documentation are liable to be cut off at any time. In such a society it is sometimes necessary to protect one's sources, so a number of the chapters deliberately do not identify them. Occasionally, where data itself would have revealed the source, it has been excluded. While this exclusion has obvious research implications, it cannot be avoided. The possible effects on the individual whose identity is disclosed cannot be underestimated in a country whose coercive mechanisms are becoming increasingly sophisticated and whose media institutions are reluctant to employ controversial figures. Besides, as Herbert Gans points out, anonymity is an established fieldwork tradition. We are more concerned with the practices within which individuals operate than with their personalities.

While emphasising the importance of theory, this series also acknowledges the need for empirical work. The ideal is, of course, a seamless integration of theory and solid empirical detail. Some of the chapters are brief, even journalistic, while others present concrete empirical data. So little critical material exists on the South African media that we considered it important to include a range of material which would stimulate much needed debate.

The critical study of the media is relatively new in South Africa; most English-medium universities only acknowledged this discipline after the introduction of television in 1975, while Afrikaans universities have dealt with it as part of their curricula in communication for a longer period. 'Black' universities don't deal with the mass media at all.

Our authors come from a wide range of disciplines — development studies, education, geography, sociology, psychology, dramatic art, history and of course, journalism and media studies.

This series draws on research being done by people working on the relationship between the media and these disciplines. Topics of importance that remain to be covered include the foreign media, sport, parliamentary reporting, crime, religion, finance and so on. Each of these has crucial implications for the maintenance and preservation of pre-liberation South African society.

The present volume concentrates on the mainstream commercial press. Chapter 1 provides a general theoretical overview of the conceptual tools applied in our analysis of the South African media throughout the series, *Addressing the Nation*. Chapter 2 traces historically the political and economic context of the South African media and should be seen as providing the framework for the chapters that follow in the three books. The majority of the remaining chapters are case studies of specific historical or contemporary elements of the South African media.

Finally, we should like to thank the following people for their contributions and criticism: publishers' referees, Mark Orkin and Ken Jubber; and others who critiqued one or more chapters: Eve Bertelsen, Paul Stewart, Kevin Cox, Gordon Pirie, Stephen Friedman, John Allen, Marion Whitehead, Denise Armour, Pam Christie, Peter Randall, Glen Collyer, Kevin Harris, Kevin Kevanny and our many anonymous sources without whose commitment to a better media industry certain chapters could not have been written. In terms of institutional help, we are indebted to the SABC for granting us access to their staff and allowing us to observe their operations during 1985 and 1986.

March 1986

K.G.T.
R.T.
J.M.

Chapter 1
A Conceptual Framework for Media Analysis

Ruth Tomaselli, Keyan Tomaselli and Johan Muller

Although the subject matter in this book covers a wide spectrum, it does not pretend to be exhaustive. Further studies need to be undertaken on the media's treatment of sport, finance, business, property, 'women' and religion, for instance. Broadcasting is even more neglected than the press in this regard and numerous avenues of research demand attention. Nevertheless, it has become clear that the reminiscences of retired editors and journalists are no longer sufficient sources of information.

Only after the introduction of broadcast television in 1976 did media studies begin to emerge as a serious, critical area of concern in South African universities. The initiation of the second and third TV channels in 1982 coincided with legislative encroachment into the operations of the press and generated intense argument by academics to the right and the left of the political spectrum. Journalists themselves — both print and electronic — have come under increasing attack as the academic debate gains momentum, and are challenged either to defend or to reassess the assumptions that have hitherto governed their professional practice. The conflict reached its most intense level in 1985 when a number of journalists resigned or were fired from a variety of newspapers because of their criticism of the way those papers were or were not reporting on township unrest, labour issues and worker stayaways.

Many early commentaries identified their academic principles with the dominant interests of the time[1], and many of the more recent studies evidence little grasp of the complexities of historical, social, economic or political relationships that have influenced the structure of the South African media. *Addressing the Nation* seeks to develop new approaches by drawing on theoretical work from sources that have hitherto been underutilised in South African analyses of the media. Our first aim is therefore to take stock of the burgeoning theories and conceptual tools that have been developed for social analysis. With this in mind we have taken account of four major strands in contemporary social theory:

i) Theories of ideology, associated with French structuralist and post-structuralist Marxism as exemplified by Louis Althusser, Etienne Balibar, Nicos Poulantzas and Ernesto Laclau;

ii) Allied tendencies in socialist-humanist cultural studies, initiated by Raymond Williams, Edward Thompson and others;

iii) The work of Antonio Gramsci, recently rediscovered by English-language academics, an oeuvre which provides insights into issues of culture and hegemony.

iv) New theories of language and signification.

Each of the four strands referred to above offers ways of thinking about the relationship of the media to the broader socio-political and economic structures of society. In our discussion of theoretical approaches we shall highlight some of the complexities of embarking on a theoretically informed analysis of the media and try to clarify and synthesize the three related concepts of ideology, culture and hegemony, which are often confused with one another. By working through the various schools of thought and taking note of their conceptual differences, we shall offer operational definitions which are the starting point for the chapters that follow. While not imposing definitions of any of these terms on the authors, care has been taken to ensure that their application is specific and defined. Obviously, different contributors will emphasize different approaches. The task of this chapter will be to provide a contextual framework for these various approaches.

Thinking about Ideology

The point of departure for Althusser's approach to ideology is how capitalist societies reproduce themselves. He places special emphasis on the necessary economic and political conditions. At all three levels within society (the ideological, political and economic), the State intervenes to ensure the optimum conditions for the reproduction of capitalist relations. This is accomplished by means of two sets of institutions. The first he calls Repressive State Apparatuses; for instance, the police, the military and the civil service. The second — the Ideological State Apparatuses — include the church, law, the institution of the family, education and the media.

For Althusser, it was immaterial whether the Ideological State Apparatuses belonged to the State or to private enterprise, since: "What matters is how they function. 'Private' institutions can perfectly well 'function' as ideological 'state apparatuses' "[2]. In so far as they also contribute to social reproduction these apparatuses reproduce submission to the rules of the established order, give currency to the world view of the ruling groups and make that perspective the 'common sense' of all the classes within the social formation.

Althusser's notion of world view, or dominant ideology, supercedes the conventional idea of ideology which sees it as 'false consciousness'. For Althusser, ideology is 'lived' and so, as far as the individual experiences it, it is real. This reality which each person lives is an image of society which gives him or her an identity and a place in that society.

Althusser goes on to say that ideology has a 'material existence'[3]. It exists as a set of actual practices in a State apparatus. It follows that each individual, through his or her 'lived relations' takes part in the practices and rituals that constitute an ideological apparatus — be it a religious organisation, a political party, a television station or a newspaper.

The identity that ideology confers upon an individual identifies him or her as a subject of a particular practice or set of practices[4]. The term 'subject' in Althusser's theory has a double sense: it points to the self-initiating aspect of activity, and it also indicates that the person is subjected to that activity. For instance, going to church identifies the subject and his or her relation to the 'higher power' of God. This participation in particular apparatuses of society involves an ideological recognition of a seemingly self-evident situation. That is, for the believer, going to church presumes beyond doubt the existence of the 'higher power'. And so paradoxically, when subjects believe themselves to be acting as 'free agents' and to be motivated only by what they see as obvious 'common sense', it is precisely at that time that they are most powerfully motivated by ideology. For the subject, going to church initiates a 'personal' relationship with God which conceals the prior internalisation of say, the Christian ideology. 'Common sense', therefore means "something that is self-evident" precisely because it stems from one's most powerfully internalised ideological precepts.

Beyond the Dominant Ideology

Althusser's theory of ideology has been indispensable in helping social scientists move beyond an idealist or mental notion of ideology. Nonetheless we need to recognise some weaknesses in his account[5]. His insistence on an abstract, ahistorical definition of ideology makes it difficult to apply his categories to concrete situations. It also stresses the rationalist side of historical materialism at the expense of experience.

In his discussion of the relationship between the economic base of society and its political/ideological superstructure, Althusser maintains that the upper floors (politics, ideology) could not "stay up" alone if they did not rest supportively on their base (economic structure)[6]. It is the upper floors — the edifice — with which he is primarily concerned, to the relative neglect of the base. Although he stresses that the economic is determinant in the last instance, Althusser runs the risk of sliding back into the idealism that he is trying to avoid.

But by far the major difficulties of applying Althusser's theory lie with his level of abstraction — which, while clarifying some theoretical issues, could have the effect of obscuring the connections between ideology and economic conditions at a specific historical moment. At best the theory allows the identification of parallels between the base and superstructure. While crises in the one can be associated with crises in the other, the causal connections are not easily pinpointed because of the bifurcation produced by the structural model.

Another limitation which Althusser himself has noted[7], concerns his tendency towards functionalism. For Althusser, ideology seems to subsume contradictions by all too neatly preparing individuals to take up their places in the social and economic hierarchy. This allocative process is presented as happening with such inevitability that it appears immutable[8]. Althusser's notion of ideology therefore emphasizes the unchanging, reproduced aspect of culture. But what about cultural change?

Ideology and Social Classes

Marxist theory defines social classes in terms of the relations of production, that is, in terms of social relations of control and subordination. On the economic level they are defined in terms of the ownership (or lack of it) of the means of production. In ideological terms they are defined in the way in which classes as a whole fulfill the roles assigned to them in capitalist society. The relationship between the owners and non-owners is by definition a conflictual one.

In order to account for social change, a theory must allow for the existence of ideologies other than the dominant one. The ensemble of 'ideological tendencies'[9] in the working class arising from its encounter with its working conditions includes an orientation to manual labour, and a concomitant stress laid on physical prowess, toughness, endurance and dexterity. The organisation of the work process under capitalism can also foster an awareness of collective power and the possibilities of industrial action.

Contrary to the impression of inevitability given by Althusser, then, the very arrangements of capitalist society can give rise to understandings which are not useful components of the dominant ideology.

For the ruling class, or the bourgeoisie, the dominant ideology serves to reassure its members that their place within the structure of society has been 'appointed by nature', or that it is the 'will of God', and that they have a 'moral duty' in their 'trusteeship' of the workers. For this class, the emphasis is on 'juridicial equality', for unequal rewards for unequal success, on the virtues of mental labour and on the belief that all objects and men have their price[10]. For them it is obvious that their task is to 'persuade' the working class to accept their conditions of exploitation as if that were the natural order of things.

Between the bourgeoisie and the workers there is an intermediate class, or set of classes, usually referred to as the petty bourgeoisie, who are neither owners like the bourgeoisie nor do they produce wealth like the workers. We are speaking here of the vast array of shopkeepers, white collar workers and the like. Members of this class see themselves as being outside the class structure, in an essentially neutral position. A dominant element of their ideology is that they should do their duty both towards their employer and their country. Their primarily classless conception of themselves reconciles them to the task of supervising the workers on behalf of the bourgeoisie and keeping the necessary administrative and cultural functions running smoothly. Most journalists fall into this category and largely unwittingly contribute to keeping the wheels of the social arrangement running, not only in what and how they write. During times when black newsvendors and deliverymen have been on strike, for example, journalists have been co-opted into selling newspapers on street corners.

Class ideologies exist in self-contained purity only as analytical constructs. Different ideologies, however defined, not only co-exist, compete and clash, but also overlap, affect and contaminate one another[11]. To talk of class ideologies as being immediately identifiable in practice is misleading, since only elements, tendencies and 'gobbets of common sense' are apparent to the observer. Since ideologies only exist in the experiences of individuals and not 'in themselves' it is more useful to consider ways in which ideologies are expressed by real people. We will use the term *ideological discourse* to denote the personal expression of the experience of people to any given situation.

How Ideological Discourse Works

The construction of particular ideological discourses is the outcome of struggles at particular historical moments. Most have a class base although this is often not immediately apparent. The maintenance of these discourses depends upon processes of affirmation and sanction. For example, discursive practices like the broadcast of the National Anthem as the closing item to each evening's television programming or the clenched fist salute of black power affirm a particular vision of a social and ideological order. Discursive sanctions on the other hand work to exclude people from the 'in' group who challenge an ideological order; for example, radical students are often described as 'dirty', 'immoral', 'ungrateful', 'unrealistic', 'arrogant', leeches on the social body[12]. This process of discursive exclusion is important to keep the purity of the group ideologically intact, and is always also an affirmation of the group and the order it promotes.

There are also three important procedures through which discourse is controlled: restriction, shielding and appropriation. The restriction of discourse refers to socially institutionalised restrictions on who may speak, how much may be said, what may be talked about, and on what occasion. These restrictions are not only seen in censorship, coercion or repression (for example, banning), but also operate through the often subtle rights and protocols governing social relationships. Journalists, for example, are usually not in a position to question their editor's definition of newsworthiness, however much they might disagree with it.

The shielding of discourse protects it from the intrusion and contamination of other potentially disruptive points of view. The main way of doing this is to 'authorize' certain dominantly positioned individuals to define the situation, Such 'primary definers' are overwhelmingly used by the media to authorize their own account of an event[13]. Cabinet ministers, for example, are always a very handy source of primary definition for the television producer. Related to this is the tactic of repetition of definitions in such a way that they become accepted as the way things are. The theme of 'total strategy' , for example, runs like a thread through ministerial speeches, civil defence exercises, television documentaries and series, radio soap operas and the sale of bonus bonds during the time they were being used to underwrite the South African Defence Force.

The appropriation of discourse compartmentalises and fragments the permissible content of discourses to certain contexts. Each discourse has its own appropriate place and time: politics, for instance, should be kept out of sport and education, as primary definers constantly reiterate. This is not to say that contradictory viewpoints do not find their way into the mainstream media, but in the total context their impact is minimised by the overwhelming solidity of accepted common sense policed by the procedures and processes of discourse.

Culture and Adaptive Responses

The second strand of social theory, 'cultural studies', has extended the traditional anthropological understanding of the term 'culture' to include an historical dimension, a dimension which seeks to account for domination as well as resistance in capitalist societies. No longer is 'culture' confined to the general accomplishments of a society; it is seen in this view as an expression of a "constitutive social process, creating specific and different ways of life"[14] within that society.

Two seminal writers in this tradition are Raymond Williams and Edward Thompson. Both consistently argue against the base/superstructure distinction and, like Althusser, offer alternative formulations for conceiving their interdependence.

Williams denies any systematic separation between culture and other social processes. He insists on the importance of relationships rather than divisions between social domains. He proposes the mediatory notion of 'experience' through which all social processes, whether economic or political/ideological, are lived[15]. Williams is concerned with the relationship between the control of culture's content and form and the economic institutions in which they are embedded. His idea of 'cultural materialism'[16] involves an analysis of literature and the media, with special emphasis on their history and the actual means and conditions of their production.

To Williams' central category of experience, E P Thompson adds the important one of 'values', a category which had been entirely neglected by both the structuralists and by Marxist historians [17]. Values are situated within classes or identifiable groups of people. By 'values' Thompson implies goal-seeking and intention, activities which vary according to class. In any social system, there are many competing sets of values, of which only one set is dominant. The concept of values serves to remind us that ideology and culture are the products of active human endeavour and not just passive reproductions of the State or its apparatuses. The major concern here is with the quality of human relationships rather than with the structuring effect of the economic/social relations of production. Thompson rejects all notions of class that refer to determining structures.

By ignoring the determinations of class, Thompson's writings, and those of socialist-humanist historians in his tradition, are best able to take account of 'class consciousness' and 'class organisation' in periods of social crisis or turbulence. On the other hand, in periods of political stability, when class conflict is relatively dormant, the dynamic of history is not adequately accounted for by descriptions of active experience alone. This is borne out in Chapter 2 of Volume 2 of *Addressing the Nation* which looks at the experiences of a wide range of producers and technicians employed by the South African Broadcasting Corporation's (SABC) radio and television services. As a result of their differing ideological positions, informants often gave conflicting accounts of the same event. The significance of the conflicts could not be ascertained from these experiential accounts alone.

Now if these theoretical strands are to be of use to media analysts, we need to clarify the ways in which the notions of culture and ideology are applied. The literature on the subject is extremely complex and often confusing[18]. Whereas the historians use the concept of culture in concrete historical studies, referring to ideology only in passing, the structuralists tend to use the notion of ideology in a rather abstract and theoretical way, and do not refer to the notion of culture at all.

Culture differs from ideology in that it implies an active effort to resolve collectively experienced problems arising from contradictions in the social structure, ways in which people act out their 'uniformities of behaviour'[19] and socially determined identities, but in their own unique and often modifying way.

A clear example of a cultural response to cultural domination was the organisation and formation of the Broederbond, a group initially outside the dominant alliance[20]. In Volume 2 of *Addressing the Nation* Graham Hayman and Ruth Tomaselli analyse the way in which the Broederbond used the SABC as a site of cultural struggle after 1938, culminating in the Afrikaner dominance of the Corporation in the 1960s. In other words, the ideology that informed the struggle was that of Afrikaner nationalism; the cultural response was the mobilisation of the Broederbond as a collective, determined attempt to adapt and ultimately mould the organs of public opinion to reflect the Afrikaner 'way of life'. In Chapter 4 of this volume Johan Muller traces the way in which contemporary Afrikaner cultural organisations — the Dutch Reformed Church, the Broederbond and the Transvaalse Onderwysersvereeniging (Transvaal Teachers Association) — have responded to internal questions of identity arising from crisis in South African society.

Hegemony: The Negotiation of Consent

Cultural forms emanating from subordinate groups are, potentially at least, antagonistic to the dominant order. The distinction between potential and actual antagonism is illuminated by Gramsci's concept of 'hegemony'.

The other key terms in his analysis of history and culture are 'common sense' and 'ideology'. To start with these last two: 'common sense' refers to "the uncritical and largely unconscious way of perceiving and understanding the world that has become 'common' in any given epoch"[21].

'Ideology' can be thought of as a coherent set of ideas which have a limited ability to transform the ways in which men live out their 'common sense'. Gramsci distinguishes between historically *organic* ideologies, and ideologies that are arbitrary, rationalistic or *willed*. The first of these has the ability to "organise human masses and create the terrain on which men move, acquire consciousness of their position, struggle, etc", while the second "only creates individual 'movements', polemics and so on"[22]. Apartheid, for example, can be thought of as being an organic ideology which has been constructed from elements of the beliefs of religious 'chosenness' and racial exclusivity. In other words, apartheid is the means by which the ruling class, or more precisely, an alliance of fractions of the ruling classes, is able not only to coerce subordinate classes into conforming to its interests, but to exert 'total authority' over the classes. This does not mean that the subordinated groups believe in apartheid, but it does mean that apartheid prevails 'for now', what Gramsci calls passive hegemony.

The composition of 'hegemony' is determined by the interests of the various class fractions represented in the ruling alliance or 'hegemonic bloc'. The power it exerts over subordinate classes cannot rest solely on force and coercion — it needs to be attained "... without force predominating over consent"[23]. The granting of legitimacy to the dominant classes must appear ideally not only spontaneous but also natural and inevitable. The complex notion of hegemony can therefore be understood as the 'unstable equilibrium' that a ruling class achieves at any particular moment. It is the mixture of force and compromise to conflicting demands that is necessary to keep the existing order intact. Winning some form of consent is a crucial element of any hegemonic order. Every such order is underpinned by a hegemonic principle.

In South Africa the hegemonic principle is, or has been, 'racial capitalism'[24] — in other words, capitalist relations overlaid by economic and political apartheid. As an abstraction, the hegemonic principle does not exist 'out there' any more than, say, the principle of gravity does. It is always embodied in an ideological discourse, which is necessarily a discourse *for* a specific set of interests. In most liberal capitalist democracies, the State ensures continued accumulation and legitimises this in the name of the 'general interest'. Universal franchise in these countries lends a modicum of credence to the belief in a 'general interest'. In South Africa there is no universal franchise, and so the most important means of general consent-building is missing from the South African hegemonic armoury. Chapter 4 examines the way in which various discourses have attempted to deal with this fact, and shows how shifting patterns of class alliance created a rift in the Afrikaner educational domain, resulting in a 'Volkskongres' which attempted to win consent for reform in education in the face of changing national priorities. Also reflecting the importance of education in obtaining 'consent' from the subordinate classes is the way the Radio Bantu School Service aimed to prepare individuals to take up their places in the productive process (see Volume 2).

Voicing Class Aspirations

Each class develops "strata of intellectuals ... which give it homogeneity and awareness of its own function, not only in the economic, but also in the social and political fields"[25]. The function of these intellectuals is to direct the ideas and aspirations of the class to which they belong or which they serve. The capitalist entrepreneur, for example, fosters intellectual 'deputies' whose function it is to formulate and express the needs of the capitalist class and to translate these into more universalised symbolic and political imperatives. In this way, the class manages not only to rule, but to make its rule seem natural and inevitable. This interest-translation role is described in Chapter 4, which shows how journalists of all persuasions, reproduce, amplify and transform the terms of common sense to create the cultural conditions for a new consent to the re-arranged hegemonic alliance.

The working class similarly develops 'organic intellectuals' from within or parallel to its own ranks who, through the organisation of work and the spelling out of political organisation, are able to direct the working class towards a more active formulation of counter-ideological discourses. This was the strategy adopted by black journalists after 1976, described in Chapter 3. Since then, the worker movement has come to speak not only for itself, but through the new COSATU super-union, for subordinated black communities as a whole.

The Struggle for the Sign

The final strand we want to pull out concerns the ubiquity of meaning in society.

All aspects of society and culture *mean* something, they possess a semiotic value. This indicates simply that we do not encounter the world directly, but always through a *representation* of the world. These representations, or signs, are governed by rules of organisation that are called *codes*. Indeed, communication could not exist without the presence of a common code. Cultural and ideological discourses are therefore sets of coded meaning, and one part of understanding them would involve some attempt to 'crack the code'. This emphasis on sign, representation and meaning has a number of very important implications for the study of culture and ideology.

In the first place, codes are always historically determined. No meaning is ever natural, necessary or neutral. The apparently spontaneous forms of common sense, culture and discourse depend for their seeming naturalness upon discursive authorizations and repetitions that the media are more often than not constructed to foster. Codes operate subconsciously. The first step in 'cracking the code', therefore, involves penetrating the naturalness of common sense and questioning the historical form of the code.

In the second place, representations are always ideological: "The domain of ideology coincides with the domain of signs"[26]. This means both that meaning is always saturated with the ideological imperatives of a society, and conversely that ideology itself has always to do with meaning. This last point is the most important. It implies that ideological struggle is also a struggle for meaning:

"The struggle between different discourses, different definitions and meanings within ideology is therefore always ... a struggle for possession of the sign"[27]. This is because the same language is used by all the competing classes in a given society. Different accents intersect in each meaning. Which one prevails depends on both the State and the stage of struggle. How one accent prevails and others are submerged is one account of the class struggle waged in ideology.

Finally, dominant meanings and codes are never invulnerable. They can be violated and overthrown, although this is never a simple process. Violations of meaning have the power to provoke and disturb, especially when these meanings are rooted in formations central to the prevailing hegemony. Social struggle is, therefore, always a simultaneous struggle for power and for the sign. They are two sides of the same coin.

Ideology, Culture and Hegemony: Towards a Resolution

A fundamental problem of structuralist theories of ideology is that they take insufficient account of change and resistance. The role they assign to ideology is that of fostering the conditions of reproduction. However, while abstractions of ideology on the theoretical level are invaluable, it is also necessary to be able to apply these analyses empirically. All the writers mentioned above make the point in various ways that despite the commanding position of the 'ruling ideas' in any social formation, a diversity of cultural elements outside the mainstream of the dominant ideology does exist. In order to be useful, any theory of ideology must make allowances for opposition, change and counter-ideologies. It is at this level that culturalist theories come into their own. By stressing the moment of self-creation, they extend our notion of ideology to include the whole spectrum of ideological and cultural expression in a concrete situation. The concept of hegemony is fundamental, too. It provides a tool with which to theorise the integration of diverse ideological and cultural strains, and to see the results of breaks and crises within the dominant consensus of society.

In conclusion, the interrelationship between ideology, hegemony and common sense can be considered in the following way: ideology ranks the elements of common sense into a specific hegemonic order, the particular 'common-sense-for-now' sometimes referred to as the hegemonic ideology of the society. This hegemonic ideology will be contested by counter-ideologies, which themselves may form part of a counter-hegemonic struggle. Above all, the clash of meanings in the state of struggle is always changing. The essays in this series attempt in various ways to show the changing stakes and forms of struggle in South Africa as they intersect in the multiple institutions of the media.

Notes and References

1. With the exception of the following: E Potter, *The Press as Opposition: The Political Role the South African Newspapers*; L Switzer and D Switzer, *The Black Press in South Africa and Lesotho: A Bibliographical Guide to Newspapers, Newsletters and Magazines, 1936-1976*; B Bozzoli, *The Political Nature of a Ruling Class: Capital and Ideology in South Africa 1890-1933*; K Tomaselli and R Tomaselli, *Ideology/Culture/Hegemony and Mass Media in South Africa: A Literature Survey*; and E Louw, *The English and Afrikaans Press in South Africa: One Press or Two?* and *The Libertarian Theory of the Press: How Appropriate in the South African Context?*

2. L Althusser, *For Marx* p 233

3. *Ibid* p 155

4. *Ibid*

5. L Althusser, *Lenin and Philosophy* pp 127-186

6. *Ibid* p 155

7. In his self-critique appended to his essay, Althusser notes that while his "few schematic theses" allow him to "... illuminate certain aspects of the functioning of the Superstructure and its mode of intervention in the Infrastructure (base), they are obvi-

ously *abstract* and necessarily leave several important problems unanswered." (*Ibid* p 183)

Two deficiencies specially mentioned by Althusser are the problems of (a) the total process of realisation of the reproduction of the relations of production to which the Ideological State Apparatuses can only contribute; and (b) the class nature of ideologies existing in the social formation.

8. R Johnson, *Three Problematics: Elements of a Theory of Working Class Culture* p 320

9. M Harnecker, *The Elementary Concepts of Historical Materialism* p 9

10. G Therborn, *The Ideology of Power and the Power of Ideology* p 57

11. *Ibid* p 79

12. *Ibid* p 83:

> ... the victim ... is excluded from further meaningful discourse as being insane, depraved, traitorous, alien, and so on. The excommunicated person is condemned temporarily or forever, to ideological non-existence: he is not to be listened to; he is the target of ideological objectivication; he is someone whose utterances are to be treated as symptoms of something else, of insanity, depravity and the like.

13. *Ibid* p 84

14. Johnson, *op cit* p 218

15. See for example, R Williams, *Marxism and Literature*

16. See *Ibid* and also R Williams, *The Long Revolution*

17. See for example, E P Thompson, *The Making of the English Working Class*. See also his seminal review of Williams' work in *New Left Review* Nos 9 and 10

18. See S Hall, D Hobson, A Lowe, and P Willis (eds), *Culture, Media, Language*, London: Hutchinson (1980). Of particular note is Hall's essay 'Recent Developments in Theories of Language and Ideology: a critical note' in the same volume.

19. H M Johnson, *Sociology: A Systematic Introduction*, London: Routledge and Kegan Paul (1961).

20. For more information on the Broederbond see J H P Serfontein, *Brotherhood of Power — an expose of the Secret Afrikaner Broederbond*; I Wilkins and H Strydom, *The Super-Afrikaners: Inside the Broederbond*; and D O'Meara, 'The Afrikaner Broederbond 1927-1948: Class Vanguard of Afrikaner Nationalism' in *Journal of Southern African Studies* vol 3 pp 156-186

21. Q Hoare and G Nowell-Smith, 'The Study of Philosophy' in A Gramsci, *Selections from the Prison Notebooks* p 322

22. Gramsci, *op cit* pp 376-377

23. *Ibid* p 80 note 49
24. J Saul and S Gelb
25. Gramsci, *op cit* p 80 note 49
26. Volosinov, quoted in D Hebdige, *Subculture: The Meaning of Style*, London: Methuen (1979), p 13
27. Hebdige, *op cit* p 17

Chapter 2
The Construction of News in the South African Media

Keyan Tomaselli, Ruth Tomaselli and Johan Muller

In the most exhaustive empirical study available on the sociology of news, Herbert Gans claims that journalists tend to identify ideology with allegiances at the extreme ends of the political spectrum. That is, as "a deliberately thought out, consistent, integrated and inflexible set of explicit political values, which is determinate on political issues"[1]. A large section of the media in South Africa views the term 'ideology' as a fixed and immutable system of ideas which is separate from, and superimposed on, the economic realities of Southern Africa. Liberal thinking argues, for example, that apartheid is an irrational and illogical system of semi-truths which is imposed on South African society by politicians[2]. It contends further that the system is economically inefficient as it limits the freedom of the market and prevents economic growth and expansion.

However, ideology, as we have seen, is not a system of ideas imposed from the outside. Rather, it is an interlinked ensemble of social, political and economic structures which permeate our everyday experiences as we have shown. In the light of this, we want now to examine how journalists mediate everyday events and social processes into an acceptable commodity called 'news'. However well-intentioned the individual journalist, seen from this perspective, news is necessarily an ideological discourse. We will go on to show how journalists participate in the social and ideological conflict occasioned by the current crisis in South African society[3].

Apartheid ideology, as a systematic credo, argues that racial separation is a natural, moral and inevitable condition predicated on cultural and racial differences and on moral attitudes. Around this rationale has evolved the entire system of apartheid with its myriad laws which ensure racial segregation. Apartheid, like all discourses is itself in a constant state of flux, constituting and reconstituting the identity of South Africans[4]. This could be clearly seen in the use between 1983 and 1986 of 'Indian' and 'coloured' continuity announcers on TV1, which paralleled the re-definition of those groups in political terms.

The flexible nature of apartheid discourse is implicitly understood by apartheid theoreticians themselves, although it cuts across the common sense of the great majority of South Africans, who perceive the inevitability of apartheid less as an argument and more as having "the same energy as a material force"[5]. It falls to the media to harness this common sense to accord with the changing imperatives of the discourse and the social order it underwrites.

Journalists and Ideological Discourse

For those who hold them, liberal and apartheid common senses are real and 'objective' in character. They are the individual's world view from the inside looking out: they are the sum of people's feelings about themselves as they go about their day-to-day behaviour. Ideologies are ongoing social processes. They are always produced, conveyed and received in particular, materially circumscribed social situations. They govern people's relations with other people and their environment: they suggest whom we shall meet and under what circumstances, with whom we shall work, play and pray[6], and with whom we may not. The ways in which we act and react to one another, the ways in which we work with one another, and the kinds of work we do, are all governed by ideology.

In other words, while ideology suggests social practice it is in turn formed and constituted by these practices. The practice of ideology may be argued to have succeeded when it has produced a 'natural attitude', when, for example, the existing hegemonic relations are not only accepted but perceived precisely as the way things ought to be and will be.

Journalists are in the business of reporting news subject to what Gans calls 'considerations', factors which shape the availability of information and suitability of news judgements. He comments that unlike sociologists, who divide up external reality into social processes, and historians, who look at these processes over longer periods, journalists see external reality as a set of disparate and independent events, each of which is new and can therefore be reported as news[7].

Journalists, in their professional claims to neutrality or objectivity, locate themselves within a particular ideology. They are not necessarily aware of this ideology nor of how it is forming and shaping their position in the world. They are able to recognise ideology in others to the right and left of themselves in the political spectrum only because it differs from their own. English speaking journalists are able to accuse their Afrikaans counterparts of being ideologues with axes to grind, and who are thereby committed to choosing and reporting stories and sources which advance Nationalist ideological interests. That they themselves are unconsciously doing the same thing is not immediately apparent to English speaking journalists even when accused by Afrikaans journalists, in turn, of advancing their own liberal interests.

Certain kinds of reality are singled out, selected from the continually on-going process of social experience, highlighted and made more important than the mundane social processes within which they repose. The event is then re-presented and sold as 'news' to a consumer public. News in this way becomes a commodity.

McDonald asserts that the most pernicious journalistic convention is the notion that a thing is not newsworthy until it becomes an event; that is, until something 'happens'[8]. Two conclusions follow from this. First, significant phenomena that are not events, such as situations, trends and conditions, go largely unreported. In South Africa for example, the continuous resettlement of blacks into shanty camps in the homeland regions are seldom reported because they have become 'conditions'[9]. Second, the context which makes an event meaningful is either not reported or is reported inadequately. This point is made by Jeff McCarthy and Michelle Friedmann in Chapter 7. They argue, amongst other things, that the context in which the state and business have co-operated in shifting the costs of housing onto blacks themselves through so-called 'self-help' schemes has been misunderstood by the media. It is incorrectly identified as a liberalising movement heralding an easing of bureaucratic restrictions, and an opportunity for blacks to gain a 'permanent stake in the urban areas'.

A second, more striking example of the press's misinterpretation of context is the way the English press reported P W Botha's liberalisation policies following the Carlton Centre conference held with businessmen in November 1979. Against a background of apparent large-scale easing of racial restrictions and the state's commitment to free enterprise and capitalist growth, amongst other things, the English press — as in the case of housing — communicated an inability to grasp the politico-economic significance of these changes. The English press declared that apartheid was 'dead' and that a 'new dispensation' was around the corner[10]. *The Star* further defended the English press by claiming that it is unable to delve instantly deeper than the event and that "in-depth analysis must come later":

"The legislation involved is often complex and it is asking too much of journalists that they should provide an in-depth analysis and verdicts on the probability of official announcements in 30 minutes or 3 hours where legal investigations may take 30 days[11]".

The extremely tight time constraints operating on the production of news must at least partially be responsible for the press's somewhat hasty judgements. However, this cannot account for the systematic omissions that are a feature of news reporting. The fragmentation is reinforced by the way news is organised into distinct 'beats' such as 'political', 'sports', 'business', 'crime', 'parliamentary' and so on. Very often news is further moulded by giving it a news angle to fit these categories or to make it newsworthy. Sally Ride, the first American female astronaut, suddenly becomes 'news' on the 'woman's page', for example.

Selection and Organisation of News

The method by which news is processed through the news organisation has been the subject of a number of studies. The filtration of information is sometimes called 'gatekeeping' or 'blocking', and accounts for specific points or 'gates' in the newsroom through which given news items may or may not be admitted. An editor who opens or closes the 'gate', choosing some news stories but rejecting others, makes an 'either/or', 'yes/no' set of choices. Such a selection process emphasizes the event rather than on-going continuities. In terms of this theory, the gatekeeper is faced with a number of separate and fully fledged versions of particular incidents drawn from 'reality'. The theory does not, however, give any idea of the processes by which the versions are created. Staffers are argued to be more sensitive to their immediate organisation's surroundings than to their environment outside the newsroom[12]. The relationships within the newsroom make news an objective in itself, a commodity which has to meet production schedules even if nothing has 'happened'. This constraint ensures the journalist's conformity to company policy since "journalists are not rewarded for analysing the social structure but for getting news"[13].

Occasionally conditions are reported, but these are often discrete features lost in the welter of news about topical events. Such coverage is usually the result of an event which is brought to light by primary news definers, such as international press agencies, authoritative sources, newsworthy persons or an individual Gans labels more generally as a 'Known'. The use of primary definers in this context exemplifies the process of shielding ideological discourse discussed in the previous chapter. As one political reporter of a daily newspaper told us:

I think that I practise a lot of self-censorship. I feel that you get bludgeoned into writing in a style. I know that if I lead with a comment from an authoritative source, be it the police or government department, the paper will snap up the story. But let my lead be from any unknown source — no matter how accurate it is or how relevant it is to whatever I was covering — they would be less keen. (Interview, 22 Sept 1982)

An example of the influence of primary definers was the sudden interest shown by the English press in Indian flower sellers in Johannesburg. Since 1973, these street traders have been working under the constraints of a tender system which gives them no security of tenure over their flower stands and forces them to pay a higher rental per square metre for unprotected pavement stalls than they would have to pay for an equivalent sized area in a plush downtown shopping complex. Because these people were Indians, and because their plight did not affect the majority of readers, this situation was not regarded as news. In March 1980 a deputation of flower sellers approached a number of prominent City Councillors for assistance. Following this meeting, the flower sellers' grievances were brought up for discussion in the Council Chambers. Through the intervention of 'Knowns', the issue had now become newsworthy. During the period from 3 to 23 April 1982 no less than eleven articles appeared in *The Star*, while two reports were published in the *Sunday Express*, one in the *Rand Daily Mail* and two in the *Financial Mail*. Then, as suddenly as the interest had been aroused, so the issue was dropped. Once the City Councillors connected with the issue ceased making public statements, the issue was no longer considered news. A journalist working on *The Star* subsequently submitted an article on the background to the crisis in which she interviewed a number of the flower sellers. The article was not published since the editor of *The Star* claimed that the issue had already been sufficiently reported and was no longer of general interest, despite the fact that no resolution has been found to the problems existing between the flower sellers and the Johannesburg City Council. The flower sellers' continuing battle with the

Council has attracted no subsequent media coverage — nor will it until some notable figure once again intervenes in the dispute[14].

Nearly all the gatekeeper studies point out that the shaping process is primarily a response to pressures placed on the journalist by the bureaucratic structure of the firm, (for example, SAAN, Argus, Perskor or Nasionale Pers) or the newsroom organisation. However, these studies do not account for the relationship between the firms and the newsrooms and the hegemonic interests which speak through the media. They identify the uncertainties surrounding the gatekeeper's decisions[15]; choice becomes the resolution of management and professional constraints. Omnipresent deadlines inevitably force a choice, as do mechanical pressures, budgetary constraints, personal experience, ethical controls, company policy, and so on[16].

The idea of 'considerations' involves the judgement of the journalist as well as editorial decisions, and attributes a more active role to the journalist than does gatekeeping theory[17]. This offers a starting point for a more comprehensive theory of news filtration which accommodates the notion of ideology and the construction of news, as well as making sense of the unconscious and unintentional conjunction which exists between the journalist who writes the article, the sub who sub-edits it, the production editor who designs the page layout, the picture editor who chooses and crops the pictures and the editor who passes it for publication. While there might, in reality, be very little personal interaction between these different practitioners, their perception of what is news and how it should be represented is common to the discourse of the newsroom. We do not want to over-homogenise this process. In fact, some behaviour defies this kind of structural logic and is purely personal and idiosyncratic. Nevertheless this is not to deny that in general the ideological standpoint of the practitioner, particularly those in real decision-making positions, must be consistent with the ultimate interests served by the particular newspapers. Journalists who question the dominant discourse find that they are deprived of the support mechanisms which would otherwise be available to them.

This withdrawal of resources is the firm's method of restriction and shielding. An experienced Cape journalist commented on this process in the following way:

> I find it very difficult to get a photographer for a lot of contentious stories. Let's take, for example, a riot in the townships. The editor is very conservative. He believes that publicity adds fuel to riots. There have been times when I have actually had to use my own car and my own camera to cover these events. That's on the photographic side. On the newsdesk, I might put in a story which is the point of view which would rub up the conservative guy on the newsdesk. I would find that he would sit on it, and it wouldn't get past him and would, in fact, miss the deadline. The result is that the story might only appear in one of our slip editions.
>
> We have to book a photographer, and if the job is, say, an animal stuck up a tree, I'll get a photographer immediately. It's almost standard that if it's a job in the townships it's a hassle for me to get a photographer. The hassles come from the picture editor. You apply for a photographer through him and, as a matter of principle, he virtually turns it down. If I motivate very strongly for a photographer, tell him I believe that there is going to be a riot — or something to that effect — he will say, "Go out, and if anything does happen phone us and we will get somebody out." Obviously, in that situation it is difficult to get to a telephone. If you do get to a phone by the time the photographer gets out there, it's all over. (Interview, 22 Sept 1982)

The reporter on the spot is not an 'authority', and is not regarded as a credible source where his/her reports conflict with the limits set by the primary definers. Many journalists interpret this as a 'lack of trust' on the part of their superiors on the newspaper. Commented a political reporter:

> I covered the first day of the riots in 1980 which were quite dramatic. There were shops on fire, flames leaping into the sky, and a lot of shooting going on. I wrote a descriptive piece which the paper did not use because they could not believe that

this was actually happening. It was only after a few days that it had become a pattern and similar reports were creeping into other newspapers, did they actually start using descriptive pieces. The news editor did not believe them. I was writing these stories overnight and he would be the first person to see them. He would snap up the factual copy or "the police spokesman said ..." but anything that I had witnessed myself and written in a descriptive way, I found was being spiked. (Interview 22 Sept 1982)

In most cases the journalists and the 'considerations' which inform their practices speak with one voice. We refer to the way in which the common sense discourse is reproduced as consensual signifying practices. This concept gets us away from the misleading notion of 'bias'. Bias implies the possibility of non-bias, or neutrality. This in turn implies that truth or reality can be apprehended by simply 'cracking the code'. *Consensual discourse* and its associated signifying practices account for the entire process of news selection from its sources and collection, through to the way in which it is structured by the journalist, rewritten by the sub-editors and arranged hierarchically within the entire body of other news items (newswhole) making up the newspaper or broadcast and consumed by the consenting public[18]. At each stage in the production and consumption of news the individual largely shares the same ideological framework, and is subject to the discursive affirmations conditioning journalistic discourse. Should she/he violate the values and assumptions implicit in the discourse, then she/he becomes subject to discursive sanctions. Journalists find it almost impossible to work outside these constraints.

The new staffer quickly comes to know what the prevailing common sense is and how company policy — which is seldom spelt out — is shaped and maintained through consensual discourse. Policy is learnt through *osmosis*, a tacit process of 'learning the ropes'. The subtlety of this process is described by a Cape Town journalist:

I find it very difficult to express what has been happening to me over the years I have been on the newspaper, but I am sure that it is happening almost daily. I know that there is a pressure on me not to step out of line. I don't know how it really came about. There is an expectancy from a person in the newsroom. You learn what it is over a long period. Then you fit into the groove. (Interview, 22 Sept 1982)

Media policy is further circumscribed by the production schedule of a newspaper or broadcasting station. Newspapers, television or radio reports occur on a regular basis: hourly, daily, weekly or monthly. This schedule encourages the media to relate mainly to 'events' which are 'reportable'. Ongoing social processes and social conditions do not 'happen' at regular or reportable intervals. Events which draw attention to themselves and which stand out from everyday experiences do. This process — identification and contextualisation — is one of the most important through which events are 'made to mean' by the media. Things are newsworthy because they represent the changefulness, the unpredictability and the conflictual nature of the world[19].

The popular press views those who transgress or threaten dominant social norms (like drug users, criminals, soccer hooligans, homosexuals, political extremists and so on) as 'outsiders'. By casting such groups in the role of 'folk devils'[20], the media serve to strengthen our degree of commitment to ideas of normal behaviour, and to create a climate of opinion that supports the operations of society's sanctioning agencies. The activities of folk devils are presented in such a way as to re-affirm the maintenance of law and order as a primary social goal. Public outrage at 'deviant' acts will only be sustained when there is a large measure of consensus about what constitutes social norms and values. In a society in which there is a crisis of hegemony, where a substantial proportion of the population does not subscribe to the same social and political norms, then the portrayal of these folk devils may, in fact, have an opposite effect: they may become folk heroes whose patterns and modes of behaviour may well be emulated, or at the very least serve as a source of inspiration for those classes or groups disadvantaged by the dominant consensus[21].

A consensual view of media communication makes it possible to account for the shaping of news in its entirety rather than in terms of the immediate options of choice described in gatekeeper studies, and brings us closer to understanding the relationship between the resulting signifying practices and the hegemonic ideology.

Situations do arise where journalists consciously refuse to accept the consensual discourse and associated signifying practices of the newsfirm and thereby situate themselves outside the hegemonic ideology operating in the wider society. Such individuals risk ostracism and discursive and material sanctions such as exclusion. Occasionally, they may provide or attempt to provide an alternative view of 'accepted reality'. Although the concept of gatekeeping is a limited one, it is used in this study to refer to the deliberate exclusion of critical information. It is the penultimate sanction to be applied when journalists or broadcasters refuse to comply with consensual discourse. The ultimate sanctions are dismissal, victimisation, or even bodily harm[22].

The Contradictions of 'Press Freedom'

While it is clear that the various external constraints as well as the internal consensual pressures to which the South African media are subject do limit its degree of independence, they cannot be said to nullify it. The English language press, to some extent the Afrikaans press, and even the SABC at times express views which are offensive to the various 'establishments' — be they in the field of politics, culture, crime, religion or morals[23]. While such 'controversial' views have resulted in the banning of a number of newspapers, and the harassment of even more, and the censuring of the SABC from party political platforms[24], there nevertheless remains a substantial degree of tolerance and latitude within the media. Notwithstanding direct state control, the SABC, for example, has or has had islands of critical expression — such as *Radio Today*, TV1's *Network/Netwerk*, some of the initial broadcasts of *Spectrum* and *Midweek* on television and, in specific instances, *Verslag*.

The importance of dissent should not be minimised. Nor should it mislead anyone into an uncritical acceptance of the rhetoric that 'the freedom of the press', and the 'opportunity for expression' provides a channel for the articulation of alternative viewpoints which have the potential of seriously challenging the existing social and political system. Nevertheless, we must bear in mind that even allowable dissent operates within the larger structure of exploitation. Freedom of expression is not rendered meaningless. But that freedom has to be set in the real economic and political context of these societies; and in that context, the free expression of ideas and opinions *mainly* means the free expression of ideas and opinions which are helpful or at least not harmful to the prevailing system of power and privilege[25].

Conclusion: Maintaining Hegemony

Racial capitalism as a social order in the South Africa of the 1980s is unable to withstand major critical disturbances either from within or without the system. To minimise the impact of such infringements, the state has had to strengthen its mechanisms of control. However, as we point out in Chapter 3, state opposition to English language newspapers has to be seen as a *secondary* consequence of the suppression of black opposition to apartheid. The coincidence of laws curtailing the freedom of the press should be seen as a secondary extension of legislation curbing black dissident activity. Such legislation is not aimed at silencing the English press *per se*, or because "30 years of executive and bureaucratic power has given the (National) party a peculiar view of its own status"[26], but rather to eliminate opposition, particularly black opposition. Insofar as the English press is prepared to articulate such sentiments, it will be subject to these laws.

These arguments point to a major contradiction in the state's relationship with the press. It seems paradoxical that the state should attempt to silence or control the press when, as we have shown, all sectors of the established media support one or more fractions of the hegemonic alliance through the maintenance of consensual discourse. One explanation for this contradiction is that the government misunderstands the socially stabilising role of the press within parliamentary democracies[27]. A more likely explanation is that in South Africa the state underestimates the degree to which it has achieved hegemonic control over the English language press, making the enactment of excessively authoritarian laws redundant[28]. Nevertheless, this over-reaction points at least to the state's awareness of the precariousness of its hegemonic balance. Most of the chapters in this book reflect on the way in which this balance is constantly being threatened on the one hand, and reinforced on the other.

Notes and References

1. H Gans, *Deciding What's News*, pp 29-30

2. See for example, E Hellman, *Handbook of Race Relations*, Cape Town: Oxford University Press (1948); and, more recently, sections of D Welsh, *Oxford History of Southern Africa*, Cape Town: Oxford University Press (1972).

3. See for example, J Saul and S Gelb, *The Crisis in South Africa: Class Defence, Class Revolution*.

4. This is implicitly understood by apartheid theoreticians themselves; for example N Rhoodie and H J Venter, *Apartheid*, Cape Town (1959), pp 19-20. These authors state that:

> ... the basic elements of the (apartheid) idea do not have a detailed series of practical equivalents in the form of concrete apartheid measures ... The *idea* represents the common synthesis of the Afrikaner's attitude towards colour. This synthesis is not a rigid structure which crystallised at a given moment and is incapable of further growth and movement".

These ideologues fulfill Gramsci's criteria for the organic intellectual, articulating the needs of classes they represent. Their position is ironically similar to that taken by writers arguing from a radical standpoint: for example, H Wolpe, 'Capitalism and Cheap Labour Power: From Segregation to Apartheid' in *Economy and Society* vol 1 no 4 (1970); and F A Johnstone, *Race, Class and Gold*, London: Oxford University Press (1970). These authors postulate that apartheid is not a literal ideology to be literally implemented, but rather a pragmatic system of organisation for the maintenance of white prosperity and supremacy.

Johnstone (*Ibid* p 130) for example, states: "Capitalist business, far from being incompatible with the system, secures high profits through very cheap, unorganised and rightless labour."

5. See G Therborn, *The Ideology of Power and the Power of Ideology* pp. 77-8

6. A leader in the *Rand Daily Mail* (8 July 1981) reported that a Coloured woman lost her membership of the Gereformeerde Kerk in Linden, Johannesburg, only a week after it had been approved by the church board, because of dissatisfaction among members of the congregation. For a historic overview of the churchgoers' conversion see C Loff, in *Apartheid is a Heresy*, edited by T de Gruchy and C Villa-Vicencio, Cape Town: David Phillip (1983).

7. Gans, *op cit* p 167

8. O McDonald, 'Is Objectivity Possible?' in *Ethics and the Press*, edited by S C Merril and R D Barney.

9. A study conducted by the Black Sash covering the period from Mr Vorster's "Give us six months" plea in November 1974 to the announcement of a general election in January 1981 highlights the values attributed by the English press to news:

> This analysis shows up a disastrous pattern of hope and let down brought about by a combination of press wishful thinking and the government's indecision, inherent reluctance, or cynicism or fear of its right wing. Sometimes the very article in which change is announced carries its own negation ... the English press, at times of announcement of change, lean over backwards to give the government the benefit of the doubt and not to emphasise negative comments — even those made by government officials.
>
> These reports reflect a desperate desire for change which is hardly reprehensible. But they seem to have had the unfortunate result of creating the impression ... that significant changes have occurred.

10. *The Star* (17 March 1981)

11. Of its identification of what was news during this time, *The Star* (17 March 1981) comments with hindsight: "The English Press does hope for change; but in any case it is its duty to report what looks like change. The promise makes news after all — on the same principle as 'man bites dog' — after so many years of no change". 'What the state represents as change', however, need not have been reported at 'face value', for its context had already been defined the previous year in the first Steyn Commission: "Governmental credibility must at all costs be maintained and strengthened and the extremely dangerous 'unfilled expectations syndrome' must be avoided". In other words, the press was told not to present news in a way which could be interpreted by black South Africans as being a harbinger of change.

12. See, for example, W Gieber, 'News is What Newspaper Men

Make of it' in *People, Society and Mass Communications*, edited by L A Dexter and D M White, pp 177-82

13. W Breed, 'Social Control in the Newsroom' in *Social Forces*, no 33 (1955), pp 326-35

14. In a rare moment of self-criticism, the *Sunday Express* (25 October 1981) published an analysis of the decay of reporting about political detentions from the front page news to "a few column centimetres, often inaccurate in detail ...". This awareness suggests that newspapers do not ignore process completely, but it is the exception rather than the rule that they acknowledge this.

15. T Dimmick, 'The Gatekeeper: An Uncertainty Theory' in *Journalism Monograph* no 37 (1974), pp 37 ff.

16. See for example, Gieber, *op cit*; Breed, *op cit*; and D M White, "The 'Gatekeeper': A Case Study: The Selection of News" in Dexter and White, *op cit* pp 160-72

17. Gans, *op cit*

18. A consensual view of media communication makes it possible to account for the shaping of news in its entirety rather than in terms of the immediate options described in gatekeeper studies, and brings us closer to understanding the relationship between signifying practices and the hegemonic ideology. *Work in Progress* (WIP) offers the example of *The Star*'s survey of the Silverton bank seige (25 January 1980). *WIP* notes that despite screaming headlines about "Killer Terrorists" and "Innocent victims of Terror", about ninety per cent of Sowetans interviewed actually responded positively to the African National Congress action. Yet, despite this, and the availability of alternative labels such as 'guerrillas', 'freedom fighters' or 'gunmen', the South African print media (with the exception of *Post*, which used 'gunmen') persisted in describing this event in terms of a seige, of a challenge to law and order, and saw it as a threat to the cohesion of nation and society. Significantly, the first Steyn Commission regarded the white press coverage of the incident as 'favourable'. The only newspaper Steyn gave a 'negative' rating was *Sunday Post*, which was read primarily by Sowetan black people. This newspaper presented the police force involved at Silverton in a 'negative' manner, revealing "a potentially unacceptable alienation of the public from the police force" (Steyn, *Report of the Commission of Inquiry into Reporting of Security Matters Regarding the SADF and SAP*, RP 52/1980, paragraphs 209-26; hereafter referred to as *Steyn Commission I*).

The substitution of nouns such as 'gunmen', 'freedom fighters' and 'guerrillas' for terms such as 'terrorists' was criticised by the Commission, and it was suggested that these 'semantic matters' should be resolved in briefing sessions with security and defence officials (*Steyn Commission I* paragraph 234).

19. S Hall *et al* (eds), *Policing the Crisis: Mugging, the State and Law and Order*, p 54

20. S Cohen, *Folk Devils and Moral Panics: The Creation of the Mods and Rockers* p 28

21. *Ibid.*

22. A case in point was that of Kevin Harris after he refused to bow to pressure from upper management to delete certain references in his TV production on Baragwanath Hospital. This programme was surreptitiously broadcast on SABC TV1 as originally edited. Despite widespread praise from the Afrikaans and English press alike, Harris was given twelve hours notice to leave the SABC. He subsequently had to take court action to secure his pension which was withheld by the SABC as punishment for talking to the press about his dismissal. Clearly, the institutional consensus had been breached and the unstated policy arising therefrom (which was directly influenced by an external source, the Superintendent of the Hospital) had been transgressed. The unusual step of dismissal was taken to establish the parameters of the Corporation's policy, which continued to be unstated.

23. A significant example in the field of religion was the radio sermon broadcast by Professor Murray Janson on 5 September 1982, in which he criticised segregation and suppression. While praised by Dr Allan Boesak, he was criticised and ostracised by some members of the Lynnwood Church where he gave the sermon. He was also attacked by Dr Andries Treurnicht, leader of the Nationalist breakaway Conservative Party who, in the light of the World Alliance of Reformed Churches expulsion of the DRC a week before, claimed that the sermon was "part of a deliberate attempt by a group of priests to justify a pattern of integration and prescribe it as a norm for South Africa". See *Rand Daily Mail* (7 September 1982). For extracts from the sermon see *Rand Daily Mail* (8 September 1982).

24. Apart from the Progressive Reform Party's continual complaints about the political leaning of the SABC, in 1982 the Corporation came under unprecendented attack from the National Party itself, which accused it of broadcasting 'party political propaganda' for the newly formed Conservative Party. This attack was made on the 8pm *News* by the Deputy Minister of Information, who was given an unusually long time to air his views as the first item on 1 September 1982.

25. R Miliband, *The State in Capitalist Society*, p 197

26. G Stewart, 'A History of Press Control' in *South African Outlook* vol 112 no 1330 (1982), p 67

27. *Ibid.* In fact, this seems to be the interpretation of the majority of commentators writing from the liberal-humanist position. The issue of *South African Outlook* quoted above is a case in point. The majority of the articles take the report of the second Steyn Commission at face value, thereby completely missing the structural factors underlying the Commission's task. On the other hand, most also mention the problem of South Africa's negative overseas image. In Pollak's book, *Up Against Apartheid*, this is a constantly recurring theme. The more significant question of what the economic implications of the 'negative image' are, is replaced with less penetrating questions, which assume that the Government is simply being bloody-minded. This structurally inadequate understanding of the role of media in society is best expressed by Michael Richman in his preface to the Lawyers for Human Rights publication entitled *Distrust in Democracy*, published in June 1982. Although not all the authors of this publication take his libertarian view, he states:

> What South Africa's present rulers have consistently failed to understand is that a truly free press is not a luxury to be dispensed with or relegated in favour of sectional and short term interests. We are a society in a state of crisis and it is precisely for this reason that we desperately need a public and a government which are well informed"(p 4).

28. See for example, the *Report of the Steyn Commission of Inquiry into the Mass Media*, RP 89/1981; hereafter referred to as *Steyn Commission II*.

Chapter 3
The Political Economy of the South African Press

Ruth Tomaselli and Keyan Tomaselli

Despite the contribution of the press to public debate in South Africa, until the early 1980s scholarly analyses were few and far between[1]. Published studies of the South African press fall into five broad categories. The first consists of the reminiscences of retired journalists and editors, which though they go some way towards reflecting the social history of their times, are of little use to the serious student looking for the structure and underlying principles determining the role and function of the press[2].

The second category is uncritical in its description of the current organisation of the South African press, and disregards the 'black' press. These publications tend to emphasize patriotism and are written by ex- or incumbent South African journalists and editors[3].

The third category recognises that South Africa is not a 'whites-only' state, and offers analyses within the orthodox western liberal framework. For example, an historical overview of the press in Africa is given by Barton, who includes a sympathetic, if somewhat brief resume of the black-oriented press in South Africa from its inception to the banning of *World* in 1976[4]. *Muffled Drums* is the title of William Hachten's book on the African press. As with Ainslie's contribution, which preceded it, it is short on explanation; and like others in this category, it lacks analysis of structural conditions.

Index on Censorship has carried a number of articles on the plight of local journalists and the growing bank of restrictive legislation, while *Journalism Quarterly* has concerned itself with wider functional issues of the media[5]. Similarly, a local journal, *Communications in Africa*, published during the early 1970s, offered mainly positivist accounts of the South African media. *Ecquid Novi*, which appeared in the early 1980s is functionalism at its worst, often publishing unscholarly articles and untheorised discussion by academics, newsmen and editors on the issues of objectivity, press freedom, journalistic ethics and the future of the press. This journal, which emanates from an academic communications department, is complemented by A S de Beer's *Joernalistiek Vandag*[6]. As one reviewer put it, the book is "a series of informal chats ... (which) ... aim to teach students to accept the way things are (i.e. apartheid discourse), to observe within these confines and to conform rather than to probe, test and question"[7].

Total Onslaught: South African Press Under Attack is the title of Bill Hachten and Tony Giffard's 1984 book. The most comprehensive to date, this work is marred by historical inaccuracies and accepts the libertarian perspective at face value. Historical determinations are reduced to the actions of individuals: for instance, General Magnus Malan devised the idea of 'total onslaught'; P W Botha does not understand the press, and so on. This personification of social processes precludes a structural analysis of the struggles[8]. Clearly written for American readers, it has limited relevance to contemporary debate in South Africa. A second book written in this vein is Richard Pollack's *Up Against Apartheid*, which sums up the underlying theme of books written within this liberal framework; namely that "more than any powerful force in the country (the English press) stands almost alone between the Afrikaner government and totalitarian darkness"[9].

Another provocative title in this third category is John Phelan's *Apartheid Media*. Writing in a sort of Orwellian journalese, Phelan tries to convey to American readers in American terms the horrors of apartheid and the contradictions of the South African media. The result lacks theoretical analysis but incorporates a dramatic narrative that cannot fail to impress the anti-apartheid reader[10].

The more rigorous works of Elaine Potter and Alex Hepple, and to a lesser extent, Lindsay Smith and others, constitute a fourth category. One of the first studies to explore questions of ownership and control was Lindsay Smith's book, *Behind the Press in South Africa*, published in 1947[11]. The contributions of Irene Ginwala and SPROCAS questioned the position of the 'courageous and outspoken English press' and its perception of democracy[12]. The gathering momentum of anti-press legislation was documented by Alex Hepple, former leader of the South African Labour Party and later Director of Research of the International Defence and Aid Fund in London[13]. Although weak on explanation, he does provide examples of legislative applications against the press. Hepple's documentation is supported by legal work done by John Dugard, Kelsey Stuart and Anthony Matthews[14]. The most searching — although now dated — analysis of the English press is Elaine Potter's study, which outlines the relationship between the white press and the South African political system[15]. This work, however, excludes an analysis of the black-oriented press which, at the time of writing, she saw as having no special significance. The mouthpiece of the South African Society of Journalists, *The Journalist*, provides useful source material on ongoing issues within the South African journalistic profession. Many of the articles take a critical and perceptive view of long-term structural changes within the industry.

Studies in the fifth category, incorporating structural analysis, have appeared only since the late 1970s. While many of the initial applications tended to be eclectic and weak on theoretical content, the early 1980s witnessed a tighter methodological approach. A pioneering work breaking with the libertarian paradigm was Chimutengwende's *The Press and the Politics of Liberation*[16]. The analysis is, however, somewhat disjointed. Of a more rigorously structured nature are Les Switzer's studies of the political influences of the media on black readers and radio listeners and media dependency in the Ciskei region. His bibliographical overview of the black press in South Africa and Lesotho is a useful source guide, although it contains very little explanatory text. Only he and Tim Couzens have written on important historical moments of the black oriented press[17].

The work published in journals like *SA Labour Bulletin*, *Critical Arts*, a special issue of the British published *Media Development* and, to a lesser extent, *Work in Progress* and occasionally in *Communicatio*, offer the most fruitful directions for further study. These empirical and theoretical analyses and documentation take account of the media within the broader political economy of the South African society, rather than seeing them as an isolated phenomenon. Articles published in these journals do not pretend to be final statements but see themselves as offering exploratory introductions to a wider contextual analysis. Nevertheless, these contributions are more significant than the majority of the publications which fall into the first three categories above[18].

This chapter aims to explore the role of the print media in relation to the overall political economy of South Africa. More specifically, it will attempt to demonstrate that the mass media articulate the ideology of apartheid which has the effect of naturalising the class-assigned roles that define the relationship between capital and labour. As a corollary, it is argued that the State's repression of the press is at its most significant on those occasions when the press articulates the needs and aspirations of the black working class majority and dissident elements within the black petty bourgeoisie.

Class Alliances in South Africa

In the last decade numerous studies have identified South Africa as a society in crisis[19]. This sense of crisis permeates all levels of society — the political (notably the increasingly obvious split in National Party unity outlined by Johan Muller in Chapter 4), the ideological (manifested, for example, in the excessive level of control and legislation exercised over the press) and not least, the economic (as seen, for instance, in the chronic recessionary conditions, inflation, structural unemployment and deteriorating labour relations that have characterised the South African economy in the 1980s).

In response to these crises, the State, as the guardian of the welfare of capital in general, has attempted to establish a coalition of interests between the politically dominant groups and the white and black middle classes. The congruence of interests between the capitalist classes and the white middle and working classes is well known and will not be dealt with here[20]. This section will explore the growth of the black middle classes and outline the State's attempts to incorporate them, while at the same time dividing them from the larger mass of black workers and peasants, particularly those in the rural and 'homeland' areas[21].

South Africa's entry into the stage of monopoly capitalism has meant a burgeoning of the non-productive positions in industry — especially those in the administrative, clerical and distributive sectors. Simultaneously, the shifting emphasis within the South African economy from the mining and agricultural sectors to manufacturing has brought about a change in capital's requirements from the working class. The primary sectors still need a large workforce whose cost of reproduction of labour power has been kept low through the mechanisms of migrant labour, geographical and job segregation[22], and whose demands must be suppressed through institutionalised repression and violence[23]. The continued expansion of the manufacturing sector, an inadequate educational structure for blacks and the rigorous application of the job colour bar in the recent past has resulted in a shortage of skilled manpower, which in turn inhibits the growth of manufacturing. Successive drives for 'suitable' white immigrants have only partially relieved the situation. Propelled by the imperatives of capital, and particularly the shortage of skilled labour, the State is encouraging the creation of middle class elements within the state-designated 'black', 'Indian' and 'coloured' 'communities'. It has been forced to relax some areas of its racially discriminatory legislation (while at the same time increasing others) in order to allow for the development of a relatively small, stable and skilled black workforce.

Urban Permanence and Co-option

One of capital's primary requirements for continued growth is the provision of more extensive educational facilities — hence the appointment of the De Lange Commission into Education, and the subsequent debate on the implementation of its proposals (see Chapter 5). Another is the provision of better housing for the strata of urban-based workers, a response that is examined in Chapter 7. These and other strategies, some of which will be outlined below, reinforce the need for skilled labour to fill the service sectors, especially in teaching, administration, nursing and the bureaucracy. In recognising the importance of this tendency of expansion, it should be borne in mind that it has been limited by the fact that these jobs have traditionally been a white preserve, especially at the higher levels, while blacks have occupied the jobs with the least power and responsibility[24].

The report of the President's Council Committee for Constitutional Affairs on an 'Urbanisation Strategy' acknowledged that black urbanisation was both unavoidable and desirable. The report calls for the abolition of influx control, and the concommitant 'Pass Laws', to be replaced by a 'strategy of orderly urbanisation'. The same theme was echoed by the State President in his opening address to Parliament, February 1986, dubbed 'Rubicon II' by the media. Influx control under 'Grand Apartheid' relies on negative sanctions, which are impossible to effectively enforce: "Illegals" who are apprehended and convicted "simply do not return to the urban areas". 'Orderly urbanisation'. on the other hand, will rely on the 'positive' use of market forces, subsidies and development, which will "encourage people to settle in suitable areas rather than forbidding them to move to certain urban areas"[25]. This increased security of workers would, it was hoped, encourage higher levels of productivity and skills acquisition. Thus these changes envisaged the development of a skilled and semi-skilled, relatively highly paid labour force with permanent urban rights, in order to break out of the vicious circle of high labour turnover — low productivity — low wages — high labour turnover. This urban accessibility is accompanied by certain limited forms of surrogate representation, notably through local government, and by improving social services such as hospitals, clinics, schools and other public facilities. These social services remain the cause of great dissatisfaction among urban dwellers, but they are far superior to those provided for their rural counterparts, constituting an important part of the state's package to induce cooperation from this stratum. Nevertheless, the outbreak of a low intensity civil war in 1984 heralded popular opposition on a massive scale among urban blacks[26].

In ideological terms, the strategy of fostering a relatively privileged black sector represents an attempt to coopt it into a collaboration with white capital. This collaboration would be based on its relatively advantaged position with respect to the broad mass of the black population, who are excluded from well paid and permanent employment opportunities, or who are subject to geographic segregation and economic repression.

Strategies to Divide the Working Class

The status of rural 'homeland' blacks is even more precarious in the light of the restructuring of the economy. The 'positive' approach to urbanisation does not however mean that urban-bound migration will be unrestricted. The phasing out of influx control will take place "in accordance with the demands of good order". The hidden agenda of the proposed legislation is that migrants may live only on 'approved sites'. 'Informal housing' on non-approved sites can be demolished under the Squatters Act which, noted, Dr Dries Oosthuizen, the Report's chairman, "applies to everyone. Black and whites. There will be no discrimination"[27]. The 'suitability' of an area will depend largely on the availability of employment and infrastructure in the area.

The attraction for workers of secure wage employment is juxtaposed to a growing awareness of their exploitation under an apartheid economic system. Even relatively privileged urban blacks have become enormously politicised by their falling rate of employment and by exposure to the SA Police and SA Defence Force occupation of the townships since October 1984, and particularly following the declaration of a state of emergency on 17 July

1985[28]. This, together with the personally close ties of many members of the middle class with the marginally employed and unemployed, accounts for their ambivalent attitude towards co-option into the 'benefits' of the capitalist system. This ambivalence will be further explored in a discussion of the ideological position of black journalists in Volume 3 of this series, *The Limits of Dissent*.

It is against such a background that the various components of the South African mass media can best be understood. In the sections that follow we shall discuss the role of the 'black' press as well as the English and the Afrikaans-language press in the service of the crumbling hegemonic alliance.

The 'Black' Press: Ideological Ambivalence

The black middle classes are only able to articulate their feelings and grievances through the commercial mass media in an indirect way, since, with the exception of a few trade union and community-based and distributed newspapers, there are no commercial newspapers, radio stations or television networks which are owned or controlled by blacks. This lack of access has been partly responsible for the channelling of grievances through school and consumer boycotts, industrial action and subversion which, because of the actions' dramatic nature, draw attention to themselves in the pages of the press.

A brief historical overview of the 'black' press will indicate the mechanisms through which this medium has come under the control of white capital, and how the many attempts to establish a truly independent 'black' press and alternative media channels have been quashed (A more detailed analysis can be found in Chapter 1 of Volume 3 of this series).

From Mission Press to Corporate Ownership

At the turn of the century, a number of African-owned publications voicing black aspirations existed. The most important of these was *Imvo Zabantsundu*, founded in

1884 in the Ciskei. *Ilanga lase Natal* was established in 1903 to serve Zulu readers, and Solomon Plaatjie published the first issue of *Koranta ea Becoana* in 1901 in Tswana and English. Other papers soon followed. These have been described as a "highly individualised, non-corporate, elite press for literate blacks drawn from rural, usually Christian, peasant communities and nascent urban areas of Southern Africa"[29]. A host of non-white political organisations were responsible for the spate of African-language newspapers in many parts of the country before 1930. All fell prey to economic restraints and/or political suppression. A second generation of radical publications came into being in the late 1940s and early 1950s. These included *Inkundla ya Bantu*, set up by the African National Congress (ANC) in 1946, *Torch* in the same year and *Spark* in 1952. All three were banned following the Sharpeville shootings in 1960. In 1931 the Bantu Press was established by two white South Africans and their first newspaper, *Bantu World*, was a forerunner of the daily, *World*. Bantu Press gradually assimilated the major surviving newspapers, including *Imvo, Ilanga* and *Evening Post*. The Argus Company realised the commercial potential of the Bantu Press, and funds provided by the Anglo American Corporation enabled it to acquire a dominant interest by 1950, and total ownership by 1963. This investment found substantial reward in the enhanced circulation figures of newspapers aimed at black readers. *World's* circulation, for example, rose from 11 000 in 1959 to 90 000 in 1968. By 1976 this newspaper's penetration equalled that of the *Rand Daily Mail* at 145 000 copies sold mainly on the Reef. This growth occurred despite the fact that the early 1960s saw a low point in black journalism as well as political militancy in South Africa[30]. Elaine Potter observes that "it was impossible for any independent African newspaper to survive the competitive power of the white-controlled Bantu Press, and indeed this was the intention"[31]. *World's* masthead announced that it was 'Our Own, Our Only Newspaper', a curious reflection of the interests attributed to the black reader, since the editorial was chiefly concerned with sensational crime, violence and sex. It avoided politics, which, said its general manager, elicited "apparently very little interest among the Bantu"[32]. *Post*, which was to replace *World* after its banning in 1976, was at that time a bi-weekly made up of similar editorial fare. This is borne out in Fred St Leger's content analysis of three newspapers during the years 1967 and 1968. Pointing out that both *Ilanga* and *World* editorials concentrated on homeland politics, he shows that *Post*, in contrast, had no political content at all:

> This reflects what appears to be to some extent a difference of policy but certainly a difference of interest between *Post* on the one hand and *World* and *Ilanga* on the other. There is also a marked difference between the policy of *World* and that of the *Rand Daily Mail*. The latter's general attitude is that the Bantustans are a sham ... whereas *World* and *Ilanga* tend to pursue the theme 'let us make positive apartheid work' — though they do not do so without reservations[33].

An exception to this compliant attitude was *Drum*. Published monthly, it flourished in the 1950s and 1960s. Though still in existence, it "gives little hint of the journalistic heights it attained in its heyday"[34]. Owned by Jim Bailey, son of Sir Abe Bailey of South African Associated Newspapers (SAAN), it ran exposés on a number of contentious issues such as the use of prison labour on farms, the brutality of prison conditions for blacks and the repressive measures of apartheid from a black point of view. Afrikaanse Pers's *Bona*, an educational magazine published in Zulu, Xhosa and Sotho, was established to counteract *Drum* and was distributed free to African Schools. This company also bought *Imvo* and *Zonk* from Bantu Press in 1964. Not content with these competitors, the now defunct Department of Information attempted to buy out *Drum* in 1977. When these efforts failed, it founded *Hit* under the control of Johnny Johnson, later to become editor of the State-funded newspaper, *The Citizen*. A second magazine, *Pace*, the most highly capitalised publication of recent times, was established soon afterwards by a front company, Hortors, in direct competition with *Drum*. However, after the exposure by the English Press of the Department of Information's illegal dealings[35], *Pace* changed hands and was finally was taken over by the Argus, through their acquisition of a shareholding in Caxtons.

Golden City Post, established in 1955 by Jim Bailey, was bought out by Argus in 1964. This paper subsequently became the bi-weekly *Post*, and then a daily to fill the gap left by the banning of *World* in 1977.

Following the closure of *World* and *Weekend World*, the Argus elevated a smaller weekly, *Post* and *Weekend Post*, to exploit the readership previously served by *World*. *Post* journalists went on strike in October 1980, calling for improved salary scales. The strike went on for two months and in terms of a Supreme Court ruling, registration of the newspaper lapsed. When the Argus applied for a condonation of the lapse in the registration or for re-registration of the newspapers, it was informed by the Government that resumption of publication would result in these newspapers being banned. This threat was designed to intimidate the Argus into reducing its operations amongst black readers. *Post* and *Weekend Post* were in turn replaced with yet another small weekly, the *Sowetan*, which is now published from Monday to Friday. Although many of the journalists who had previously worked on *World* and *Post* continued with the *Sowetan*, the Argus managing director commented: "The company's activities in the black newspaper field will, however, be considerably reduced as a result of the closure of the *Post* newspapers ..."[36].

Golden City Press was launched by Bailey and SAAN in early 1982 to fill the gap left by the banning of *Weekend World* and *Sunday Post*. Run from Bailey's *Drum* offices, it was printed by Perskor. The paper, which reproduced the sex, violence and gang war formats of the 1950s, experienced financial difficulties. Chris Day, seconded by SAAN to resolve these problems "turned *Golden City Press* round by making it a Kaizer Chiefs propaganda sheet that began to attract some attention in the townships"[37]. He also introduced a Friday edition to capitalise on black interest in horse racing. By November 1982, the paper's sales reached 100 000 to surpass its chief rival, *The Sowetan*. Bailey considered that Day had now done his job and sent him back to SAAN. The amount of R3 million was reportedly needed to keep the newspaper afloat during its loss-making months. In an attempt to push the issue of control, SAAN, who were rumoured even at that time to be closing the Extra editions of the *Sunday Times* and *Rand Daily Mail*, gave Bailey an ultimatum of either resigning as executive manager or facing the total withdrawal from *Golden City Press* by SAAN. Bailey refused to resign and SAAN subsequently withdrew from the venture. The paper closed on 31 January 1983. On 2 February, after an acrimonious wrangle over the copyright of the name, Bailey brought out a new paper identical in all respects under the masthead of *City Press*.

A year later, Raymond Louw, formerly of SAAN, took over as joint general manager and Percy Qoboza was recruited as editor. On 5 April 1984 *City Press*, *Drum* and *True Love* were sold by Bailey to Nasionale Pers. Perskor as printers of these publications had been given first option, but were unable to raise the necessary finance. Nasionale Pers was seen as the faithful voice of the Cape National Party which "is the party of total onslaught, of Nkomati, of tricameral parliaments, a party dedicated to winning hearts and minds ... and destroying those it can't win." Naspers needed an established and well accepted 'black' newspaper since "the one thing missing from total strategy (was) a credible voice with which to win the hearts and minds of this country's black (African) townships"[38].

Prior to this move Nasionale Pers had bought into black media in 1982, acquiring Chain Publications which produced five knock-'n-drops delivered to 125 000 homes in the PWV area. *City Press* has grown enormously under Nasionale Pers and by the end of 1985 reached 154 000 readers. The circulation increased substantially from the middle of 1984 as attested by the 34 per cent growth rate during the period July to December 1984, and the further 21 per cent increase over the period January to June 1985. This growth occurred under the editorship of Qoboza and was no doubt spurred by the paper's vociferous anti-apartheid stance.

Besides the urban-based publications, there have been a number of black-owned or managed newspapers published in the homeland areas which "stress ethnic consciousness, which ideologically is compatible with apartheid"[39]. These newspapers are usually published in the vernacular and are careful not to criticise homeland policies or leaders. Those deviating from a bland and noncritical stance are soon forced out of business. A case in point is the Transkei weekly, *Isasizo*, which was banned in 1977. This newspaper reappeared as *Isizwe* in January 1978 and was banned six months later for publishing adverse political comment. The publisher moved to Lesotho where he has set up that country's first commercial news service.

Analysis of conditions leading to the demise of the church-funded *The Voice* indicates that legislative control is only one factor in the viability of newspapers, particularly black-oriented papers. Editor of *The Voice*, Revelation Ntoula, experienced difficulty in finding typesetters willing to work on the publication, in obtaining National Press Union accreditation, and in contracting with a professional distribution agency. The Springs Advertiser agreed to print *The Voice* provided that all articles had been vetted by a legal adviser prior to publication. To add to these problems, only one advertising broker agreed to deal with the paper, and only two years after its establishment was the paper able to secure a distribution deal. This fell through almost immediately when the editor published a front page article predicting the election victory of Robert Mugabe's ZANU Party in Zimbabwe.

The only rural-based newspaper which attempted to penetrate the urban areas was *Nation*, mouthpiece of the Zulu political movement, Inkatha. It ceased publication in March 1979 after nine consecutive bannings. These two examples serve to underline the impossibility of an independent black press following a critical, if not radical, stance in the present politico-economic situation. *The Nation* was replaced by *Clarion*, a much more sober monthly. January 1986 saw the launch of *The New Nation*, a fortnightly published by the South African Catholic Bishops Conference and edited by Zwelakhe Sisulu.

The Limits of Black Editorial Control

The black press under the 'protection' of the white publishing companies is virulently anti-apartheid, but not necessarily anti-capitalist. These newspapers not only face State intervention but are also subject in varying degrees to white editorial policies. Using the example of *World*, we shall discuss the movement of editorial control from white overseers to black journalists themselves and the structural limitations of this control. In the first half of the 1970s both the ownership and control of the *World* newspaper was vested in the Argus management. The content of the newspaper was decided by its white editorial director in consultation with the black editor, M T Moerane. This content reflected the editorial director's view that readers now "wanted crime, sport and funeral news and were not overtly interested in political or international news." The editor, Moerane, was more idealistic but had little or no ability to determine the policy of his newspaper[40]. This put him in a contradictory position. Because of his membership of the Soweto professional elite (doctors, lawyers, businessmen, journalists) he felt duty-bound to campaign for the upliftment of his community of readers but at the same time he found himself answerable for the lack of a wider social and political awareness on the part of his newspaper. Moerane was unable to fulfill the expectations of his own social class and it is therefore not surprising that journalism under his editorship generally fell short of the standards aspired to by the more radical Black Consciousness movement.

A Lesotho poet associated with Black Consciousness in South Africa, Njabulo Ndebele, voices this criticism, castigating the black community for being 'obsessed with capitalist values and sharing in the oppression of blacks': "The journalists are worse ... The strategy of this (black) press is to make feeble attacks on apartheid as an indication that it is on their side"[41]. Black journalists working on *World*, and those employed on other white-owned newspapers, became increasingly disillusioned with the conciliatory policies adopted by the editorial staff. The belief in the need for a more committed stance was articulated in the establishment of the Union of Black Journalists (UBJ) in January 1973. The UBJ is described by Patrick Lawrence as "a black consciousness union (which) sought to mobilise black journalists and synchronise their aspirations with those of the broader black community"[42].

The appointment of Percy Qoboza as editor of the *World* in 1974 brought no immediate change to the situation, but early in 1976 Qoboza visited the United States as a Nieman Fellow and returned with a greater determination to fight for the black cause. His return coincided with the months which were to lead up to the outbreak of violence on 16 June 1976.

The extensive scale and geographical spread[43] of the disturbances made nonsense of the idea that blacks 'have little interest in politics'. Reflecting this event, the changed editorial content of *World*, together with a more incisive marketing strategy and the production of a morning edition, led to a dramatic increase in circulation. At the time of its banning on 19 October 1977, St Leger suggests that *World* was "more widely-read and ... more influential than almost all other newspapers, black or white, in South Africa"[44].

The long-brewing conflict between Qoboza and the white editorial director culminated in the latter being transferred to another newspaper. Thereafter, editorial policy was vested in Qoboza. This period ushered in the beginning of black editorial control on white-owned newspapers. In a wider context, these developments underlined the importance of black journalists in the whole of the newspaper industry. Their contribution during the mid-1970s is described by Qoboza:

> When the Soweto riots raged in earnest, the black journalists were there right in the middle of the crossfire. Because his white colleague was refused entry into the black areas, and because of the dangers that faced whites in general, it fell on the shoulders of the black journalists to keep South Africa and the outside world informed about what was going on there[45].

While both the *Rand Daily Mail* and *The Star* had a number of black journalists in their employ, the Afrikaans newspapers were caught unprepared, since — with the exception of the *Transvaler*, which had one black reporter — these newspapers were unable to obtain first-hand reports of the township events. The extent of *Beeld*'s predicament, which followed directly from their narrow understanding of what constituted 'news' for white readers, is illustrated by the following anecdote:

> So desperate was *Beeld* that it gave one of its black messengers a camera with the aperture setting and the shutter speed taped up and sent him into Soweto on the first day of the uprising with instructions to click when he saw something exciting. The man came back with good photographs and a dramatic eye witness account of the rioting. He was promptly placed on the editorial payroll[46].

Qoboza espoused a cautious Black Consciousness viewpoint in some of his editorials during 1976: "Editorial concern had switched from what may be seen as the peripheral to the central issues of South African politics, and from co-operation to uncompromising rejection of the institutions of apartheid"[47]. Qoboza was among the first newsmen to conduct an interview with the Soweto student leader, Tsietsi Mashinini. The resulting article cannot, however, be seen as an endorsement of Mashinini's views since it was headed with a passage explaining that "all sorts of people have been expressing their views and opinions on the student demonstrations ... but little has been heard from the people most concerned, the students themselves"[48].

During this period black journalists were harassed by the police, culminating in the detention of thirty black journalists without trial, including Qoboza, who was held for eight months. In a study which monitored gatekeeping processes on *World*, *The Star* and *Rand Daily Mail* during the Soweto uprising, Marion Whitehead described techniques of intimidation: the taking down of names by police, the confiscating of press cards and car keys, the ordering of journalists to report to the police station, question sessions, arrests, detentions and assault. *World* had five reporters detained, the editor interrogated for eight hours, and the highest number of telephone calls from the Minister of Justice, containing a mixture of threats, demands and requests[49].

Although at the time the 1976 disturbances seemed to mark a turning point in the editorial control of *World*, in retrospect it did not put forward a radical point of view and the "consensus theme which underlay much of the 1968 editorial writing was still present to some extent in 1976"[50]. Editions of *World* and *Weekend World* have been described as a "crisis sheet, doing little more than recording day-to-day happenings with a modicum of comments"[51]. Nor were newspapers exempt from the editorial process whereby the final presentation of the story coincided more closely with the views of the white media managers than of the reporters themselves. In her study of the three daily newspapers, Whitehead comments:

> On *The Star* the policy was a conservative 'middle of the road' style of news presentation; on the *Mail* it was slightly to the left and the newspaper was more willing to print controversial stories provided they fitted into conventional news story formats; the *World*'s treatment of news coincided most closely with the original copy submitted by reporters[52].

During their stand against the inequities of the apartheid system, especially during 1976 and 1977[53], the journalists, all part of the relatively advantaged petty bourgeoisie, maintained an ambivalent attitude towards the needs of the black working class: "While most ... sympathise with Africanist ideals ... they also reflected the burden of a generation that had grown up under apartheid, internalised its values and sought security in its benefits"[54]. This ambivalence is further compounded by the frustrations felt by many black journalists with regard to newspaper policy and job prospects. Qoboza, for example, refers to:

> the rising wave of criticisms black journalists are throwing into the white oriented establishments. Many of these journalists are beginning to say that there is a conspiracy on the part of some editors to discourage stories which the white community will find unacceptable or unpalatable. They see this situation continuing unless black journalists can exercise positions of real influence in the policy of the paper[55].

Qoboza's own position of influence, however, was not without its contradictions. Comparing him to the previous white editorial director who 'wanted to play it safe', a reporter on *World* declared: "Mr Qoboza talks my sort of language ... but when it comes to the crunch I sometimes feel a guilty stab against my editor. He is also one of the big money boys and walks to the tune"[56]. This dissatisfaction on the part of black journalists, together with their increasing harassment, the banning of *World* and *Weekend World* and the detention of Qoboza, led to their increasing radicalisation.

Salary scales are another point of contention, black journalists arguing that they are discriminated against in comparison with their white colleagues. Few black journalists working on the white-oriented papers are permanently employed. This occurred even during Allister Sparks' editorship of the *Rand Daily Mail*.

The Government onslaught against black journalists continues to the present, sharpened by the Media Workers Association of South Africa's pledge to uphold what they call 'commitment journalism' which, amongst other things, rejects ideological controls such as the principle of 'objectivity'. This philosophy, together with their grassroots support amongst unskilled media workers and deliverymen, places them in a powerful position *vis-a-vis* management and sets them against the white-owned English liberal press and the State[57].

MWASA's militancy is in spite of the realisation that it could never mirror working-class grievances or even the black majority view [58]. However, the Government has deemed MWASA sufficiently dangerous to warrant the banning of successive leaders. The Association was the subject of a vicious, but confused, attack from the second Steyn Commission which painted it as functioning as "shock troops for the revolution"[59].

The Steyn Report's heavy-handed recommendations regarding the 'captive black press' seemed to be entirely inappropriate and superfluous at a time when this press had been weakened by successive closures and financial bankruptcies. The newspapers serving black readers that do survive are all firmly under the control of white-owned parent companies and are, if only from a purely economic point of view, unlikely to espouse a radical discourse. Struggles within the media institutions continue, however. A managerial directive from Nasionale Pers to the editorial staff of *City Press* a few weeks *before* the declaration of the state of emergency on 17 July 1985 instructed that unrest reporting had to be reduced by 50 per cent. A content analysis of the paper at that time suggests, however, that this instruction was largely ignored by the editor and staffers.

The English-Language Press: Limited Opposition to Apartheid

The English-language press is dominated by two groups, Argus and South African Associated Newspapers (SAAN), with the former owning forty per cent of the latter. The shareholders of these two companies are predominantly financial and investment concerns traditionally associated with the mining industry; most notably Anglo American and Johannesburg Consolidated Investments (JCI). With the changing structure of the economy, the pattern of ownership and control has adjusted to give greater weight to capital from the manufacturing sector. Considering the composition of the holding companies and the directors who serve them, it is not surprising that the English-language press is closely associated with the aims, objectives and interests of the hegemonic bloc as a whole. This convergence of interests should not be viewed in the mechanistic fashion in which the English-language press is seen to be 'controlled' by individuals such as Harry Oppenheimer, John Martin and more recently Gordon Waddell. A more useful understanding of how ideology permeates from business into the media is provided in Chapter 2. This point needs to be stressed here since conventional wisdom, as well as certain published sources, insist on inferring a personal connection between powerful industrial magnates and press managements. This explanation trivialises the complex relations and multiple contradictions that govern the press's relationship to capital[60].

As we have argued, the white-owned black press is not

36,50%	Anglo American	
	Standard Bank Nominees	
	(Tvl) (JCI)	20,99%
	Abercom Nominees	8,60%
	JCI Officials Pension	
	Fund	1,90%
	JCI Employees Pension	
	Fund	1,60%
	Sharestock Nominees	1,00%
	Anglo (below 1%)	2,40%
6,00%	S A Mutual	
20,20%	Argus Pension Fund	17,30%
	CNA Gallo	2,90%
4,50%	Hillfam Investments (Pty) Ltd	
1,70%	Security Nominees	
1,60%	Legal & General Volkskas	
6,40%	South African Associated Newspapers	

Argus Printing and Publishing Co Ltd
The Cape Argus, The Star, Pretoria News, Daily News, Natal Mercury, Weekend Argus, Sunday Tribune, Sunday Star, Sowetan, Ilanga, Post Natal, Diamond Fields Advertiser, Cape Herald, etc.

75%	Afmed
	Modern Media Promotions (wholly owned by Moolman Coburn & Partners)
	50%+1 share
	Argus Printing and Publishing Co Ltd
	50%-1 share
11,00%	Argus Printing and Publishing Co Ltd
11,00%	Moolman Coburn & Partners

Caxton
Pace, Style, Top 40, Benoni City Times, Boksburg Advertiser, Boksburg Volksblad, Bolksburg Sun, Germiston Courier, Germiston Koerant, Berea Mail, Highway Mail, Vereeniging and Vanderbijlpark News, West Rand Times en Weslander, Roodepoort Record, Brixton Telegraph, Northcliff and Blackheath Times, Randburg Sun, South Coast Sun, Sandton Chronicle, Rosebank and Killarney Gazette, North East Tribune, Southern Courier, Krugersdorp News, Eastern Express, Kempton Express, Alberton Record, Edenvale News, Highveld Ridge, Randfontein Herald, Verwoerdburg News, etc.

17,85%	Anglo American	
	JCI	12,75%
	Standard Bank Nominees (Tvl)	5,10%
19,90%	Barclays National Nominees (Advowson Trust)	
1,50%	66 Marshall Street Nominees (Union Acceptances)	
2,30%	Ned-Equity Insurance Co	
2,90%	SAAN Pension Fund	
1,30%	Colonial Mutual Life	
1,10%	L H Walton	
37,20%	Argus Printing and Publishing Co Ltd	
4,90%	Robinson and Co	

South African Associated Newspapers Ltd
Sunday Times, Cape Times, Business Day, Financial Mail, Eastern Province Herald, Evening Post, etc.

Independent newspapers:
(Some may have small shareholdings of SAAN or Argus)
The Natal Witness, The Daily Dispatch, New Nation, The Weekly Mail, Grocott's Mail, The Leader, The Graphic, City Times, etc.

in a position to articulate the needs and aspirations of the real opponents of apartheid, the black working class. This has led to the English-language press being cast in the role of the opposition by default. It is Potter's thesis that in the period before 1948, and the years immediately after, the National Party and the then United Party vied with each other to be the real custodians of white interests. The National Party strategy was one of Afrikaner cultural and political exclusivity, which meant the exclusion of English-speaking elements and, more particularly, a legitimisation of the notion of racial purity. Since the opposition United Party, and latterly, the Progressive Federal Party, together with the English section of the white press which supported them, seemed to be less hostile to blacks than were the National Party and the Afrikaans press, the English and thus, by default, the English press were seen as opposing apartheid [61]. With the entrenchment of the Nationalist regime, the English-language press's view of itself as the public representative of black interests has become more deeply ingrained. This myth has been given additional credibility by the second Steyn Commission, which described this press as a "perceptual Goliath"[62] causing irreparable harm to intergroup relations[63] and aiding an "unholy alliance" of external forces attacking South Africa. The Commission was, however, aware that in the absence of black representation on the SABC or the Afrikaans press, the English press is the only outlet available to blacks. Despite its allegations, therefore, the Commission was obliged to concede that the English press had done a good job of articulating black aspirations in the absence of a "truly independent black press"[64].

It is our argument, however, that this opposition to apartheid is structurally limited, since the English press is owned by white capital and therefore has vested interests in maintaining the conditions conducive to the continued accumulation of capital, based on an exploitative division of labour. In summing up the English press's opposition to apartheid, Potter writes:

> In opposing apartheid the English press stressed the economic impracticability and expense of implementing the doctrine. In representing the interest

of the African, the English press expressed its concern for the 'underdog' a concern based on a paternalistic desire to guide the development of the African and ensure his commitment to the values it upheld[65].

In contrast to the English press's liberal discourse, this book takes the view that apartheid is not an illogical and irrational ideology hinged on racial and cultural differences, but is rather an externalisation of the class struggle in a capitalist society historically divided by race. There are, furthermore, many tenets which are common to both Nationalist apartheid and its liberal counterpart, the most important of these being the need to develop a black middle class as a skilled stratum of the workforce. In this connection, newspaper readers are told that hard work and productivity are the source of higher material rewards. The bitter irony is that in an economy which has been, and still is largely based on cheap labour rather than high productivity levels, the black worker has had to contend with long hours of arduous labour, excessive commuting distances and a disrupted family life in order to survive at all. Hard work, if not higher levels of productivity, is no stranger to the black working class. Insofar as white English-language newspapers deal with the needs of blacks at all, they normally concern themselves with the issues of housing, transport, recreational environments and education — all factors which contribute to the stabilisation of an urban workforce. During the latter half of 1985, however, this press in particular extended its coverage to unrest, educational and consumer boycotts, and allegations of police brutality. Even the daily press started to differentiate between different groups in the black opposition. Both the *Sunday Star* and *Sunday Tribune*, for example, have carried articles by black organisational spokesmen and strategists including the United Democratic Front (UDF) and Azanian Students Movement (Azasm). The *Cape Times* even tempted providence by publishing an interview with Oliver Tambo, President of the ANC[66].

Prior to 1985, the occasional stories of widows and orphans and the unemployed were supplemented by pleas for the fulfillment of basic human needs in campaigns such as Operation Snowball and Alexandra Uplift. In the former, the *Rand Daily Mail* publicised its humanitarian attempts to collect blankets and warm clothing for the underprivileged of all races (though mainly black) prior to the onset of winter. *The Star*'s Alexandra Uplift operation was a much more ambitious project run in conjunction with the State-appointed Alexandra Liaison Committee. Additional support came from the Urban Foundation, a philanthropic trust financed by large-scale business to ameliorate the lack of facilities which were a significant factor behind the 1976 riots. As such, Alexandra Uplift should be seen as a reformist response catering to middle class elements already domiciled in the urban area. While the campaign itself cannot be criticised, it needs to be pointed out that both in terms of motivation and effect Alexandra Uplift and other similar campaigns conducted by the Urban Foundation and endorsed by the English-language press, had much in common with Nationalist Government policy: namely, the creation and stabilisation of a broadly based black middle class to fulfill the needs of the commercial and manufacturing sectors[67].

The structural causes of the conditions of poverty are seldom probed, and the plight of destitute urban blacks has been treated in a humanist and piecemeal fashion, although this does not necessarily indicate that all reporters are unaware of structural processes behind black poverty. In addition to the common sense of newsworthiness which dictates that events are of greater importance than processes, there are 'human interest' stories. These are seen to operate outside ideology. One journalist explained:

> There is certainly in the press a sort of press ideology, if you like, an ideology of what is news and what isn't. And in many ways, not on a political or social level, simply on an empirical level. People are only interested in reading so-called human interest. I can write a 1000 word treatise on the biggest pass-law crackdown in the history of mankind, and putting it in all sorts of perspectives, and using all sorts of hyperbole, and everyone at (the press) conference, everyone who runs the paper would be to-

tally bored by it. If I go down to the Black Sash office and produce two guys who've been endorsed out of the area and get two pictures of them, then they want to splash it all over the front page and put up posters about it. They argue that if you want people to identify with victims of things like these, then you've actually got to show them the victims, and have a tear-jerking story about how the guys got five kids to feed, and so on. That's perhaps where I mean inconsistency. If I write about a major structural development in labour, I have to hustle like mad to sell the story to them.

Rural Images: Disease, Drought and Disaster

Rural blacks are particularly neglected by the English-language media. The early 1980s, however, saw more reporting on the distressed conditions in the homelands. This increased attention may in part be due to the unprecedented scale of resettlement which the press was unable to ignore during this time. The sources of this information, paradoxically, emanate from the urban, rather than the rural areas. In the wake of large-scale displacement of people, chronic unemployment, the ubiquity of poverty and the high cost of living in the homelands, large numbers of people sought illegal accommodation in the cities. This situation gave rise to the burgeoning of squatter camps like Crossroads, Nyanga, Langa and the Winterveld. The fact that people were prepared to live under appalling conditions within these shanty towns was indicative of the conditions from which they had fled, and to which they feared to return. The existence of these camps was largely neglected by the press until the brutal police action at Crossroads and Nyanga, both on the outskirts of Cape Town. At the latter, the newsworthiness of the 'event' was enhanced by a tour of visibly emotional United States congressmen, reported in bold front page headlines[68].

Awareness of conditions in the homelands was further stimulated by several outbreaks of highly contagious diseases such as cholera and poliomyelitis during 1981/2. Such epidemics evoke an emotional response from white readers, especially when these infections can impinge on the (white) cities. Most reports concern themselves with particular events and news stories are triggered off by academic, official and authoritative sources like Parliament, conferences, recently published studies and homeland development corporations. However, this news decays fast and is eclipsed by news on the homelands which emphasizes questions of border reajustments, debt settlement, casinos, the construction of inappropriate development projects like international airports, excessive use of power by government officials and, to a lesser extent, resettlement — in other words, news which is perceived to have serious economic implications for the political economy. Certain types of news, like continued reports on disease, for example, are seen as a danger to dominant interests, particularly when they emanate from non-official sources. An example of direct State interference in the processes of news gathering and reporting concerns the poliomyelitis outbreak during the period August 1981 to May 1982. In July 1982, the *Rand Daily Mail* wrote: "The Department of Health has clamped down on publicity about poliomyelitis at the same time it blames the spread of the disease on complacency and ignorance"[69]. It is significant that in the three months prior to this editorial, the *Rand Daily Mail* had not published a single article on the outbreak. The tone of the editorial nevertheless indicates a sense of indignation at what is seen to be an infringement of press freedom.

Other attention-getting events include droughts, influx of refugees from neighbouring countries, white rural exoduses and the spectre of terrorist infiltration in the areas denuded of white farmers. All these 'events' trigger off a perception of an area to be investigated and it is only then that the press examines the conditions which have been extant all the time. The outbreak of poliomyelitis in the northern Transvaal rural areas in mid 1982, for example, was the impetus for a two-part investigation in KwaNdebele by *The Star*, entitled "The Cinderella Homeland"[70]. Not fortuitously, official estimates of the number of children affected by the disease, as well as an alarming appraisal by a university medical professor, pointing out that the notifiable cases were the "tip of the iceberg", were given considerable prominence. The leader article which coincided with the second instalment unwittingly identified the media's event-orientated interest in homeland conditions at the particular conjuncture in its headline: "Polio Reveals a Crisis Area"[71]. The ongoing structural causes behind this condition are telescoped into an event, that is, a 'crisis' happening *now*.

Five weeks later (3 August), *The Star* reported on the findings of a medical students' conference in Cape Town under the headline: "Ten a Day Die of TB Says Expert"[72]. Two days later (5 August) a report emanating from the same conference noted that "Resettlement (is) Blamed for Outbreak of TB"[73]. At the same time as the first report (3 August) was an article on page ten which pointed to the near starvation levels of income to be found in Lebowa and Venda[74]. Most of this article consisted of an interview with an official of the Lebowa Development Corporation who, despite evidence to the contrary, insisted on the development potential of this homeland region. A more penetrating appraisal of the situation appeared in the report on 5 August. This article, spread over two pages, investigated the "Generation Raised on Disease and Hunger". Researched by the newspaper's own staff, it uncovered the devastation in the northern homeland areas which manifested itself in malnutrition and polio. Once again, the leader article, entitled "SA's Third World" was concerned with the same issues[75]. These examples serve to show that reporting on conditions in the homelands is sporadic and comes in the wake of official and authoritative sources of information. Apart from the two clusters of interest in the homelands, only one other report on unemployment, which was gleaned entirely from the Annual Report of the Corporation for Economic Development, appeared in the two month sample of *The Star*[76]. Except for information emanating from Parliament, Government or official sources, the *Rand Daily Mail*'s coverage of homeland conditions was even more sparse during the same sample period.

In an interview with the authors in 1980 the editor of an English Sunday newspaper was asked about the lack of attention paid to conditions in the homelands. He denied that this news area had been neglected, but qualified his remarks by saying that it was relatively less important than the urban areas:

> ... because there are relatively fewer people there. I think our problems actually begin in the urban areas. Our problems are in Soweto, rather than with the underpaid farmhands. I would actually suggest that proportional to the importance in the scheme of things we devote too much space to underpaid farm workers, and semi-slave labour in rural areas. Not that I am saying it is unimportant[77].

In contrast, John Mattison takes a more critical approach to the function of the English press, reflecting that it "should be investigating the social and economic as well as the political effects of the homeland policy ... investigative reporting of this type is far too rarely presented"[78].

When considering the English press's coverage of the homeland areas it must, however, be borne in mind that such news gathering is achieved despite considerable constraints. There are few journalists located in the homeland regions and those who do venture into these remote areas have to contend with a lack of telephones, telex machines, slow postal services, poor roads, and so on. More serious, however, is the very real sense of non-co-operation and, in some cases, outright intimidation by the homeland authorities. One Umtata-based journalist describes the lengths to which the Transkei Government went to control what was written about that territory:

> There are always threats of detention. For instance, the first time I met George Matanzima (it was at the time Peter Honey was in detention), he said, 'You had better be careful, otherwise you will be in the same position that Peter Honey is'. About every fortnight the journalists are called in by Brigadier Ngceba (Chief of the Security Police) to discuss something or other: 'You must report favourably on what the Transkei Government is trying to do, it's in the interests of the people,' and so on. On specific reports, he calls them in regularly to chastise them. The other way they harness reporters is by using

them as state witnesses in political trials on the basis of reports that they write ... (when) journalists report speeches the Security Police use the report of the speech written by the journalist and turn the journalist into an informer. ... So it is not in the people's interest to talk[79].

Labour Reporting: Using the Gaps

Exceptions to the rule that newspapers report on events rather than processes do occur. This is extremely uneven, however, with some newspapers and individual reporters being more conscious of causal connections than others. The practice of labour reporting is one such exception. A Cape-based labour reporter interviewed was aware of the primacy of 'newsworthiness', but felt that labour reporters were, to some extent, exempt from strict newsroom pressures, because the editorial decision-makers were not entirely *au fait* with the labour situation. Managements were therefore unable to appreciate the extent to which labour reporters were unable to employ discursive practices to communicate the processes underlying an event. While obeying the dictum of quoting from authoritative sources like management, for example, they would attempt to put across the viewpoint of the workers as well:

> You have got to write it in (the newspaper's) paradigm. You have got to be helluva careful not to use words or phrases that you might think but to try to get other people to say them so that you can quote them[80].

As previously noted, the extent of awareness of the importance of these issues varies, both in individual reporters and newspapers: "The freedom to report from a class-based analysis also depends on the position that you get to in the newspaper and the sort of credibility you have got with the editor"[81]. Although labour reporters spearheaded process-oriented reporting in the decade following the mid-1970s, the closure of many newspapers in 1984 and 1985, the extended consumer boycotts, labour stayaways, and politicisation of trade union activity in the context of a press under seige may well see the demise of the labour beat as it developed in the decade prior to 1985. The first nail in the coffin of this beat came with the closure of the *Rand Daily Mail*; the second was the establishment of *Business Day*, which replaced it in April 1985. Phillip van Niekerk, the labour reporter for *Business Day*, resigned when his report of a massive Witwatersrand labour stay-away over the death in detention of Raditsela was replaced by a story playing down the stay-away. In an unrelated development, three reporters on *The Daily News* in Durban resigned over that newspaper's paltry coverage of the formation of the massive Congress of South African Trade Unions in late November 1985. While this paper has no labour beat as such, the issue was seen as a labour one.

While the Sunday or weekend press provides longer-term perspectives and overviews, only the *Weekly Mail*, established in April 1985, consistently offers process-oriented analysis, putting events into broader social and economic perspectives. Despite our basic argument that the commercial press is locked into serving capital in general, it should not be thought of as a monolithic body which forces an equal conformity on all journalistic practices. As an interviewee explained:

> I think one of the most important things about the newsroom is the contradictions of society which are reflected in the newsroom at all levels. Because there is an overriding view which the newspaper takes and overriding interests which they represent does not mean that there are not gaps in the newsroom to actually get other voices across and reflect other interests as well. The newsroom is just a bed of contradictions. The contradictions allow one to get one's stories in[82].

Usually, reporters who are assigned to a specific beat — for example, labour, education, crime, and so on — have far more autonomy than those who work within the general newsroom. However, this does not guarantee that journalists covering these beats have *carte blanche* to present their material in any way they please. An education reporter explains how her efforts at uncovering the structural ramifications of the De Lange Report into education were thwarted:

When the De Lange Report came out I was in touch with a lecturer at the University of Cape Town who had done extensive research — in fact he was employed to help De Lange and help the University to formulate its response to De Lange. He said that the Report was basically designed to streamline apartheid education. ... A lot of people were feeling that — educationists outside the mainstream, people in the townships, academics. I did the story. It was one that I pushed. It came in four or five days after I submitted it. It was cut fairly substantially and it was used very far back in the paper. It was never commented upon.

I am sure that other reporters did take that angle but I am aware of only one other, major, very well done story, criticising De Lange. It was published in the *Sunday Tribune*. This was a major document which was not given a proper airing because the newspaper was in favour, and the white Opposition was in favour of the Report[83].

Press reaction to the Volkskongres held in the wake of the De Lange Report and how the congress was designed to engineer consent for the recommendations of the Commission is dealt with in Chapter 5.

State Intervention and Harassment

It is our thesis that the English-language press does not provide a serious threat to the social and economic relations in South Africa. Nevertheless, its limited resistance to Government policy has met with fairly severe repression. State intervention into 'press freedom' correlates closely with the press's intermittent efforts to articulate the views of the black majority which are thought to be a challenge to the maintenance of stability in Southern Africa.

The *Rand Daily Mail* was traditionally considered the most 'liberal' of the English newspapers, and repeatedly came under attack from the Government for its defiant stand against the Nationalist regime. The occasional intensity of this conflict is shown in a front page article signed by the then editor, Laurence Gandar, entitled: "Take Care Mr Vorster"[84]. A continuous and acrimonious exchange between the *Rand Daily Mail* and the Government, mediated through the Afrikaans press, preceded strong Government action against the *Mail*. In July 1965, the *Mail* published a series of articles outlining the abuse of black prisoners, which sparked off demands for an immediate Government enquiry. The police responded by raiding the offices of the paper and confiscating further material. The informant on whose evidence the articles were largely based was immediately banned and charged with making false statements. He was found guilty under what some felt to be irregular court procedures. Gandar, together with the *Mail*'s reporter, Benjamin Pogrund, was accused of "Running a campaign to vilify the Prisons Department, of publishing one-sided reports, and of rejecting information favourable to the prisons"[85]. They were charged under the Prisons Act, and three years later found guilty. Although minimal penalties were imposed, the case was of great importance in clarifying the contradictions of a 'free' press in a repressive state. The crippling legal fees were certainly also a deterrent against further contentious stories[86].

A second important example concerns the *Daily Dispatch*. This newspaper's investigation into the death and detention of Steve Biko is well known, as is the subsequent banning and exile of its editor, Donald Woods. The action taken against Woods was far harsher than that imposed on Gandar, and was implemented without recourse to law. One reason for this, apart from the increased use of extra-judiciary methods with which 'State security' has been enforced during the last decade, was the growing influence of the *Daily Dispatch* as a black-orientated news medium. Writing in 1975, Potter noted that:

> it was not realised ... except by a few ... that the *Daily Dispatch* had, at the same time as the *Rand Daily Mail*, published the prison conditions articles which had had ... serious repercussions for the *Rand Daily Mail*. Like the *Rand Daily Mail*, the *Daily Dispatch* saw itself as a 'crusading newspaper', but unlike the *Rand Daily Mail*, the *Daily Dispatch* editor,

Donald Woods ... suffered few repercussions, mostly because the paper was so small[87].

Potter almost prophetically goes on to observe that: "On the other hand, attempts by the *Daily Dispatch* to increase its non-white readership in the Transkei are likely to make its policies more radical as well as to bring it under closer government surveillance"[88]. In an interview in 1976, Donald Woods claimed that the *Daily Dispatch* encouraged the expression of dissent in Black Consciousness groups in the hope that eventually their policies might be incorporated into the peaceful options open to all South Africans[89].

As Potter correctly foresaw, the *Daily Dispatch* did increase its circulation in the Transkei and Ciskei with a concomitant radicalisation of its political agenda. This expansion coincided with an undeclared state of emergency which had existed since June 1976 and which culminated on 19 October 1977 in the detention of numerous opponents of the government, along with the banning of sixteen organisations connected with Black Consciousness. Amongst these was the South African Students Organisation (SASO), whose president was Steve Biko, and the Union of Black Journalists[90]. On that date too, banning orders were issued on *World*, Donald Woods, and Beyers Naude of the Christian Institute, for their support of Biko and the Black Consciousness movement[91]. The editor of *World*, Percy Qoboza, was also detained. Subsequent to his release, Woods fled to London and later to the United States as a political refugee.

In the wake of Woods' departure, the *Daily Dispatch* toned down its political stance considerably. An Umtata-based journalist tells of his experiences as Transkei correspondent for the *Daily Dispatch* in the period following Woods' banning:

> On my appointment I was told that my function was to report news. News was defined more or less as utterances of the Transkei Cabinet, crime, Kei politics, the opening of agricultural schemes, hydroelectric projects, etc. which could fall into developmental coverage. I was told to write a favourable report, for instance, on the opening of an irrigation scheme which is a total disaster. We were

kept under very tight control because (the newspaper management) were afraid of being banned. They knew how sensitive a lot of issues were. A significant amount of the stuff that I wrote was spiked and most of the rest of it was doctored. Matanzima knew that the *Daily Dispatch* was afraid of being banned and this had the effect of self-censorship on the newspaper. Every day in Parliament, George Matanzima would say: 'The *Daily Dispatch* reporter sitting up there writing nonsense about us — we will ban the newspaper, we will detain you'[92].

Despite its attempts to comply with the requirements of the Transkei bureaucracy, the *Daily Dispatch* was banned in that territory in April 1980 for a period of three weeks following a report on the arrest of 200 people in the aftermath of an alleged assassination attempt of Kaiser Matanzima. That the banning order was of a temporary nature was due to the fact that the *Dispatch* was the only regionally circulated newspaper and its banning created a vacuum: Government tenders could not be publicised and there was no vehicle for the utterances of members of the Transkei Cabinet. On the other hand, the financial viability of the *Daily Dispatch* was threatened by a drop of approximately twenty per cent in circulation and by the loss of advertising revenue, particularly from Transkei Government offices[93].

Extras: 'Black' News in 'White' Newspapers

Five of the national daily and weekly newspapers — *The Star, Rand Daily Mail, Sunday Times, Daily Dispatch, Sunday Tribune, Sunday Star* and *Rapport* — carry (or carried) special supplements, generically known as Extras, aimed at black readers. The first newspaper to undertake this venture was the *Rand Daily Mail*. The genesis of the *Mail Extra* is informative.

During Benjamin Pogrund's time as African Affairs Reporter on the *Rand Daily Mail* prior to 1963, blacks were employed on a 'tip-off' basis only. In that year, the first black journalists, Laurence Mayekiso and Sidney Hope, were appointed. Gradually, the coverage of African affairs took on the format of *Township Mail*: "We used to do page 3. It began within the paper as ordinary news and later became a separate edition"[94].

The contradictions that were outlined earlier in our analysis of the English press were manifested here in the *Rand Daily Mail*: on the one hand it was a liberal and integrationist newspaper, on the other it presented segregated news. This is clear in its publication of a separate edition for blacks, as well as Pogrund's rationale explaining its existence: "Total integration is obviously desirable, but are our readerships ready for it?"[95].

Initially, the separate edition replaced the shares page with a full page of 'black' news. In all other respects, the newspaper remained identical to the Late Final edition. By 1970, this edition was selling approximately 20 000 copies a day and a small corps of black journalists had begun to form. The *Township Mail* was restructured and renamed *Rand Daily Mail Extra* in 1973. The front page of the 'white' Late Final was moved to the shares page and replaced with black-orientated news, as were the financial pages. More important, however, was the limited degree of autonomy assigned to the *Extra*, with a greater use of black reporters and photographers and the appointment of a black sub-editor. Nevertheless, the *Extra* remained a makeshift and disjointed publication. It was redesigned in 1979. At the time, editor Allister Sparks commented:

> It was not (previously) a comprehensive, fully adjusted edition of the paper. Black readers felt it was a second class paper. We are now replacing a number of pages, including two feature pages and two sports pages. Nothing is done on the cheap and it is now a full-blown edition change"[96].

Similarly, *The Star Africa Edition* replaced two or three pages of 'hard news' with pages carrying township, black show business and sports news.

The reaction to Extra editions by black readers is equivocal. Percy Qoboza, for instance, called the *Mail Extra* and, by implication, other special editions, a 'monumental insult' to blacks[97]. In an uncharacteristically perceptive editorial, *The Citizen*, which was never slow to denigrate the *Rand Daily Mail*, pointed to the dilemma facing the latter: "What is happening is that the *Mail* is already too black for white readers but not black enough for black readers". Furthermore, noted *The Citizen*:

> Black Consciousness leaders jibe at the idea of the *Mail* providing a special edition for blacks as if its main edition is not good enough for them. They feel that this is a kind of condescension, a form of discrimination, since it means that what is good enough to be printed in the *Mail Extra* is not necessarily good enough to be read by all the *Mail*'s readers including whites[98].

Any clash of ideals between the professedly non-racial standpoint of the *Rand Daily Mail* and the publication of the *Extra* edition is overcome by the very real financial benefits derived from it. Circulation had always been the prime factor behind the establishment of Extras; the *Sunday Times*, for example, launched an Extra edition to counteract the strong appeal among coloured readers of the *Rapport Ekstra*, which threatened its dominant position in the marketplace[99]. While the Extras may contribute to the Government's dislike of the more liberal newspapers, they have not been singled out for the same extremely authoritarian treatment as has been dispensed to newspapers wholly aimed at a black readership[100].

The Press War:
Aunty Argus' 'Orrible Appetite[101]

Argus made an unsuccessful attempt at buying a 65 per cent share of SAAN in 1978 which was prevented by an invocation of the Monopolies Act. From that time the Argus made slow, but effective incursions into the control of SAAN.

By 1981 Argus owned 39.9 percent of SAAN. Despite their strong interlinks the two groups struggled for dominance in the press market place from the early 1980s. The 'gentlemen's agreement' which had existed between them was that the morning and Sunday papers would be the ambit of SAAN, while Argus would be left to the evening weekly papers.

By 1983, three terrains in this 'war' could be identified:

first, clashes between the Saturday and Sunday papers; second, takeovers and consolidation; and third, diversification of interests.

"Sundays are no Longer SAAN Days"

The Durban based Argus-owned *Daily News* and the Johannesburg *Star* were the first evening papers to appear on Saturday mornings, with publications known as the 'Sunrise' editions. The former set itself against the *Natal Mercury*, while the latter took on both the *Rand Daily Mail* and Perskor's *The Citizen*. SAAN responded by cutting the Saturday price of the *Mail* to 10 cents and upgrading the paper, usually very thin on Saturdays. This boosted the latter's readership from 110 000 to 166 000 but cost the company R2 million extra in losses.

The *Sunrise Star* included a property tabloid which was aimed at siphoning off advertising from the *Sunday Express*, which had an almost total dominance of the estate agency market. In order to achieve this, massive discounts were offered on property advertismeents: "in a single morning the *Express* lost almost all of its property clients"[102].

SAAN challenged Allied Distribution's right to carry two morning newspapers (i.e. the *Mail* and the *Sunrise Star*) at the same time. When SAAN's court action against Allied failed, SAAN and Robinson (the publisher of the *Mercury*) set up their own distribution company the following year called Mercury Distribution.

The battle for the marketplace intensified when Argus launched a Sunday edition of *The Star* in October 1983. This newspaper broke the dominance of the *Sunday Times* in the employment advertising market in the Witwatersrand area. *The Journalist* expressed the opinion that "This Press War is not really about editorial at all. It is a war of the advertising departments and the better sales staff and distribution teams will win"[103] SAAN reacted by lavishing the *Express* — the forgotten poor sister of the *Sunday Times* — with cash "for the first time in its history"[104]. The *Express* had protected the *Sunday Times* from further Sunday competition, and now it functioned as a buffer between the *Sunday Star* and the

Sunday Times, in an attempt to prevent the former stealing advertisements from the latter. This effort was wasted, however, as it came AFTER *The Star* had already won over the property advertisers.

The *Express* was relaunched in a new larger format but was unable to re-establish its place in the market. It did not reclaim the property market advertising lost to the *Sunday Star* and a survey indicated that the paper had cavalierly done away with one of its major attractions: its tabloid format. With the closure of the *Mail* in April 1985, the *Express* merged with *The Sunday Star* which took over some of its staff as well. Despite this, more than a hundred of the country's best journalists found themselves unemployed.

Centralisation and Control

In the two year expansion from 1979 to 1981, Argus made inroads into the country and suburban press, free sheets and jobbing printing. In December 1979, it bought a substantial share of Caxton Press, a profitable Johannesburg printing house, specialising in knock-'n-drop suburban weeklies. At that time Caxton published eleven free sheets with a combined circulation of 250 000. Argus and Caxton expanded their partnership by buying the glossy black magazine, *Pace*, the 'upmarket' *Style*, the pop magazine *Top Forty* and *South Coast Sun*. During the following two years they acquired a half share in Hortors, controllers of some of the biggest printing works in the country. Argus also bought various regional papers including the lucrative *Highway Mail* and other free sheets.

SAAN acquired a 100 percent shareholding of the *E P Herald* and *Eastern Cape Post*, both Port Elizabeth newspapers, through the formation of Eastern Province newspapers, a wholly owned subsidiary directly incorporated into SAAN in 1984.

In September 1984 the Bailey Trust sold its shares in SAAN to Johannesburg Consolidated Investments (JCI), an Anglo American subsidiary mining company which had considerable holdings in the Argus. SAAN informed its staff that the shares were in "friendly hands", ignoring the consequences of a concentration of ownership and control. Gordon Waddell, chairman of JCI, stated that the war between SAAN and Argus had to stop, that joint cooperation between regional papers was necessary, that competition for the same markets with the similar 'broad sweep' of news was not viable. It is not known, though there has been considerable speculation, what part the Argus company as a major shareholder played in the eventual decision to close the three SAAN newspapers[105].

In October 1985 Argus took effective control of the *Natal Mercury* by acquiring a 55 percent share of the newly formed Natal Newspapers. Robinson retained 30 percent and editorial control, leaving SAAN with 15 percent. This was done to 'save' the *Mercury* from extinction and, reportedly, to prevent the possibility of asset-stripping on *The Mercury*. The government, however, was again perturbed at the takeover[106].

A precursor to further mergers can be found in the 'rationalisation' talks between the Argus and SAAN relating to printing in Cape Town and the Transvaal during the latter half of 1985. As has been their consistent policy SAAN denied speculation of a merger, but given their previous track record, such a possibility is not unlikely. While all the signs indicate "that in a few years Argus will control the English-speaking commercial press, either through the effective destruction of SAAN, or through greater control of it"[107], the managing directors of both SAAN and Argus "denied that a full merger of the two companies is in the pipeline ... at least in the short term"[108].

Diversification into broadcasting and information

The move by newspapers into broadcasting and the information industry is a worldwide phenomenon. In South Africa, Argus led the way with investments in film production, strengthening its holdings in CNA-Gallo and purchasing a half share of INFO, a computer based data service. INFO has negotiated with the SA Press Association (SAPA) for its supply of news and hopes to make this available via telephone and eventually through television screens.

All the newspaper groups bought shares in Bop-TV in 1982 which is broadcast in English and Tswana to Tswana speaking areas in the Witwatersrand. Despite SABC-TV attempts at jamming the blanket reception of this signal, spillage into white areas does occur, bumping up the mean income of the ratings.

Subscription television (STV) is to be launched in the middle of 1987 in South Africa as a whole. The joint shareholding consortium, M-NET, is made up of Nasionale Pers, SAAN, Argus and Perskor (18 percent each) and the Natal Witness and Daily Dispatch (1.75 percent each). In July 1985, the consortium relinquished 30 percent of its shares to the SABC in exchange for 30 percent of the advertising revenue of TV4. While the SABC gets 30 percent of both subscription fees and advertising revenue of STV, M-NET does not receive a proportional income from SABC licences[109]. The timing of the announcement, two days after the closure of the *Rand Daily Mail*, *Sunday Express* and *Soweto News* is surely more than coincidence, a point that will be developed in the next section.

The Demise of the *Rand Daily Mail*: A Lesson for the Marketplace?

Of all the English-language newspapers, the *Rand Daily Mail* had the strongest reputation as a 'liberal' mouthpiece. Under the editorship of Lawrence Gandar from 1957, it became the principal voice of dissent among the country's major publications[110]. This in turn attracted a full frontal attack from the state:

> ... ceaseless, often vicious, government propaganda began moulding white public opinion to accept that the English-language press in general, and the *Rand Daily Mail* in particular, by championing the cause of blacks ... was endangering the security of the whites[111].

The SAAN board of directors in a tactical move to placate government hostility sacked Gandar in 1966, replacing him with Raymond Louw. Louw followed the same pioneering editorial policies and he too was relieved of his post in 1977. His successor, Alister Sparks, himself a liberal, was dismissed in 1981. While Sparks' ability as a writer and political analyst were never in doubt, "senior men in SAAN's hierarchy believed Mr Sparks's style of making writing a priority meant many administrative chores tended to be pushed aside"[112].

The profitability of the *Rand Daily Mail* was given a huge boost in 1976 when it was able to take advantage of its large black editorial staff to cover the 1976 Soweto disturbances more effectively than its opposition. This rise in circulation occurred in the face of the introduction of broadcast television for the first time to South Africa. From 1977, when Sparks was brought in, however, circulation figures fell. Despite the fall in *The Citizen's* readership following the Information 'scandal', the *Mail's* circulation only improved with the introduction of a computerised racing guide at the end of 1978. In July the following year, a price hike to 15 cents started a downward trend, which was exacerbated by a further increase of 10 cents to 25 cents in June 1980, making the *Rand Daily Mail* the most expensive daily in the country. Sales plummeted to 100 000, but picked up slightly after July 1980.

SAAN, in a desperate effort to turn around the financial affairs of the *Mail*, appointed Tertius Myburgh as editor of both the *Rand Daily Mail* and *Sunday Times* with Ken Owen as managing editor of the former. As far back as 1981, rumours concerning the future of the *Mail* were rife. Among the possibilities discussed in the newsrooms — if not the board rooms — was the imminent closure of the *Mail*, the changing of the *Mail* to a morning financial, becoming a newspaper aimed at an entirely black readership or even being changed into a central subbing depot for coastal newspapers[113].

The new partnership of Myburgh and Owen lasted only eight months before it gave way to the editorship of the paper by Rex Gibson, previously editor of the *Sunday Express*. *The Journalist* summed the situation up thus: "A source close to the top of the RDM put its crisis in a nutshell — a defeated staff working for a defeated paper in a defeated corporation"[114].

SAAN, however, was publically more optimistic. In August 1983 managing director Clive Kinsley announced that although the *Rand Daily Mail* had lost substantial sums of money the SAAN board stated "quite clearly that closure of the *Mail* was not an option it will consider. Nor will the board allow the character of the newspaper to be changed"[115]. A plan for revamping the *Mail* included the supplement named *Business Day* which appeared from 4 October 1983. This revitalisation followed an in-depth investigation into the future of the *Mail* by two consultants from the London based *Financial Times* who suggested that apart from immediate steps to restructure management and marketing strategies, the *Mail* should adapt the paper to a dual market: businessmen and blacks, thus exploiting the newspaper's inherent strengths.

In spite of the five years of crisis management of the paper the *Rand Daily Mail* ceased publication on 30 April 1985. In its place appeared *Business Day*, upgraded as a fully fledged financial daily, and aimed at the more prosperous section of the *Mail's* readership equation. The demise of the *Rand Daily Mail* on 30 April 1985 was not unexpected. Rumours of the shutdown, and/or transformation to a financial daily had been persistent for the previous four years. The reasons advanced by SAAN were that the group as a whole was in financial difficulty, and that the *Rand Daily Mail* had accumulated a R45 million loss over the previous ten years. Independent auditors, hired by the South African Society of Journalists (SASJ) confirmed SAAN's losses, but reported that "management incompetence is largely responsible for the mess the company finds itself in at the moment"[116]. A remarkable turnabout for a company which only a few years previously had been placed in the top ten best run companies. The SASJ, in an editorial in *The Journalist* suggested that at least part of the loss was incurred in "fighting the phoney Press War" between SAAN and Argus.

A more immediate cause of the closure was the non acceptance of the *Rand Daily Mail* by the 'market'. This statement needs to be carefully qualified. The *Financial*

Times survey found from 1976 to 1983, the ratio of black readers to white had shifted from 43:57 to 72:28 percent. Koos Roelofse, in an argument drawing on the model of 'stages of mass media development' which underlies the racist discourse of the South African advertising industry, argued that the *Mail* had "two markets", and dominance of neither[117]. He based this conclusion on the dualistic assumption that the white press "is already in the Modern phase, with saturated mass publications, decreasing readership and an increasing commitment to specialisation and diversification", while "black publications are in the Transitional phase, with a great potential for mass publications due mainly to increasing literacy and rising levels of income". The *Mail*, he argued "had positioned itself in a no-man's-land between a sophisticated white market and a developing black one"[118]. Ideology too, played a significant part. To dismiss cavalierly as does Roelofse, Rex Gibson's comment made to *Die Burger*[119] that the government was responsible for the demise of the *Mail* as an "emotional outburst in the place of rational reflection", and posit instead a reductionist "curve of stages of media development" is naive. This kind of analysis not only disregards contextual processes, but it operates from ideological assumptions which take the discourse of 'the Market' at face value[120].

The split in readership lay at the heart of the *Mail's* dilemma. Advertisers had not been prepared to accept the changing readership profile of the *Mail* despite SAAN's attempt to persuade them of the logic of class — rather than race — targeted marketing strategies. In expanding its readership, the *Rand Daily Mail* was not necessarily obeying the dictates of the 'free-enterprise market'. Indeed, at the time of the *Mail's* death the circulation was rising and advertising had improved by 24 per cent. Steven Friedman, a former labour journalist on the *Mail*, noted somewhat cynically: "If the Market killed it (the *Mail*) ... it was not because people didn't want the product but because certain types of people — richer and whiter people — didn't want it"[121]. The tone of Friedman's article, and others in the same issue of *The Journalist* suggested a conspiracy:

> ... the *Mail* and *Express* were not killed by the mar-

ket at all, but by something — or, to be more precise, some people — a great deal more visible and closer to the boardroom where the decision to kill it was made ... if (the paper) is attracting both (readers and advertisers), and is losing money, the fault may just lie with its managers — those who are responsible for making sure readership and advertising a paying proposition[122].

Former *Rand Daily Mail* political reporter Anton Harber took the analysis one step further:

... there can only be two reasons why they (SAAN) chose to throw the *Rand Daily Mail* title out of the window and start from scratch (with *Business Day*). First, they wanted to clear out the *Rand Daily Mail* staff and give the new *Business Day* editor, Ken Owen, a free hand to build up a staff from nothing.

The only other possible reason is to get rid of the political and journalistic tradition of the *Rand Daily Mail*. Neither of these are economic reasons. Both point to a desire to get rid of the *Rand Daily Mail* tradition and form a more conservative newspaper[123].

Perhaps the most chilling observation on the closure of the *Mail* came from Professor John Dugard:

A bare few weeks after the decision of the SAAN board to close the *Mail* and the *Sunday Express* we ... are informed that the Government has granted a concession to a newspaper consortium — including SAAN — to operate TV5 — the new subscription service.

It is surely asking too much of the South African public not to connect these two events. Indeed everything now falls neatly into place. It seems more than probable that the *Mail* and the *Sunday Express* were the price that SAAN had to pay for inclusion in the TV5 consortium.

... This conclusion is supported by the State President's outburst of pleasure over the closure of the *Mail*.

This link would also explain the decision of the SAAN board to close its most anti-Government newspapers in Johannesburg and continue with the *Sunday Times* and *Financial Mail* which are both close in thinking to the new alliance between big business and Government ... the reason for the closure of the *Mail* and *Express* is now out in the open. And we, the South African public, know how far the new alliance between big business and Government is prepared to go[124].

The significance of the agreement between the newspaper groups and the SABC lies not only the the more-than-symbolic burying of the hatchet between the English and Afrikaans press groups (indeed between the two Afrikaans press groups themselves) but also marks the alliance of the English press with the SABC. Noted *The Weekly Mail*, "The newspaper industry's spirited criticism of the SABC has suddenly been stilled"[125]. More significant still is that the press groups are prevented by the SABC from providing news or public affairs reporting on STV. This component will be retained exclusively by the SABC. This emasculation of the press' *raison d'etre* would seem to be the first coherent attempt on the part of the state to induce what it calls 'consensus journalism' and 'broader South Africanism'.

In assessing the role of 'the Market', mismanagement and boardroom manoeuvres in the death of the *Rand Daily Mail*, the *Sunday Express*, the *Soweto News* (all SAAN papers) and *The Herald* and *The Friend* (Argus), sight should not be lost of the ideological implications that were an inevitable by-product of economic imperatives. Afrikaans and English dominated capital has increasingly merged over the previous decade because of adjustments occurring in the political economy and a commitment to 'free enterprise' by the Botha administration since the Carlton Centre conference held in November 1979. English reformist capital had been overtaken by the state's so-called 'new dispensation'. It is not insignificant that the *Mail* and *Express* were the only two white-oriented Transvaal newspapers which had played a key role in the Information Scandal expose and had advocated a "No" vote in the 1984 referendum on the introduction of a tricameral parliament. English dominated capital appeared no longer to need newspapers which were hypercritical of the state acting on its behalf. As the chairman of JCI, Gordon Waddell, put it to Pat Sidley, President of the SASJ: "Van Zyl (Slabbert, then leader of the PFP Opposition) and his friends in Cape Town are more concerned about the politics. In this office, Ma'am, we're concerned about the bottom line"[126].

The closure of the SAAN papers occurred against growing emphasis from the government on the discourse of 'consensus journalism'. The SASJ, in a message to the SAAN board predicting the closure of the *Mail* and *Express* pointed out that ...

> In an era when the present Government is requiring of journalists an anathema called 'consensus journalism', we are particularly fearful that this may come about, not because of Government pressure, but because of shareholders and directors reacting rashly to economic pressure — leading to decisions which silence voices of protest in their publications[127].

Paradoxically, barely a few months after the demise of the *Mail* and *Sunday Express*, even the more conservative elements of the English press, *Business Day*, *Sunday Times*, *Financial Mail* and *Finance Week*, were castigating the government in the wake of the appalling economic consequences of the declaration of the State of Emergency. Within hours of the State President's 'Rubicon' speech telecast to the world on 17 August 1985, the Rand dropped drastically, the international disinvestment campaign intensified, and international banks foreclosed on international loans, placing South Africa in its worst financial crisis ever. The English press, particularly *The Cape Times*, *The Sunday Tribune*, *The Star* and *Sunday Star*, *City Press* and *The Weekly Mail*, exposed a government that had lost control of its reform programme, and worse still, its police and security forces. The *Mail* had been killed, but many of the conditions it had reported on over the decades could not be wished away so easily. The sheer extent of the crisis of hegemony experienced by the government and the intensifying threat by the African National Congress and internal opponents of apartheid kept the events at the forefront of press exposure. Where the *Mail* sought to expose oppressive conditions hidden from the public view, the more conservative English-language press that remained was again fighting a battle on behalf of capital in general as the state seemed to have abrogated this task by enacting reform too late and too slowly. Despite this new found criticism, it is probably fair to say that the cutting edge of English language journalism was lost with the death of the *Mail*. The surviving newspapers relied increasingly on official and authoritative sources, largely ignoring eye-witness accounts which contradicted official police reports on disturbances, amongst other things[128]. As ex *Rand Daily Mail* political reporter Anton Harber put it, "If nothing else, the *Rand Daily Mail* ensured that its competition could not totally ignore these areas. Now that it has disappeared as competition, there is no reason why other newspapers should worry about missing such stories"[129].

The *rapprochement* that developed between the press groups in the early part of 1985 is indicated by the appearance of *Positive Prospects*, a once-off supplement published by the Argus group in April which set out to "restore the balance" (of reporting on unrest). *Positive Prospects* was sponsored by 18 companies offering a glowing description of South Africa's future potential. Clearly aimed at reassuring foreign and local investors, the publication was a mere hiccup in the chaos that was beginning to unfold. This was followed by Nasionale Pers's *City Press Prospects*, a fortnightly supplement first published on August 18. Entirely aimed at a black readership, it was "specifically designed to bring our people and the business community closer together ... It contains many stories about the opportunities people can take advantage of, as well as stories of successful people".

Politics and the Afrikaans Press

A thorough going analysis of the Afrikaans press has yet to be published. In the section which follows we offer a few tentative pointers in this direction. We do not claim that our observations are in any way definitive, but in the absence of a more comprehensive historical critical work they are offered to provide a context against which Chapter 4 can be read.

Contrary to popular belief among English-speaking South Africans and some scholars of the media, the Afrikaans press is not a monolithic undifferentiated publicity arm of the National Party. Before South Africa became a Republic, the Afrikaans press was, it is true, loath to criticise the policies and direction of the party to which it owed its allegiance. This press then saw itself as a specialist extension of the National Party's communication system: "Hence government's messages were directed primarily and often exclusively to the 'Volk' whose interests it represented and to whom it was responsible"[130].

All the major Afrikaans newspapers were founded with the aim of propagating the views of various precursors and branches of the National Party, including the Afrikaner Party. Unlike the English press, which was financed with corporate capital[131], the capitalisation of the Afrikaans newspapers was initially made possible by a large number of small investors, each of whom was personally approached in order to raise the necessary finance. By 1953, for example, *Die Burger* was registered in the names of 3 239 shareholders. The largest of these was Santam/Sanlam, a consortium of Cape-based Afrikaner enterprises which was created with the intention of consolidating small capital[132]. Afrikaanse Pers was also financed largely through the supporters of the National Party in the Transvaal, as well as by direct sponsorship from the Party itself[133]. Wepener, for example, states:

... no Afrikaans newspaper of importance was started merely as a commercial venture. Especially the earlier Afrikaans newspapers were all pioneer organs designed to promote certain ideas and today they are still closely tied to the cultural and political life of the Afrikaner. Therefore, don't be surprised that the Afrikaans newspapers are today still bound to the National Party. The very circumstances of their origin brought this about[134].

By 1948 the Afrikaans press had achieved its greatest ambition and the next ten years were spent in the consolidation of the Afrikaner power base. While the

1,40%	Afrikaanse Persfonds	
7,60%	S A Mutual	
7,92%	Liberty Life	
2,10%	Zylvos Edms Bpk	
1,30%	Fairheads Nominees	
2,20%	W & E Barclay	
11,40%	Anglo American	
	Standard Bank (Tvl)	
	(Pty) Ltd (JCI)	
	Barclays National Nominees	
11,69%	Sanlam	
	Mercabank	7,30%
	Murray & Roberts	4,39%

Vaderland Beleggings

22,00%	Bonuskor	
14,78%	Afrikaanse Pers	
	Perskor Nominees	5,00%
	Afrikaanse Persfonds	4,68%
	Afrikaanse Pers (Pty) Ltd	4,00%
	Afrikaanse Persfondsraad	1,19%
9,27%	National Party of Transvaal	
4,21%	Volkskas Trust	2,13%
	Volkskas Pension	2,08%
4,00%	Koopkrag Bpk	
3,38%	Christiaan de Wet Fonds	

Dagbreek Trust Bpk

17,60%	Sanlam	
40,40%	Federale Volks Beleggings Bpk	12,10%
	Federale Seleksies Bpk	12,10%
	Nasionale Persfonds	6,00%
	Jan Marais Nasionale Fonds	3,50%
	Metropolitan Homes Trust	5,20%
	Assura Bpk	1,50%

Nasionale Pers Bpk
Beeld, Die Burger, Die Volksblad, City Press, Seipone, Fair Lady, Huisgenoot, Cosmopolitan, Landbouweekblad, Carleton and Fochville Herald, Potchefstroom Herald, Vaalweekblad, Wes Transvaal en OFS Herald, Ooste Standaard, etc.

43,60%	Vaderland Beleggings
14,00%	Dagbreek Trust
4,60%	Murray and Roberts
1,60%	Nedbank Nominees (Sage Holdings)
2,30%	S A Mutual
2,00%	Barclays National Nominees (Anglo American)
2,30%	Liberty Life
1,40%	Volkskas Nominees

Die Afrikaanse Pers (1962) Bpk
Trading as PERSKOR
Transvaler, Vaderland, Rapport, The Citizen, Imvo, Zabantufundu, Tempo, Eastern Transvaal Advertiser, Wes Transvaal Rekord, Noord Transvaal Rekord, Middelburg Observer, Witbank News, Vista, etc.

Trading as Republican Press (wholly owned subsidiary)
Scope, Thandi, Bona, Rooi Rose, Your Family, Family Radio and TV, Radio en TV Dagboek, Farmers' Weekly, Garden and Home, Living and Loving, Femina, 14 picture comics, etc.

National Party was in opposition it could count on the uncritical support of the Afrikaans press since there existed a symbiotic relationship between the two. This is illustrated by the identification of the National Party with *Die Burger* during the editorship of Dr D F Malan, who was at the time the leader of the Cape National Party. Reminiscing over Dr Malan's seeming inability to distinguish his role of editor from that of prime minister, Weber recalls that:

> *Die Burger* remained the familiar and trusted advisor of Dr Malan, to the extent that a contemporary Minister once complained, probably not without good reason, that at the *Burger* we sometimes knew more of Dr Malan's plans than some of his cabinet![135]

By the late 1950s, however, it was clear that there were differences between an unequivocal support for an entrenched Government and the building up of a cultural entity under perceived attack. For the first time, elements of the Afrikaans press were prepared to challenge the leadership of the National Party. It should, however, be stressed that any opposition to the National Party by an Afrikaans newspaper has revolved around the *application* of apartheid policy rather than the principles involved.

A highly significant instance concerned *Die Burger*'s campaign for "The principle ... that Coloured voters must be permitted to elect white or brown members"[136]. During the second half of 1960, *Die Burger* carried many articles presenting the case for the reappraisal of Coloured policy. Prime Minister Verwoerd's position was voiced repeatedly through the *Transvaler* (which he had previously edited) and centred on the notion that coloured representation was the thin end of the wedge and a dangerous step in the direction of integration, leading to the engulfing and destruction of whites. The public debate between these two newspapers and other prominent Nationalist figures represented the first open argument in the National Party for more than thirty years.

In December of that year, Verwoerd announced a 'New Deal' for the Coloureds, which consisted of the appointment of a Minister of Coloured Affairs, the extension of the Coloured Council and other economic and educational programmes. The subsequent inability of the National Party to come to terms with the so-called 'Coloured Question' is evident in the rejection by coloureds of surrogate representation. *Die Burger* surrendered unconditionally, although it could not hide its bitterness and disappointment. Yet at no stage of this protracted and unprecedented debate did *Die Burger* envisage its suggestions as being counter to the broad aims of apartheid.

Like the SABC news commentaries, Afrikaans newspapers act both as reporters of Government policy and as harbingers of change and adaptation. In this connection, Domisse notes:

> Over the years the best Afrikaans newspapers have frequently acted as scouts and pathfinders toward new policies. In this they are often ahead of the government. *Die Burger* foretold the new policy toward blacks in the fifties, the run-up to the Republic, and the movement toward equality in human relations in the sixties. The current official policy of 'moving away from discrimination' was foreshadowed nearly twenty years ago when *Die Burger* showed severe impatience with 'petty apartheid'. Newspapers took the lead in the battle against the right-wing Hertzogites in the late sixties. More recently the trend-setting newspapers such as *Beeld, Die Transvaler, Rapport* and *Die Burger* are often far ahead of the government concerning elimination of racial discrimination, consolidation and development of the black homelands, accommodation of the coloureds and Indians, home rule for urban blacks, and better living conditions and economic opportunities for them. The views of these papers on differentiation and multi-nationalism are aimed at getting the support of a majority of moderates of all groups[137].

Despite the rhetoric of verligtheid[138], Dr Willem de Klerk, editor of *Rapport*, former editor of *Die Transvaler*, and an important figure in the formulation of National Party discourse noted that:

> The Afrikaans newspapers do ... to a greater or lesser degree — set their face against a politics of total

integration. The concept of separate development as a *leitmotif* for our politics still remains a prominent policy of the Afrikaans press. This appears in the strong emphasis placed on self-determination, an own living space for each group, and an own education[139].

As is well known, the problem of each group having its 'own living space' sees its fulfillment in the homeland areas and the loss of South African citizenship for the majority of the country's inhabitants. 'Self-determination' has been translated into a series of proxy representations in the form of the now largely defunct urban councils, management committees and homeland governments. For advocates of the 'willed' National Party ideology, these institutions represent 'reform': "The way in which the Afrikaans press currently supports the reformist path comes over clearly in its advocacy of the idea of bringing together coloureds, Indians and whites within one state, with a mixed government based on separate local authorities"[140].

De Klerk goes on to describe the three levels on which the Afrikaans press contributes to "the cause of reform": first is its publication of "unvarnished statements of fact regarding our political situation". He points to the "heavy ... emphasis ... on the reality of numbers, economic demands and international involvement", which through prominent and consistent publication attune Afrikaners to responsible choices that will help solve problems rather than be ideologically determined[141]. This reformist discourse is being entrenched through what Therborn refers to as 'shielding', that is, the repetition of the preferred discourse to the exclusion of alternative formulations. This is apparent from de Klerk's second point that "there is a well-nigh intolerant approach to the *verkrampte* attitude". Verkramptes have been largely excluded from the mainstream of newspaper discourse and are reported as a threat to nation and society.

The Afrikaans press succeeds in projecting *verligtheid* as the image of the responsible Afrikaner and *verkramptheid* as the deviant, the dubious and the self-deceptive, even the stupid. *Verligtheid* has obtained an party' ('money party') and the ascendancy of reformist discourse within the Party is clearly indicated by Jooste. Though he insists that *Die Patriot* is not simply 'an official Party mouthpiece', Jooste does avow that "*Die Patriot* supports the Conservative Party as the most effective political organisation in the entire conservative movement"[144].

Traditionally, a division has existed between the Cape and Transvaal arms of the National Party, with the former being more verlig than the latter. Afrikaans newspapers have long been the site of struggle between the two major divisions, with Nasionale Pers supporting the Cape National Party and Perskor the Transvaal National Party. The present struggle dates as far back as the premiership of Verwoerd, who was adamantly opposed to the establishment of a Nasionale Pers newspaper in the Transvaal, hitherto the stronghold of the more conservative Perskor Group. The suggestion emanated from P W Botha, then a director of Nasionale Pers, and Fanie Botha, previously a journalist with Nasionale Pers and later Minister of Labour. The Bothas' idea was blocked, however, since at that stage they did not have the political clout to carry the suggestion through.

When Vorster became prime minister, the establishment of a Nasionale Pers newspaper in the Transvaal was again mooted, while Connie Mulder[145], a director of Perskor, was in favour of launching an English-language newspaper to compete with SAAN and Argus. This latter proposal was not acceptable to Nasionale Pers and was not pursued until the setting up of *The Citizen* by the Government under a front company. Vorster's compromise proposal was to allow for the establishment of a Nasionale Pers newspaper in Pretoria, and for Perskor to cease publication of its two dailies in that city, *Hoofstad* and *Oggendblad*[146]. This proposal was not acceptable to Perskor either. Nevertheless, Nasionale Pers moved into Johannesburg, setting up *Beeld* in 1965. As a result, the site of conflict was extended from the state to include the two newspaper corporations as well.

In the ensuing struggle for circulation and, in order to ensure advertising revenue and viability, Nasionale Pers heavily subsidised its new newspaper. Perskor responded

image of decency, respect and credibility, particul
the Afrikaans press.

This interpenetration of the sites of discursive
tion is a theme which is further explored by Johar
in his study on press reactions to the Bloen
Volkskongres, and Hayman and Tomaselli's cha
the South African Broadcasting Corporation in V(
Suffice to say at this point that the Afrikaans pr
the forefront of articulating a reformist strateg
has brought it into conflict with right-wing el
who are frustrated by their exclusion from a n
communicating their preferred discourse.

The early 1980s saw a crisis in the Nationa
which culminated in the breakaway of the right
form the Conservative Party in 1982. This new
grouping, and the previously constituted H
Nasionale Party, have been largely dependent o
conservative non-commercial publications for e:
The lack of a widely distributed medium throug
to articulate their viewpoint has been a considera
drance in the propagation of extreme right-wing
Writing shortly before his dismissal as editor
Transvaler, Dr Willem de Klerk suggested that i

> ... doubtful that a fully-fledged daily newspape
> be launched by the Treurnicht/Marais camp.
> an undertaking is too expensive and risky as a
> vestment. Without the financial and other su
> of extensive interests that Perskor and Nasi
> Pers enjoy, such a newspaper would face a dif
> time. Those conservative Afrikaners are thei
> likely to remain dependent on propaganda s
> like *Die Afrikaner* and *Die Patriot* — unle
> course, they could infiltrate and hijack one (
> proper newspapers in the Afrikaans field[142].

Both 'sheets' folded after a short while.

Writing at the same time, Christoffel Jooste, tl
of *Die Patriot*, avers that his paper "was started t
vacuum which has been left in Afrikanerdom's
bulwark by the defection to liberalism of]
Afrikaner's) own moneyed elite, his press, and
ernment"[143]. The mistrust of the National Party a

with the appointment of more verlig editors in the persons of Dr Willem de Klerk to the *Transvaler* and Dr P G du Plessis to *Hoofstad*. Thus the introduction of the Nasionale Pers newspaper, backed by the traditionally more enlightened Cape wing of the National Party and following a self-consciously reformist policy, led to a parallel — if temporary — liberalisation of the opposition Perskor newspapers. With the dismissal of De Klerk it appears that Perskor has returned to its old strategy of backing the more conservative elements of Afrikanerdom.

In an open letter to De Klerk in the *Sunday Tribune*, Alister Sparks, fired from the *Rand Daily Mail* in 1981, drew attention to the similarities of their respective dismissals:

> Two newspapers losing money in a hopelessly overtraded market where the losses all round are immense, but in these cases aggravated by years of erratic and unimaginative management.
>
> Nasionale Pers is much more slickly run than Perskor in every managerial respect, just as Argus is more competent than SAAN[147].

The change in the distributions of the two major groups, Nasionale Pers and Perskor, is in part a result of the changing structure of ownership and control, with a concomitant dilution of regional loyalty. By 1980, the shareholding of the Afrikaans press was characterised by a consolidation under the aegis of large-scale pension funds. It is particularly noteworthy that many of the traditionally 'English' financing and pension funds have bought into the conservative Afrikaanse Pers (which includes Perskor) and Vaderland Beleggings. These two corporations together own *Die Transvaler*, *Oggendblad*, *Rapport* (fifty percent share with Nasionale Pers) and *Die Vaderland*. The major shareholder of the competing Nasionale Pers, which owns *Beeld*, *Die Burger* and *Volksblad*, is Sanlam.

Until the publication of Robin McGregor's *Who Owns Whom in the Newspaper Industry*, which appeared at the same time as the second Steyn Commission Report, it was supposed that only the SAAN and Argus Companies were owned by large-scale capital. McGregor's revelations to the contrary were not anticipated by the Steyn Commission, whose major recommendation — that no single investor be allowed to own more than one per cent of the total shareholding of any particular newspaper — was deflated almost immediately. The Commission's apparent objective was to render impotent the Anglo American Corporation's indirect proprietorship (and suspected control) of SAAN and Argus. This proposal would have opened the possibility of penetration by Afrikaner capital into the English press[148]. It appears that, realising the complications that this suggestion would have for the Afrikaans press, the Government judiciously ignored this recommendation.

Although we have argued that the English press indirectly supports the capitalist relations of production on which apartheid is based, the Steyn Commission and the Afrikaans press take a different view. While the major newspapers within the Afrikaans press may be described as reformist, and perhaps even 'liberal'[149], commentators within the Afrikaner establishment are insistent on their sense of 'responsibility' which they see as being of a higher order than that of their English-language counterparts. This is the implicit message behind Arnold de Beer's statement that:

> There is, however, one point of difference between the Afrikaans press and a few English newspapers in this country. The Afrikaans press has always made it clear that change in South Africa should not occur through revolt, violence or revolution and that this should be avoided and prevented at all costs[150].

This implied correlation of the English press with "revolt, violence or revolution" is made even more strongly by De Klerk, who notes that the English dailies with their "great mass of black and brown readers" and their influence on the views on South Africa held by the "outside world", are encumbered with a serious responsibility in "the demand for Press patriotism". The emphasis and nuances of these newspapers, according to De Klerk, "unfortunately often give evidence of the opposite":

> In over-emphasising the negative aspects of South

Africa, with under-emphasis of the positive, I feel that they are often guilty in this respect. There is often a fanatical wilfulness, even a wantoness, to be found in their columns, a one-sidedness and venom that looks suspiciously like an internationally oriented attempt to destroy South Africa's delicate balance ...

What applies to the English press, applies as well to those newspapers which have blacks as their target market. With their kind of partisan politics, it is easy to overstep the mark and sow the seed of revolutionary agitation[151]

Emphasis on the 'positive' by the Afrikaans press results, however, in a totally skewed picture of repression in South Africa. One pertinent example relates to press reporting during the state of emergency in the latter half of 1985. A comparison of Sunday papers in particular shows an Afrikaans press in the form of *Rapport* which simply continued as if nothing was wrong with the country that a better 'media image' couldn't put right, blaming all of South Africa's ills on communists, agitators and misinformed international opinion. While *Rapport* was complaining that the police were powerless to act against unlawful elements destroying the township in the face of international opinion, the English press, particularly the *Sunday Tribune* and *Sunday Star* consistently drew attention to the excessive violence, torture and over-reaction of the part of the police in their brutal manner of restoring 'order' to the townships.

In summary, this section has concentrated upon the relationship between the Afrikaans press and the National Party. The emphasis should not obscure the press's importance in the reproduction of capital in general, and Afrikaner-based capital in particular. As was mentioned in Chapter 2, most critics tend to argue the distinction between emphasis on the economy (the English press) and ethnic concerns (the Afrikaans press)[152]. This argument is valid on a superficial level only, for we have shown that apartheid — the so-called ethnic rationale — has decided benefits for capital. Even the most sacrosanct of cultural values, Christian national education, has important economic implications. While not denying the importance of ideology and culture, the economy, as Althusser puts it, is determinant in the last instance.

The Legislation of Coercion and Consent

The harassment of both black and white oriented newspapers and their staffers has been the subject of numerous articles[153], few of which place this intimidation within the broad context of the State's reaction to resistance against it.

Our thesis that state opposition to English-language newspapers should be seen as a secondary consequence of the suppression of black opposition to apartheid is further supported by an overview of the main areas of legislation applied to the press. All the major laws curtailing the freedom of the press are also those which most effectively restrict the activities of black groups opposed to the Government. This thesis is not held by all commentators on the South African press. Barton, for example, writes of the National Party: "When that Government came to power in 1948, it had every intention of emasculating the English-language press, in the same way as it had just politically emasculated the English-speaking community"[154]. That it took so long to accomplish this is ascribed by Barton to the amateurishness of the new regime, unfamiliar with administrative procedures of government. In agreement with Barton is Joel Mervis, who sees the restrictions being extended to Afrikaans newspapers as well: "The irresistable truth is that any oppressive or restrictive action against one section of the press has direct repercussions on the freedom of every other section. And once the corrosive, undermining process begins, it cannot be halted"[155].

These viewpoints on the growing momentum of persecution applied to the English-language press neglect the wider ramifications of the legislation in question. They also miss the complex means by which an ideology is disseminated through the media. In contrast, we intend to demonstrate that the enactment of the 'minefield' of legislation alternates between moments of co-option, followed by coercion, as the Government tries to balance force with consent.

The first and broadest of the legislative acts to appear was the Suppression of Communism Act of 1950. This Act was instrumental in banning the left-wing newspaper, *The Guardian*, in 1952; its successor, *Spark*, in 1954, and its reappearance under the name *New Age* in 1962. Examples of other restrictive legislation are the Public Safety and Criminal Amendment Act of 1953, which was the direct result of the press's coverage of the 1952 Defiance Campaign; the Riotous Assemblies Act of 1956 and the General Law Amendment Act of 1962, which made it impossible for a newspaper to campaign against social inequalities in South Africa or to write anything that could be interpreted as inciting hostility between the various racial groups. The Prisons Act of 1959 arose directly from an article written in *Drum* which revealed the conditions of non-white prisoners in the Johannesburg Central Prison[156]. This Act formed the basis of charges against the *Rand Daily Mail* six years later. The Police Amendment Act was added in 1978, and was rationalised by *Beeld's* statement that "South Africa faced a total onslaught and it was necessary for the press to be disciplined".

In the wake of the Information Scandal, the Advocates General Bill was introduced in Parliament in 1979. It included a controversial section prohibiting the publication of articles concerned with public corruption and maladministration before the information had been vetted by an Advocate General. This Act arose out of the exposé by the English press of the Department of Information's illegal activities, including the state's attempted purchase of SAAN through Louis Luyt, the subsequent clandestine setting up of *The Citizen, Pace, Hit* and the attempted purchase of shares in foreign broadcasting and newspapers. Ironically, though this exposure totally discredited PW Botha's main rival for the Premiership, Connie Mulder, Botha pushed the Bill through Parliament in great haste. In an unprecedented development, the Afrikaans press stood firmly with the English press in opposing this section of the Bill. Faced with this united resistance to the restrictive measures, and the publicity given to its denunciation by the SABC Staff Association[157], the Bill was modified before being passed as law. In its final form, it prevents comment or reports on any matter formally under investigation by the Advocate General. Furthermore, this official may not be insulted, disparaged, nor may his investigation be anticipated in a manner calculated to influence his findings.

Opposition to the Advocate General Bill prompted an awareness of the need to create a climate of consent before introducing further restrictive legislation. This was the prime purpose of setting up the Steyn Commissions which reported in 1980 and 1982. In the wake of the second Report were three pieces of legislation which, together, provide a matrix of coercion under the guise of 'voluntary' censure. The first of these, the Internal Security Act (No 74 of 1982) prohibits the circulation and debate of ideas relating to alternative social, political and economic policies for South Africa. A second Act, the protection of Information Act (No 84 of 1982) repealed the old Official Secrets Act, to which numerous additional clauses had been added. These have been augmented in the new law, which prohibits the obtaining of 'forbidden' information and its disclosure to any foreign state or 'hostile organisation' — as defined by the State President — either within or outside the country. The forbidden information could be anything relating to the defence of the Republic, any military or security matter for the prevention or combating of terrorism or any other matter which the journalist knows — or reasonably should know — may directly or indirectly be of use to a foreign state or 'hostile organisation'. Serious implications for newsgathering are the Minister's powers to declare any place or area a 'prohibited area', which could include not only security installations but also schools, factories and other economic and industrial sites. The identification of such sites is not defined or publicised and may unwittingly be violated by journalists. Once an area has been proclaimed a 'prohibited place' any person who approaches, inspects, enters, passes over or is in the vicinity of such a location for any purpose "prejudicial to the security or interests of the Republic" shall be guilty of an offence.

The third control mechanism is an amendment of the Registration of Newspapers Act (No 92 of 1982). This amendment offers newspapers the choice of falling under the Publications Act of 1974 and thereby being under the direct control of the Directorate of Publications (the State censorship machinery), or subjecting themselves to the code of conduct and disciplinary powers of the Media Council. This body complements the National Press Union of South Africa and came into being through the Press's attempt to stave off excessive Government interference by creating its own self-policing body. The NPU had itself previously enforced a comprehensive degree of self-discipline on the press. A provision stating that none of the members of the new Council will be appointed by the Government lends credence to the view that it is an independent and voluntarily constituted organisation. Although the Act stipulates that the Council shall be an independent and voluntary body, nonetheless, it derives its power from statutory recognition.

Coercion is not, however, the only tactic used by the State to harness the press. After 1976 the Government's strategy with regard to the English-language press's proxy on behalf of black interests was to buy it out. Consequently, through an Information Department front man, industrialist Louis Luyt, the Government at first tried to purchase the *Natal Mercury*. When this failed, an offer was made for SAAN. Though a second bid was well above the listed market price, shareholders, fearing a right wing incursion, fought it off by forming the Advowason Trust.

The government responded by launching a morning daily, *The Citizen*, under the control of Luyt. The choice of a morning newspaper is not insignificant for, in part, it was designed to provide opposition to the troublesome *Rand Daily Mail*[158].

The tradition of a 'free' English press was the perfect cover under which to present seemingly 'objective', 'balanced' and 'fair' reporting of Southern African events. Apart from its primary function of persuading English-speaking South Africans to a more sympathetic view of apartheid, if not direct Party membership, *The Citizen* was the centrepoint of a proposed chain of international media channels which spanned at least three continents[159]. The objective was to foster a climate overseas which would be unresponsive to protest emanating from dissident elements within South Africa, thereby counteracting the criticism of governments hostile to South Africa's apartheid policies.

The above section has argued that there is a discernible pattern in the Government's strategy towards the English-language press. When co-option fails, it introduces legislation to coerce it. With the introduction of each successive stage of legislation, the threshold of co-option is raised, followed by further coercion as the perceived crisis escalates. The result is that the long term ability of the press to articulate alternative viewpoints is increasingly curtailed. The legislation prior to 1976, for example, was inadequate to cope with the crisis which manifested itself in the Soweto riots of that year. Extreme coercion — banning of newspapers and editors, detentions of editors and journalists — was followed by a period of co-option as the government first tried to purchase a section of the English press, and when this failed, to set up its own newspaper. In the wake of the limited success of this strategy, further coercive measures followed in the form of the Advocate General Bill. The Steyn Commissions set the climate for further co-option in the form of a Media Council and the 'voluntary' self-censorship that such a body implies. Simultaneously, three Bills were rushed through Parliament in 1982 which provide the most comprehensive arsenal yet to be deployed against the press[160].

The strategy of co-option is not misunderstood by all practitioners of the media. Before the release of the first Steyn Commission Report in 1980, Alister Sparks, then editor of the *Rand Daily Mail*, correctly predicted that the 'total strategy' would include pressures on the press to secure its co-operation in the 'national interest', and draw it into the system. Sparks stated: "We already see a proliferation of liaison committees between the press and various government departments; and I see these becoming the instruments of this new form of news manipulation"[161]. This prediction saw its fulfillment in 1985 with the establishment of a Bureau for Information under the control of the Assistant Minister of Foreign Affairs and Information. Their first directive was the banning of cameras (print, movie and television) from 'unrest' areas falling under the declaration of State of Emergency. This followed the refusal by the police to provide names of detainees, or to provide information on detentions other than through the Police Directorate of Public Relations in Pretoria. Where at the start of the emergency, information was made available several times a day, after a while the Police reduced this to once a day. This prevented conflicting information emanating from the unrest areas themselves and made it almost impossible for reporters to verify eye-witness reports. The result was that the authoritative reports are usually the only version to be published.

While maintaining their credibility as an opposition press, the English-language newspapers are, nevertheless, under the indirect control of government-approved media policy. These laws apply, of course, in equal measure to the Afrikaans press. There is, however, less chance or necessity of this legislation being applied to the Afrikaans press, since it functions well within the hegemonic consensus, although it is, at times, highly critical of the National Party itself[162].

Restrictions of Readership and Revenue

Many of the ideological trends identified in the foregoing sections can be ascribed not only to the discourse of the newsroom, but also to the structural limitations placed upon newspapers as commercial enterprises in capitalist society. Financial success, and therefore the viability of the newspaper, is not guaranteed by the revenue derived from subscriptions and newsstand sales, but rather by the revenue derived from advertising.

In all capitalist societies, newpaper markets are strongly stratified by income levels. A relatively small number of high-income readers is more valuable to advertisers than a large number of low-income readers. In South Africa, market stratification is more complex: not only is there the added dimension of language, but in a real sense, that of race too.

Socio-economic segments have traditionally overlapped with those of race, since few blacks would be considered to have the spending power of middle or upper stratum whites. However, with the shift in the economy outlined earlier, more urban-based blacks are being incorporated into a consumer-oriented way of life. There has been a concommitant shift in most of the major white orientated newspapers to intercept this growing readership through the publication of Extras. In contrast to most publishing groups, which tended to rely on the notion of white readers constituting the backbone of potential advertising revenue, SAAN took a more aggressive marketing stance. It actively promoted to manufacturers and their advertising agencies the concept of an integrated consumer public, which it dubbed the 'new consumer'. This market was classified in terms of income levels rather than race. It was not entirely coincidental that the identification of the new consumer followed the 1976 Soweto disturbances. The concept was seen as a revolutionary one on the South African marketing scene. Although a number of advertising agencies adopted the idea, one journalist observed that not only did advertising agencies wield immense influence on the press, but very often operated under racial rather than rational market economic assumptions:

> Advertising agencies, and to a certain extent, their clients, often make assumptions which are not, in my view, economic assumptions; they are not class assumptions, they're racial assumptions. Anybody who looks for structure, at the kind of developments in the economy, in the urban areas, will see that the kind of market you ought to be into at the moment, is the black market. Because there is going to be a limit to the amount that whites can consume. Now (most advertising agencies) are interested in how many white readers you've got and how many white women readers you have got. Those are the main issues.

SAAN invested a great deal of time and effort and held big seminars and all sorts of things to try and push this 'new consumer' idea (and) they have the figures to back it up. But (there was resistance towards it). The market does not decide what a good newspaper is, because the market is not interested in one and a half million black readers, the market's interested in 50 000 white business readers. So, in other words, the kind of classic free market theory that you take your product to the market place and if the populace likes it, then you make a profit, and if the elite don't like it, you lose.

A second marketing constraint that works against white-oriented newspapers actively attracting black readers, is that in the eyes of advertisers they do not attract a definable target audience:

> The *Mail* has had ... the problem with advertising agencies that they look at you and say you've got a bit of the whites, you've got a bit of the coloureds, you've got a bit of the Asians, you've got a bit of the blacks — you haven't got the biggest share of any of them. So, we're not reaching any market.

The media in South Africa thus have to overcome a double set of restrictions if they are to remain financially viable. This obviously has a direct bearing on the kinds of issues which receive prominence in the press. Appraising his own newspaper, one journalist noted:

> I think my newspaper covers most of the important issues. What it does at the same time is that it relegates those important issues to minor stories inside the newspaper, and the front page of the paper and all the glamour space and so on is given over to what you and I would probably see as trivial. And therefore it very much reflects white concerns; for example, white news values (imply) that cricket is more important than influx control, etc.

The economic constraints faced by the media industry are thus an important factor in determining the ideological stance of individual newspapers. In analysing the media it is important not to make the prior assumption that the press is a free agent within society. Both legislative and economic constraints are in part responsible for the press taking a stance which does not adequately reflect black concerns, worker concerns, or concerns of the poor in rural areas.

Finally, despite the visible lack of authoriterian control within the news institution, what is published very often depends on the idiosyncratic preferences of the editor. These preferences are sensed by staffers — particularly sub-editors — through the socialisation of staffers in the media institution as a whole. One editor of a large Sunday paper, for example, does not like gays or stories about death. Such items — if they do escape the gatekeeping mechanisms of the paper — are usually buried on the inside pages.

Conclusion

This chapter has attempted to outline the political economy of the South African press and has argued that all sections of this industry — white-owned, black-oriented press, the English- and Afrikaans-language newspapers — support the hegemonic bloc in different ways, emphasising different fractions within it. The English-language press and the black-oriented press owe allegiance to the dominant fraction, while the Afrikaans press supports the ruling fraction.

There has been a narrowing over the years of the ideological gap between the English and Afrikaans newspapers, as a result of the latter's reformist stance. Legislative coercion, the reluctance of distributors to handle sales of black newspapers like *The Voice*, and the inability of newspapers on the fringe of the establishment to obtain advertising, together with the general narrowing of political differences in the country as a whole, have resulted in a readership that is hostile to interpretations outside the preferred discourse. Even if the media have not entirely succumbed to co-option, the indications are there that large portions of the white reading public have. Without reader support, it is going to be even more difficult for the white press to articulate an oppositional viewpoint in the years to come.

Notes and References

1. This is not to deny that work has been conducted by South African universities. The work done tends to be highly descriptive and often consists of endless extracts reproduced from newspapers, interspersed with a few lines of indignant comment on the supposed anti-Afrikaner stance taken by the English press. These theses are characterised by unsubstantiated personal opinion and lack theoretical framework of any sort. See for example, J de Villiers, *South African Community and its Newspapers*, Ph.D thesis, Department of Sociology, University of the Orange Free State (1976); and G J Pienaar, *Perssensuur en Staatsveiligheid*, D.Phil thesis, Potchefstroom University (1968).

2. See for example, A Sampson, *Drum: A Venture into the New Africa*; F Flather, *The Way of an Editor*, and S Pienaar, *Getuie van Groot Tye*.

3. See for example, J P Scannel, *Keeromstraat 30*; I Benson, *The Opinion Makers*, Pretoria: Dolphin Press (1977); and *Ecquid Novi*, which takes a generally simplistic and highly conservative approach. See especially L le Grange, 'Persverantwoordelikheid Gesien van die Kant van die Owerheid' in *Ecquid Novi* vol 1 no 2 (1980), pp 139-49. Much of this fanatical discussion is disguised under the rubric of 'professionalisation' of the practice of journalism. Another example is A de Beer, 'Die Professionalisering van die Joernalistieke Koerantberoep in Suide-Afrika' in *Communicatio* vol 3 no 1 (1977), pp 9-14. 'Intercultural Studies' is another obscured category under which apartheid ideology is legitimised. See for example, B Piek, 'Die Rol van Interkulturele Kommunikasie in Nasionale Ontwikkeling' in *Communicatio* vol 2 no 2 (1981), pp 48-59.

4. F Barton, *The Press in Africa — Persecution and Perseverance*

5. W A Hachten, *Muffled Drums: The News Media in Africa*; R Ainslie, *The Press in Africa*, London: Gollancz (1966). Published in *Index on Censorship* are W A Hachten, 'Black Authors Under Apartheid', vol 8 no 3 (1979), pp 43-8; B Pogrund, 'The South African Press', vol 5 no 3 (1976), pp 10-16; J Lawrence, 'Censorship by Skin Colour', vol 6 no 2 (1977) pp 40-3. *Journalism Quarterly* articles include T Brown, 'Free Press Fair Game for South Africa's Government' (Spring 1971), pp 120-7; C A Giffard, 'South African Attitudes Toward News Media' (Winter 1976), pp 653-60; T Brown, 'Did Anybody Know His Name? U.S. Coverage of Biko' (Spring 1980), pp 31-8; C A Giffard, 'Circulation Trends in South Africa' (Spring 1980), pp 86-91; and C A Giffard, 'The Impact of Television on South African Daily Newspapers' (Summer 1980), pp 216-23.

6. A S De Beer, *Joernalistiek Vandag*

7. See F Rautenbach's review in *Critical Arts* vol 2 no 3 (1982)

8. W Hachten and C A Giffard, *Total Onslaught.* The discussion proceeds without any reference to Moss, 'Total Strategy', O'Meara, 'Muldergate', or Saul and Gelb, *The Crisis in South Africa.*

9. R Pollack, *Up Against Apartheid: The Role and the Plight of the Press in South Africa.* Of an even more extreme nature is M Broughton, *Press and Politics of South Africa,* Cape Town: Purnell (1961). In logic as contorted as he uses to explain the irrationality of apartheid, he states, for example, that the Afrikaner nationalist has elevated the State to a level higher than justice, trust and moral obligation:

> These are the non-logical, myth centred, dogmatic bases of nationalism. They give strength, substance and potency to the historical, organic, religious and psychological origins of apartheid. It is from these sources that it draws its 'realness' and from which springs the energy enabling its exponents incessantly to construct vaster, more intricate and complicated structures, regardless of the availability of means to make them work and of administrative resources to apply them. The elaboration and multiplication of these structures has become an end and a pursuit in themselves.

10. John Phelan, *Apartheid Media*

11. H Lindsay-Smith, *Behind the Press in South Africa*

12. I Ginwala, 'The Press in South Africa', *Index on Censorship* vol 2 no 3 (1973), pp 27-39; SPROCAS, *Toward Social Change,* Johannesburg: SPROCAS (1971).

13. A Hepple, *Censorship and Press Control in South Africa.* Also see *Press Under Apartheid,* published by the International Defence and Aid Fund in London.

14. J Dugard, *Human Rights and the South African Legal Order,* University of Witwatersrand, Johannesburg: Centre for Applied Legal Studies; K Stuart, *The Newspaperman's Guide to the Law;* A Matthews, *The Darker Reaches of Government: Access to Public Information about Public Administration in Three Societies,* Cape Town: Juta (1978). Also see S Adelman, J Howard, K Stuart and A van Eeden, *The South African Press Council — A Critical View,* University of the Witwatersrand, Johannesburg: Centre for Applied Legal Studies (1979).

Afrikaans language books on the subject of the press and the law include S A Strauss, M J Strydom and J C van der Walt, *Die Perswese en die Reg,* Pretoria: Van Schaik (1964); and, by the same authors and publishers, *Die Suid-Afrikaanse Persreg* 3rd edition (1976).

15. E Potter, *The Press as Opposition: The Political Role of South African Newspapers*

16. A Chimutengwende, *The Press and the Politics of Liberation*

17. L Switzer, *Politics and Communications in the Ciskei;* and

'Mass Communication in a Transitional Society' in *The Ciskei*, edited by N Charton, London: Croom Helm (1980). Also see his bibliographical guide to the black press written in conjunction with D Switzer, *The Black Press in South Africa and Lesotho*.

18. See for example, Media Study Group, 'MWASA — Trying to Set Deadlines' in *South African Labour Bulletin* vol 6 no 6 (1981), pp 24-9; Alan Fine in the same issue, 'Allied: Round Two', pp 30-6; 'The Allied Publishing Dispute' in *Work in Progress* no 12 (1980), pp 1-3; 'Allied Publishing' in *Work in Progress* no 12 (1981), pp 46-7. Exploratory articles in *Critical Arts* include: L Switzer, 'Steyn Commission I: The Press and Total Strategy', vol 1 No 4 (1981), pp 41-5. See also the special issue, vol 2 no 2, on 'Press and Broadcasting in Africa'. Articles of a structural nature include K G Tomaselli and R E Tomaselli, 'Ideology/Culture/Hegemony and Mass Media in South Africa: A Literature Survey', pp 1-26; C Doherty, 'The Wits-Koornhof Debate: Is There Really a Difference Between the English and Afrikaans Presses?', pp 39-49, and J McCarthy and M Friedmann, 'Black Housing, Ideology and the Media in South Africa 1970-1979', pp 51-66; P E Louw, ' "Consensus Journalism": A Critique with reference to the Dialectical Paradigm'.

19. See, for example, S Clarke, 'Capital, Fractions of Capital and the State: "Neo-Marxist" Analyses of the South African State' in *Capital and Class*, no 5 (1978); D O'Meara, ' "Muldergate" and the Politics of Afrikaner Nationalism' in *Work in Progress* no 22 (supplement) (1982); C Simpkins, 'Measuring and Predicting Unemployment in South Africa' in *Structural Unemployment in South Africa* by C Simpkins and D Clarke.

The identification of this crisis in capital is not restricted to scholars of the left. The chairman of Sanlam, Dr A Wassenaar, published a virulent attack on 'Afrikaner Socialism', claiming that South Africa was eroding free enterprise and the capitalist base of the economy. See A D Wassenaar, *Assault on Free Enterprise: The Freeway to Communism*, Cape Town: Tafelberg (1977). The subsequent ascendance of P W Botha to the premiership was a "clear victory for capitalist interests in the Nationalist alliance" (O'Meara, *op cit* p 16). Wassenaar's book was intended to stir things up within the party to bring about economic reforms.

20. See for example, R H Davies, *Capital, State and White Labour In South Africa 1900 — 1960*; and Stephen Gelb and Duncan Innes, 'Monetarism's Double Bind' in *Work in Progress* no 36 (1985).

21. Our use of the term 'black middle classes' incorporates workers from the administrative/bureaucratic, service and manufacturing sectors of the economy. No distinction is made between productive and non-productive as is, for instance, outlined by E Olin-Wright in 'Class Boundaries in Advanced Capitalist Societies' in *New Left Review* no 98 (1967).

22. See, for example, M Legassick, 'Legislation, Ideology and

Economy in Post-1948 South Africa' in *Journal of Southern African Studies* vol 1 no 1 (1974); and H Wolpe, 'Capitalism and Cheap Labour Power: From Segregation to Apartheid' in *Economy and Society* vol 1 no 4 (1974).

23. M Legassick, 'South Africa: Capital Accumulation and Violence' in *Economy and Society* vol 3 no 3 (1974); M Lacey, *Working for Boroko: The Origins of a Coercive Labour System in South Africa*, Johannesburg: Ravan (1981); and J Rex, 'The Compound, Reserve and Urban Location' in *South African Labour Bulletin* vol 1 no 2 (1974)

24. See H Wolpe, *Changing Class Structure: The Emergence of an African Petit Bourgeoisie*, privately circulated (1976).

25. President's Council report, *An Urbanisation Strategy for the Republic of South Africa* Chapter 9, paragraphs 150 and 152. For a brief summary of the content and implications of the Report see D Hindson, 'Urbanisation and Influx Control' in *Work in Progress* nos 40 and 41 (February and March 1986).

26. A searching analysis of exposing and describing the events in the black townships during the early months of the 1984-1985 unrest is provided in the Catholic Bishops' Conference publication *A Report on Police Conduct during the Township Protests, August-November 1984*.

27. Quoted in *Sunday Tribune* (15 September 1985) p 9

28. For an account of the unrest in the Durban area see Black Research Institute, *Unrest in Durban*, University of Natal Durban (1985); and M O Sutcliff and P A Wellings, *Attitudes and Living Conditions in Inanda: The Context for Unrest?*, University of Natal (1985). The State of Emergency was lifted in March 1986.

29. L Switzer and D Switzer, *op cit* p 4

30. F St Leger, 'The World Newspaper 1968-1976' in *Critical Arts* vol 2 no 2 (1981), p 28

31. E Potter, *op cit* p 48

32. Quoted in F Barton, *op cit* p 176

33. F St Leger, 'The African Press in South Africa' in *Communications in Africa* (no number or date), p 23

34. G Addison, 'Drum Beat' in *Speak* vol 1 no 4 (1978) p 3. A most informative publication on this magazine is *The Beat of Drum*, published by Ravan and Drum. It is an omnibus of photographs, articles and reminiscences on a "Magazine that documented the rise of Africa". See also D Rabkin, *Drum Magazine (1951-1961)* and the works of black South African writers associated with it. One of the earliest publications dealing with *Drum* is A Sampson, *op cit*.

35. For further information on the 'Information Scandal' which became known as 'Muldergate', see M Rees and C Day, *Muldergate: The Story of the Info Scandal*; Pollak, *op cit* chapter

3; and R P B Erasmus, Commission of Inquiry into Alleged Irregularities in the Former Department of Information. The Commission accumulated 11 000 pages of evidence and testimony and issued three reports: *Report* (December 1978); *Interim Report* (March 1979); and *Supplementary Report* (May 1979). Also see R Gibson, 'The Information Scandal in Retrospect' in *Proceedings* of the Survival of the Press and Education for Journalism Conference, Grahamstown: Department of Journalism, Rhodes University, August 1979, hereafter referred to as *Proceedings* of Survival of Press Conference.

36. *Proceedings* of the Survival of the Press Conference.

37. *The Journalist* (February 1983), p 3

38. *The Journalist* (May 1984), p 6

39. Switzer and Switzer, *op cit* p 17

40. See G Addison, *Role of Black Journalists in the Soweto Uprising of 1976*, unpublished paper, Department of Journalism and Media Studies, Rhodes University (1977), pp 56-7

41. Quoted in Addison, *Ibid* p 54

42. P Lawrence, 'Black Journalists: A Tough New Force' in *Rand Daily Mail* (6 November 1980)

43. For an analysis of the diffusion of temporal and spatial patterns of unrest see R J Fincham and G J Ward, *The Geography of Protest: Diffusion of Unrest Through South African Urban Centres, 6 June to 8 September 1976*, unpublished paper delivered at the Media and Change Symposium, University of the Witwatersrand, Johannesburg (August 1977).

44. St Leger, *op cit* (1981), p 27

45. P Qoboza, 'The Press As I See It', paper presented at the conference on the Survival of the Press and Education for Journalism. Published in the *Proceedings* of Survival of the Press Conference.

46. See Addison, *op cit* (1977) p 23

47. St Leger, *op cit* (1981) p 34

48. See *World* (August 1976)

49. M Whitehead, *The Black Gatekeepers: A Study of Black Journalists on Three Daily Newspapers Which Covered the Soweto Uprising of 1976* Honours thesis, Grahamstown: Department of Journalism, Rhodes University, pp 112-5.

50. St Leger, *op cit* (1981) p 35

51. *Ibid* p 37

52. Whitehead, *op cit* p 130

53. Whitehead, *Ibid* points out that one of the difficulties in her research was the fact that a number of key journalists who reported the 1976 unrest were in detention while a number of others had fled the country at the start of the 1977 detentions.

54. Switzer and Switzer, *op cit* p 18

55. Qoboza, *op cit*

56. Quoted in Whitehead, *op cit* p 69

57. See for example, Media Study Group, 'MWASA — Trying to Set Deadlines' in *South African Labour Bulletin* vol 6 no 6 (1981), pp 24-9.

58. See Switzer and Switzer, *op cit*

59. *Steyn Commission II*

60. Harry Oppenheimer was the immediate past chairman of the Anglo-American Corporation. Benson, *op cit* particularly implies a direct connection between Oppenheimer and the English press. Other authors who allude to the connection are J J van Rooyen, 'Die Pers is Vry, Maar Ook Nie' in *Ecquid Novi* vol 1 no 1 (1980), pp 16-28; and P J Cillie, 'The Conditions for a Free, Vigorous and Reasonable Press in South Africa' in *Ecquid Novi* vol 1 no 2 (1980), pp 67-80.

John Martin was the managing director of the Argus Company, as well as of Central Mining Investment, Crown Mines and Rand Mines. He was also a director of City Deep, ERPM, Geldenhuys Deep, Modderfontein B Mines and eleven other firms related to mining. Hence Lindsay-Smith's comment that "It has been the policy of the greater part of the daily press that *ipso facto* whatever is best for the gold mines is best for South Africa" (*op cit* p 73).

Gordon Waddell is Chairman of Johannesburg Consolidated Investments (JCI) who have large shareholdings in both SAAN and Argus. His involvement in the closure of the *Rand Daily Mail* in 1985 has been the subject of much speculation in journalistic circles. See for example, *The Journalist* (April 1985).

61. Potter, *op cit* p 170

62. *Steyn Commission II* p 838

63. The study of 'inter-group' and 'inter-cultural' relations has become an overriding obsession amongst conservative scholars, some universities and the HSRC. It is important to note that these heavily-funded research programmes which were initiated by the HSRC in 1981 tend to build dominant assumptions into their research designs. For an outline of the programme, see H C Marais and L Dreyer, 'HSRC Investigation into Intergroup Relations: The Programme and its Financing' in *Communicare* vol 3 no 1 (1982), pp 3-7.

64. *Steyn Commission II*

65. Potter, *op cit* p 170

66. *Cape Times* (November 1985)

67. See for example, *The Star*, which continues to conduct such campaigns as The Star Seaside Fund, Alexandra Uplift, Teach, and Starline. The last, while aimed at a more general readership, was mostly concerned with the consumer-orientated correspondence of Soweto residents. Addison points to the merits of the various educational supplements, notably Operation Catch-Up, People's College and, later, Learning Post, at a time when many black pupils boycotted schools and studied privately. He also warns of the danger that such 'development journalism' may become "like charity — a way of short-circuiting demands for meaningful change". See G Addison, 'New Themes and Strategies for Journalism in South Africa' in *Proceedings* of Survival of the Press Conference.

68. For an elaboration of the media coverage of the Nyanga squatter camp see K G Tomaselli, 'Editorial: Some Notes on this Volume' in *Critical Arts* vol 2 no 2 (1981), p (i)

69. *Rand Daily Mail* (16 July). This paper reported that between August 1981 and May 1982, 185 people died of the disease, while 46 164 were treated for it.

70. *The Star* (29 June 1982)

71. *The Star* (30 June 1982)

72. *The Star* (3 August 1982)

73. *The Star* (5 August 1982)

74. *The Star* (3 August 1982)

75. *The Star* (5 August 1982)

76. *The Star* (14 July 1982)

77. Interview with Rex Gibson on 19 November 1980.

78. J Mattisonn, 'Strategies for Survival of the Press in the 1980s' in *Proceedings* of Survival of the Press Conference.

79. Interview with authors, November 1980.

80. Interviewed on 22 September 1982.

81. *Ibid*

82. *Ibid*

83. Interview with authors, September 1982.

84. *Rand Daily Mail* (23 October 1962)

85. Barton, *op cit* p 203

86. The legal costs of the particular case have been estimated at approximately R500 000 (Barton, *op cit*).

87. Potter, *op cit* pp 158-9

88. *Ibid*

89. Switzer, *op cit* (1979), p 12

90. Other organisations banned on the same day were the Black Parents Association, the Black Women's Federation, the Border Youth Organisation, the Christian Institute, the Eastern Province Youth Organisation, the Medupe Writers Association, the Natal Youth Organisation, the Union of Black Journalists and the Western Cape Youth Association.

91. See G M Gerhart, *Black Power in South Africa: The Evolu-*

tion of an Ideology, p 313, for an account of the bannings and their connection with white party politics.

92. Interviewed in November 1980.

93. B Streek and R Wicksteed, *Render Unto Kaiser: A Transkei Dossier*, Johannesburg: Ravan (1981), p 298

94. Quoted in G M Stewart, *The Development of the* Rand Daily Mail *as an Intercultural Newspaper*, Honours thesis, Department of Communication, University of South Africa, p 33

95. *Ibid* p 34

96. *Ibid* p 37

97. Quoted in S Motau, 'Writing for Black Readers — Responsibilities, Obligations and Problems for the Black Journalist in South Africa' in *Communicare* vol 2 no 2 (1981), p 45

98. *The Citizen* (12 December 1980)

99. Motau (*op cit*) takes as his point of departure the supposition that the Extras "would serve as cross-cultural instruments to bridge the 'ignorance gap' by facilitating the free flow of information between the races" (p 40). Although providing a critique of this position, he nevertheless sees it as the desirable and normative value and offers numerous suggestions for overcoming their failure in this regard.

100. As was mentioned in the discussion on the white-owned black press, individual reporters from both the *Rand Daily Mail* and *World* were harassed by the police. See Whitehead, *op cit* pp 113-5

101. *The Journalist* (July 1981), p 1

102. *The Journalist* (March 1983), p 3

103. *The Journalist* (March 1984), p 3

104. *Ibid*

105. *The Journalist* (April 1985), pp 5-7

106. *The Journalist* (November 1985), p 9

107. *Work in Progress* no 6

108. *The Journalist* (November 1985), p 8

109. *Financial Mail* (12 July 1985)

110. Stanley Uys, 'A Silenced Voice' in *Index on Censorship* (August 1985)

111. *Ibid*

112. *The Journalist* (1981) p 6

113. *Ibid* p 7

114. *The Journalist* (February 1982) p 3

115. *The Journalist* (August 1983) p 10

116. *The Journalist* (April 1985) p 3

117. K Roelofse, 'Rand Daily Mail: Die dood in perspektief' in Communicatio vol 11 no 2 (1985), pp 30-37

118. Ibid p 30

119. Die Burger (18 March 1985)

120. Roelofse op cit

121. The Journalist (April 1985)

122. Ibid. See also Work in Progress no 36 (1985)

123. Work In Progress no 36 (1985), p 5

124. John Dugard in a letter published in the Rand Daily Mail's final edition (30 April 1985)

125. Weekly Mail (26 July 1985)

126. The Journalist (April 1985), p 6

127. Ibid p 13

128. K G Tomaselli and R E Tomaselli, Media Reflections of Ideology, Durban: Contemporary Cultural Studies Unit, University of Natal (1985)

129. Work in Progress no 36

130. Potter, op cit p 162

131. For a historical analysis of the shareholding of both the English and Afrikaans presses, see R McGregor, Who Owns Whom in the Newspaper Industry, Purdy Publications (1981).

132. D O'Meara, 'The Afrikaner Broederbond 1927-1948: Class Vanguard of Afrikaner Nationalism' in Journal of Southern African Studies vol 3 no 2 (1977)

133. J W van Zyl, Report of the Commission of Inquiry into the Press Annexure IV, Pretoria: Government Printer (1953), p 213

134. W Wepener, 'The Role of the Afrikaans Press' in Proceedings of the Survival of the Press Conference.

135. P A Weber, Keeromstraat no 30

136. Die Burger (23 July 1960)

137. E Domisse, 'The Changing Role of the Afrikaans Press' in The Afrikaners, edited by E S Munger.

138. This word translates as 'englightenment', as opposed to 'verkramp', which means 'arch conservative'. The former was first used by De Klerk to identify reformers within the National Party.

139. Quoted in Rand Daily Mail (2 September 1982). This paper reproduced extracts from a longer article which was later published in Issue (Spring 1982).

140. Ibid

141. Ibid

142. W De Klerk, 'Newspapers Need to be More Patriotic' in Issue (Spring 1982) pp 9-10

143. C Jooste, 'Back to Basics for the Afrikaner' in *Issue* (Spring 1982) p 24

144. *Ibid*

145. Mulder was later 'excommunicated' from the National Party because of his involvement in the Information Scandal.

146. *Oggendblad* has since ceased publication because of financial difficulties, while *Hoofstad* was discontinued in 1983. See chapter 4 for further details.

147. *The Journalist* (September 1982), p 3

148. The implications of this proposal are dealt with in K G Tomaselli and R E Tomaselli, 'Steyn Commission II: How to Separate Out Truth from Fact' in *Reality* (May 1982), pp 14-15

149. Jooste, *op cit* p 23

150. A de Beer, 'Afrikaans Press Enjoys Freedom Within Limits ...', *South African Outlook* vol 110 no 1308 (1980), p 6

151. De Klerk, *op cit* p 9

152. H Adam and H Giliomee, *The Rise and Crisis of Afrikaner Power*

153. See Qoboza, *op cit*; Whitehead, *op cit*; Addison, *op cit* (1977); and Pollak, *op cit*.

154. Barton, *op cit* p 98

155. J Mervis, 'Can Press Freedom Survive in South Africa?' in *Proceedings* of the Survival of the Press Conference.

156. The Minister of Justice, Dr C R Swart, referred to a photograph published in *Drum* which revealed black prisoners being forced to dance around the Johannesburg Prison in the nude, to prove they were not hiding anything such as knives or drugs. See *Hansard* (5 March 1959) cols 148-9. Sampson, *op cit*, recalls an incident from first hand experience, and his book includes a copy of the offending photograph.

157. The denunciation sent by telegram was the result of timeous political manoeuvring by liberal staffers who had captured the SABC Staff Association.

158. This is argued by A Sparks, 'The Press Out On A Limb' in *Proceedings* of the Survival of the Press Conference.

159. The Department of Information tried to buy shares in the *Washington Post, Sacramento Union* and ITN-TV. Already in operation was *To The Point*, based in Holland, while negotiations were in progress to acquire a French magazine in France and to establish one for French-speaking West Africa, based in Zaire.

160. State intervention is a coercive response only used in crises of hegemony. It is not, as Barton suggests, an inexorable working out of the grand strategy formulated on the National Party's ascendance to power. Neither is government 'backing off' a response to NPU attempts to 'put its house in order' in conjunction

with pressure from Reagan, the Afrikaans press or whatever else as is suggested by Hachten and Giffard (p 86). These authors do not see this coercive consent inducement as a cyclical strategy used by the state to force conformity during times of hegemonic crisis. This press-centred analysis is, therefore, largely unable to examine the mosaic of politico-economic relations which leads the state to hammer the press on some occasions, but not on others. It is not a case of 'backing off', but of responding as and when necessary.

161. Sparks, *op cit*

162. See for example, Pollak, *op cit*. In contrast is de Beer, *op cit*. De Beer sees the relationship between the press and the National Party as 'a case of independence-within-bounds'.

Chapter 4
Press Houses at War: A Brief History of Nasionale Pers and Perskor

Johan Muller

The class rifts felt at every level of Afrikaner institutional life in the late 1970s and early 1980s left their mark on the Afrikaner media too. Opposing interests that had been cobbled together by Christian nationalism in a remarkable feat of consensual organising began, in this time of generalised crisis, to separate out again with a vengeance. Publishing policy of the major press houses, beholden to the National Party since 1948, was called into question; nervous employees falsified circulation figures; publishers took one another to court; two established dailies disappeared, another moved from Johannesburg to Pretoria, and a major editor was sacked. All this happened in the period roughly between February 1982 and February 1983.

In this chapter I want to contextualise these events, to uncover some of the historical roots of conflict, and to show how these indicators of rupture can be understood not simply in terms of ideological differences, but in terms of political allegiance, economic mobilisation and class struggle. This is not intended to be an exhaustive history of the Afrikaner press. My main aim will be to give the context of development of the two publishing houses, Nasionale Pers (Naspers) and Perskor, and to show how the conflict in 1982 and 1983 between their two major dailies in the Transvaal, *Beeld* and *Die Transvaler* respectively, is firmly rooted in this context.

North Versus South: 1915-1981[1]

There has always been a simmering animosity between the smooth, cultured and affluent southern nationalists in the Cape and the rougher, poorer, less culture-conscious northerners in the Transvaal. There have been many hypotheses advanced to account for this difference. Some see it as a difference in political or ideological style. A Naspers senior executive put it this way: "In general we favoured a softer, more liberal implementation of apartheid. This was anathema to the Transvaal nationalists"[2]. Adam and Giliomee speculate that the century of colonisation experienced by the Cape had left its patina of gentility on the southerners as well as giving them practice in the ways of civilised resistance[3].

There may be elements of truth in these positions. An additional difference lies in the relative class composition of Afrikaners in the Cape and in the Transvaal. The Cape Afrikaners had greater numbers of wealthy farmers, urbanised and prosperous professional people and emergent capitalists in their ranks. The Transvalers starting off from a predominantly rural base, were proletarianised and urbanised by social forces in the first two decades of the century, resulting in a large, destitute white working class eking out an existence in the cities. In 1900, ten per cent of Afrikaners were living in the towns; by 1926, this number had grown to 41 per cent[4].

As we shall see, Afrikaner nationalism very often meant economic mobilisation. For the Transvalers, this was mostly a matter of survival, but for the Cape nationalists, it was a way to improve their capital accumulation. For both of these two, the greatest threat was the possibility of proletarianised, unemployed whites seeking common cause with proletarianised blacks in a militant non-racial workers' movement. Economic mobilisation through the channel of an ethnic nationalism was the resultant strategy. Newspapers were needed to voice this strategy, and every important Afrikaner newspaper was founded in this period for this purpose. But because divergent provincial class interests undergirded the strategy, nationalism created continual tension between the Cape and the Transvaal. This tension is mirrored in the relations between the press in the two provinces, then and now. I shall look briefly at how this came about.

In the messy, confusing history of Afrikanerdom from 1915 until the Nationalists came to power in 1948, three political events stand out. The first is General Hertzog's breakaway from Louis Botha in 1912 and the establishment of the first National Party (NP) in 1915. At the same time, there was a 'rebellion' of nationalists against Smuts's decision to join imperialist Britain's 1914 Great War. The second is the Fusion of 1934, when future prime minister Dr D F Malan led his 'gesuiwerde' or purified nationalists — (G)NP — out of the pact that had fused the white political parties into the United Party (UP) under Smuts and Hertzog. The third is the split between Smuts and Hertzog, and Smuts taking South Africa into the Second World War on Britain's side. The second election after the war swept the UP out of power and the nationalist alliance under Malan into the position of political power that it holds to the present. All three of these events had their impact upon the Afrikaner press.

In the Wake of the Rebellion: 1915-1934

The year 1915 saw the birth of three Afrikaner newspapers, each with its own circumstances and destiny. *Het Volksblad* was the first to come out, in March. It had grown out of the Dutch weekly *Het Western*, first published in 1904. It remained a weekly, published in Potchefstroom, then moved to Bloemfontein in 1916. It became a daily in 1925 and can claim to be the oldest Afrikaans paper. Although it was published by the Hertzogite Nasionale Pers, and was adopted by the Free State (G)NP after Fusion, this paper never made much of an impact on the political scene since it was not nationally distributed. In 1982, its daily circulation was not much more than half that of *Die Transvaler, Die Vaderland* and

Beeld, its main northern competitors. It was edited by van Rhyn from 1925 to 1948, when Dr D F Malan gave him a Cabinet post.

In July 1915, a far more significant paper, *De Burger*, came out in Cape Town. *De* (later *Die*) *Burger* was then and is now the flagship of Nasionale Pers and is the major voice of Cape nationalism. It was established by wealthy professional men who wanted a medium to express their political voice as well as to mobilise capital productively.

In 1903, a Dutch literary weekly, *De Goede Hoop*, had come out under the editorship of advocate J H H de Waal. By 1913 or so, de Waal was having problems with his publishers, who objected to the 'political' (nationalist) sentiments he was expressing under the pseudonym of Jan van Rozenburg. He discussed his problem with his friend, the shrewd advocate Willie Hofmeyr, who held a meeting in December 1914 which was attended by wealthy professionals and even wealthier wine farmers. With the generous assistance of the wine farmers, notably the brothers Marais and Pieter Neethling (Albert Hertzog's maternal uncle), *De Burger* was floated and De Nasionale Pers Beperk registered in May 1915. A suitable editor proved something of a problem, but Dr D F Malan was called from the pulpit to edit the paper. His first editorial in July made a strong pledge to strengthen and lead the nation (i.e. the Afrikaners) along the path to national unity[5]. Two months later, when General Hertzog convened the first Cape NP Congress, Malan was elected its first leader.

Mobilising capital in Afrikaner nationalist terms proved extremely unpopular in anglicised Cape Town, and English capital responded by calling for an advertising boycott of *De Burger* in 1917. This was a least in part a response to *De Burger's* role in co-ordinating a financial aid society (Helpmekaarsvereeniging) to assist destitute Afrikaners and disadvantaged and imprisoned rebels against Smuts's war effort. As was to happen two decades later with the press-orchestrated 'Act of Rescue' to assist the 300 000 poor whites mainly in the Transvaal cities, much of this money found its way into capital investment rather than into poor relief. Indeed, the resourceful advocate Hofmeyr, who was by this time already Naspers's chairman and the organising secretary of the Cape NP, formed Santam (Suid-Afrikaanse Nasionale Trust Maatskappy) in 1918 for just this sort of purpose. Sanlam (Suid-Afrikaanse Lewensassuransie Maatskappy) followed a year later. The aim was clear: to co-ordinate the money resources of Afrikaners into central funds so that it could be converted into productive capital[6].

The third paper to appear in 1915 was *Ons Vaderland*, founded in Pretoria in September by Noordelike Drukpers Maatschappij Beperkt, with General Hertzog and his two main supporters, T J Roos and N C Havenga, as the controlling shareholders. Indeed, of all the Hertzog-inspired papers started in this period, the bi-weekly *Vaderland* was the only one to remain loyal to Hertzog after Fusion. This was a significant point, for it meant that the nationalists backing Malan's (G)NP had no voice in the Transvaal after 1934.

In 1916, the Transvaal Hertzogite NP recognised *Ons Vaderland* as its official organ, under the editorship of Oost. In December 1931, Afrikaanse Pers Beperkt was registered. It immediately incorporated Noordelike Drukpers and shortly thereafter *Ons Vaderland*, which then changed its name to *Die Vaderland*. All the signatories to this incorporation were Hertzog Cabinet ministers, with the sole exception of his ubiquitous son, Albert Hertzog.

In this period of Hertzogite power, all these papers provided varying degrees of support and backing for him. By far the most significant paper of the period was *Die Burger* and its powerful Naspers publisher. Naspers epitomised the economic and political alliance between Cape capitalist farmers and a group of professional men around Hofmeyr[7]. *Die Vaderland*'s Afrikaanse Pers, aligned as it was to the politically more liberal Hertzog group, was paradoxically to become the backbone of the conservative Perskor empire of the North. Its time was still to come.

The Ruptures of Fusion: 1934-1939

By the late 1920s and early 1930s, the plight of northern Afrikaners forced to the cities had appreciably worsened. The mines had become the State's greatest source of income (a third of its revenue by Fusion), but these in turn wished to cut costs, especially during the early 1920s. The way to do this, reasoned the mines, was to decrease their reliance on white labour, which they considered overpaid, and to employ black labour instead. The upshot was the white miners' strike of 1922, brutally repressed by the State, which could not afford to alienate the mines. The mines, as a result, reduced white wages, and these did not return to their pre-1922 level during Hertzog's rule. The State's response was to implement a white preferential labour policy in the public sector, and during this time large numbers of Afrikaners flooded into the Railways (the single biggest employer of white labour in the country) and State-created concerns like Iscor (Iron and Steel Corporation). A large, relatively poorly paid Afrikaner working class came into being in this way in the Transvaal.

The North never possessed the entrepreneurial skills that enabled the southerners to mobilise Cape finance so effectively. Adam and Giliomee think this was because the southerners were "rather more mature and self-confident than the Northern Afrikaners"[8]. It is more likely that it was simply because the latter had no capital. Neither did the northern professionals have access to the northern farmers and their capital as the southerners did to the southern farmers. The small investment concerns like Sasbank (Suid-Afrikaanse Spaar- en Voorskot Bank) and AVBOB (Afrikaner Verband Begrafnis Ondernemings Beperk), based largely on worker savings, could never hope to become productively viable.

But what the North did have was the Broederbond (or Bond), the major mobilising body for Afrikaners in the North by the 1930s. Economic mobilisation was one of their priorities, but this largely petty-bourgeois body was more interested than were the southern capitalists in power. Nevertheless, they were the major impetus behind the establishment of Volkskas (People's Bank) in 1934 — with all the board positions filled by Bond Executive Council members, Albert Hertzog included.

The previous year, 1933, the Bond had established a journal, *Koers* (meaning direction or course), with the specific aim of attacking the evils of imperialism and economic domination by English capital. The political columnist of *Koers* was L J du Plessis. His position in the Bond was that of "Political Commissar", and with J G Strijdom, D F Malan and C R (Blackie) Swart (two future prime ministers and a future State president!), he formed a 'parliamentary group' advising the Bond on political matters. As it happens, du Plessis, Malan and Strijdom, at one time or another, all served on controlling boards of what was later to become Perskor. The slow northern press coalescence had begun. Ironically enough, it needed a spark of southern enterprise to get it going.

Having been parted in 1915 over the war issue, the Depression and the crisis over the gold standard brought Hertzog's NP and Smuts's South Africa Party together in 1934, fused into the United Party (UP). Nationalist wisdom in the Cape had it that Hertzog had sold out to imperialistic mining interests and 'Hoggenheimer' (see Chapter 5). They could afford this opinion since the centralisation of agricultural capital in the Cape was still reasonably sturdy. In the event, the Cape NP was the only provincial party to go with Malan and his new (G)NP. Both the OFS and the Transvaal National parties fused into the UP. This left the Bond as the major organising body for nationalist interests in the Transvaal. *Die Burger* of course remained with Malan and the (G)NP. *Die Volksblad*, which had been waging a mutual aid and economic mobilisation campaign throughout the 1930s via the column of Dominee Kestell, decided to back Malan as well — a wise, indeed necessary move, since they were firmly under the control of Naspers by this time. *Die Vaderland* in the Transvaal had little option but to back Hertzog, since it was practically owned by him. In the wake of Fusion then, the nationalists were left without a press 'voice' in the Transvaal.

This had not escaped the notice of Willie Hofmeyr. Returning from the crucial 1935 (G)NP congress at Middelburg by train, Hofmeyr, Malan and others hatched the plan for a northern 'voice'. Convening his wine farmers in Stellenbosch in September — by then, Hofmeyr had also managed to centralise their capital into the KWV (Ko-operatiewe Wynbouers-Vereeniging) — Hofmeyr secured backing for a new publishing venture, Voortrekkerpers, which was registered in March 1936. Hofmeyr and Malan's idea was to balance Cape finance with non-Naspers control, so that the northerners would not feel too manipulated by the South. Not that Hofmeyr was about to forgo any control, though. He was to be the chairman of Voortrekkerpers, Malan was to be a board member, and so was Strijdom, leader of the Transvaal (G)NP. To clinch the matter, there was, over Strijdom's strong objection, to be a Cape editor for the new paper, *Die Transvaler* — young Stellenbosch social psychology professor H F Verwoerd. This was to be Hofmeyr's biggest mistake. From the very first editorial in October 1937, in which Verwoerd lambasted Jewish meddling in Afrikaner financial affairs and advocated deporting all Jews, the two clashed. The pleasantly surprised Strijdom changed his opinion of the new editor. Hofmeyr resigned after only two years, withdrawing some of the Cape capital.

Verwoerd's outspoken views antagonised not only Hofmeyr but also English (largely Jewish) financial and mining capital in the Transvaal. As happened with *De Burger*, *Die Transvaler* was hit by an advertisement boycott. Swallowing their pride, Voortrekkerpers appealed to Hofmeyr for assistance. Wanting full control, Hofmeyr offered to buy all their shares at a greatly reduced price. A furious Strijdom turned him down. It was roughly at this time that Hofmeyr's Sanlam began making overtures to the Transvaal farmers to attract their capital for investment. In the context of South Africa being dragged into a second world war on imperialist Britain's side, at the tail end of a depression which seemed to the northerners to affect everyone but the mines, Cape agriculture and emerging secondary industry, it is no wonder that the northerners developed a deep mistrust of the South, of its press and its finance power. As O'Meara says: "There emerged within the Transvaal (G)NP and Bond a lasting bitterness against, and suspicion of Hofmeyr, Die Nasionale Pers, *Die Burger*, Sanlam and, to a lesser extent, the Cape Party[9].

This was the situation on the eve of the war: growing antipathy to the southerners on the part of the northerners, a strong southern press serving nationalist and capitalist interests, and *Die Transvaler* beginning to find its republican feet under the fiery Verwoerd.

Towards the Capitalist Republic: 1939-1947

Just five years after Fusion in 1939, the UP split on the war issue. Hertzog and Malan joined forces in a Herenigde Nasionale Party (HNP), leaving Smuts on his own to conduct the war and the country. The petty-bourgeois Bond saw its chance to unify Afrikaners against the war on a republican ticket, and were the principal matchmakers for the HNP. The war was initially strenuously opposed by the farmers, who had a good trading relationship with the Third Reich at the time, but the war industry boosted their position considerably, and in three years, the gross value of all farm products rose by sixty-seven per cent[10]. This meant that the bourgeoisie as represented by the Bond had to mobilise 'Afrikaner' interests if they were to advance their own.

The two major events of this period were the first Economic Volkskongres, convened in October 1939 by the Bond front organisation, FAK (Federasie van Afrikaanse Kultuurverenigings), and by Sanlam and the Reddingsdaad Bond (RDB). Despite their mistrust, the northerners had begun to realise that only a national economy mobilisation would enable them to stabilise their own position. There were important differences between the Bond and Sanlam, but these were rhetorically papered over by L J du Plessis' slogan of 'Volkskapitalisme' (people's capital), which was to make an alliance of workers, petty bourgeoisie, farmers and capitalists. Sanlam's Louw and other capitalists were undoubtedly in it for the profits they would get from centralising capital, which would enable them to become independent of agriculture by the 1950s. Nevertheless, the Kongres emphasized the crucial importance of agriculture, the permanence of an Afrikaner proletariat and the need for unions, all bound together by Afrikaner nationalism,. In other words, as editor Verwoerd stressed in his address to the Kongres, the strategy needed was a means to achieve political and economic power for the 'volk'.

Collecting all 'loose money' and re-investing it in commerce and industry to generate industrial capital was the economic strategy. It never really worked. What did work was the awakening of a financial 'spirit' amongst Afrikaners. This was achieved primarily by the Kongres offshoot, the Reddingsdaad Bond (RDB). It had two important tasks to fulfill. The first was to inculcate a notion of 'common interest' in the 'volk', something difficult to do since Afrikaner workers had already developed a healthy suspicion for all employers. The second was to patch up the proliferating differences in Afrikaner politics.

As mentioned before, the extremely weak (G)NP in the Transvaal (Strijdom was their only MP before 1939) meant that the Bond was the major, though extra-parliamentary, organising body in the Transvaal. The war had precipitated a number of varieties of extreme anti-imperialism and republicanism. In 1940 a Bond committee chaired by L J du Plessis with, amongst others, Dr Piet Meyer and Verwoerd, had convened to draft a republican constitution. This was unveiled at the 1941 HNP congress which elected Malan as new 'Volksleier' (People's Leader). It is probably no exaggeration to say that the Draft Republican Constitution was a neo-Nazi document produced in part as a rejection of Smuts's war effort. *Die Burger* led a campaign against the draft. Malan similarly opposed it. Verwoerd and *Die Transvaler* unsurprisingly supported it. The 'volkseenheid' (people's unity) platform of the HNP was in mortal danger.

In the event, a small though powerful group behind the draft was scapegoated, and the HNP united to destroy it. The Ossewa Brandwag (OB) had been formed in February 1939 by Colonel Laas, soon to be replaced by the old Administrator of the Orange Free State and self-confessed Nazi, Dr J van Rensburg. He established for himself a powerful group within the Bond, including du Plessis and Meyer. Indeed, Meyer became its propaganda chief.

It may seem strange that Malan, Strijdom and Verwoerd combined to destroy the OB, but the answer lies in the fact that the OB was jeopardising the RDB's economic mobilisation strategy. Seeing that the HNP was hesitating to support the OB-inspired draft, the OB distributed it in pamphlet form, to the intense annoyance of Malan. Its extremist petty-bourgeois *modus operandi* had alienated the farmers as well as the southern financiers, and the farmers' rising prosperity had started a drift back to Smuts. The economic strategy, still in its infancy, was jeopardised, but combined efforts managed to re-unite the HNP and by the 1943 elections it had established itself as the leader of nationalist politics, now also in the Transvaal. It was only to consolidate this position in the 1948 election victory — thanks to the extra-political unificatory work of the RDB. Indeed, this had been a time of extra-political organisation.

Consequently, the daily press during this time kept a low profile, supporting its local leaders and parties and only occasionally getting into interprovincial battles. The major mobilising work was done by the two economic journals of the time, *Volkshandel* and *Inspan*, both edited by the energetic Meyer. Through these journals, Meyer managed to win support for the RDB and capitalist centralisation by a curious anti-capitalist rhetoric. It was an anti-capitalism which embodies nearly all of the presuppositions of capitalism — private property, initiative, profit, worker stability and control, and so on. It was expressed in such a way that even the militantly anti-capitalist Mine Workers Union, now under the control of Albert Hertzog, could support it. The whole discourse had been successfully welded together by the ideology of Christian nationalism. And herein lay the RDB's greatest success — it had adjusted Afrikaner workers and petty bourgeoisie to capitalism and had ensured the necessary climate of sympathy for the centralisation and segmentation of agricultural capital, enabling finance companies like Sanlam to invest in commerce and industry. It would not be long before the northern petty bourgeoisie saw what they had given birth to[11].

A Giant Awakes

The Hertzogite Afrikaanse Pers Beperk (APB) and its main Transvaal organ *Die Vaderland* had remained loyal to the small Hertzog offshoot party, the Afrikaner Party, formed by APB board member Havenga. In the year immediately prior to the momentous 1948 election, nationalist feeling was running high. Willem van Heerden, *Die Vaderland*'s editor since it had become a Johannesburg afternoon paper in June 1936, left the paper in 1947 over a 'disagreement with management'. With him left *Die Vaderland*'s advertising manager, one Marius Jooste. Together they established Dagbreekpers Beperk with Jooste as the managing director. Van Heerden was to edit the Sunday *Dagbreek*, which first appeared in June 1947.

There are a number of curious aspects to the founding of Dagbreekpers. In 1947 the OB was in control of a press corporation interestingly enough called Perskor. Perskor was incorporated into the larger OPSA (Onafhanlike Pers van Suid-Afrika) on the initiative of Piet Meyer, and OPSA provided some of the capital, but not enough of it. Jooste then approached various English business and mining concerns, including Strathmore Investments. Strathmore had controlling shares in a Labour Party Sunday called *Weekblad*. This became incorporated into *Dagbreek* when Strathmore, negotiating under their subsidiary Scotia Press, obtained the controlling shares in Dagbreekpers. In the wake of an extremely vituperative campaign waged by the OB against English 'imperialist' capital — indeed, vituperative enough for the OB Stormjaers (Stormtroopers) to attempt to whip Verwoerd for writing anti-OB editorials in *Die Transvaler* (Verwoerd's legendary rhetoric reportedly dissuaded them) — it is indeed strange that OB capital should join hands with the hated English mining capital in Dagbreekpers.

The first board of Dagbreekpers had Strathmore fairly solidly represented by T Scott, C W Roper and J C McIntyre, with three of the remaining four seats filled by Jooste, L J du Plessis and van Heerden. The Strathmore representatives had insisted that *Dagbreek* should support no political party, and this neutrality clause was written into the articles of Dagbreekpers. Afrikaanse Pers responded promptly to the competition, and brought out *Sondagnuus* in July 1947. The paper was not a success, and it was incorporated by Dagbreekpers five months later. The resultant Sunday became *Dagbreek en Sondagnuus*.

It was soon apparent that Jooste the empire builder ('die boumeester')[12] planned to consolidate a voice for northern nationalists, and a conservative voice at that. Political neutrality would not be maintained for long. In 1951, Jooste formed Dagbreek Trust Beperk, a controlling subsidiary within Dagbreekpers. Through all the subsequent mergers and changes of name, Dagbreek Trust remains today the controlling body within what is now called Perskor. In the 1953 general election, *Dagbreek en Sondagnuus* openly supported the NP, much to Strathmore's annoyance. Jooste then offered to buy out Scott and Roper, leaving the lone McIntyre on the new board alongside Strijdom, Verwoerd, Schoeman, de Klerk (at one time or another, all prime ministers or Cabinet ministers), du Plessis, Jooste and van Heerden. From then on, Dagbreekpers officially supported the NP.

In Search of the 'Real' National Party

The meaning of this support was simply a question of nationalist fervour. The unity fostered by the RDB in the 1940s had created the conditions for the nationalist class alliance which brought the NP to power in 1948. Each class grouping of this alliance — the Transvaal, Cape and OFS farmers, specific segments of white labour, the Afrikaner petty bourgeoisie (strongest in the Transvaal) and the emergent capitalists of the RDB — had its own different interests, and for each apartheid promised a different set of advantages[13]. Influx control kept black labour on the farms and out of competition with white workers. The migratory labour system kept black workers reasonably unorganised and wage structures low for capitalists and the petty bourgeoisie, who depended at this time on agricultural and capitalist prosperity for their own. Regionalist animosities were at a minimum by 1948. But the emerging dominant fraction of Afrikaner capital would soon polarise capitalist and petty-bourgeois interests, and this polarisation would once again manifest itself in part as a North-South conflict.

The 1950 second Ekonomiese Volkskongres (Economic People's Congress) marked the ascendance of Afrikaner finance capital, which began to flourish under NP rule as never before. Volkskas investments doubled between 1948 and 1952[14], and State intervention strengthened the Afrikaner finance houses in many ways. It was not long before Afrikaner and English capital began to co-operate in joint ventures (like the Anglo-American and Federale Mynbou venture to control General Mining and Finance Corporation, or Gencor, in 1963) and to demand labour policies from the State in opposition to Afrikaner worker and petty-bourgeois interests.

Afrikaner politics in the late 1950s and 1960s saw a renewed outcry from the North against the 'geldmag' (money power) of the South (primarily Sanlam and Rembrandt). Once again, *Die Burger* and Nasionale Pers vocally supported Cape interests against northern 'provincialism' and by Verwoerd's assassination in 1966, the conflict between the southern (and some northern) capitalists, and the northern 'verkramptes' had burst into the open. It is in this context that Jooste's organisational efforts should be seen. He had correctly perceived the rise of southern capital and the need for a strong northern voice to articulate Afrikaner worker — and especially petty-bourgeois — interests. Consequently in July 1962 Afrikaanse Pers merged with Dagbreekpers, forming the powerful Afrikaanse Pers Beperk (1962). This brought *Die Vaderland* and *Dagbreek en Sondagnuus* together into the same stable. Nasionale Pers were not slow to perceive the need for a 'verligte' voice in the Transvaal, and in October 1965 they launched the Sunday *Die Beeld* amid bitter controversy. This was a major national effort on the part of Naspers, and *Die Beeld* was printed simultaneously in Cape Town, Bloemfontein and Johannesburg.

A circulation battle ensued between *Die Beeld* and *Dagbreek en Sondagnuus*, a battle neither of them could really win. Jooste, in the meanwhile, steadily consolidated his empire. In 1967, APB (1962) absorbed the Cape weekly *Die Landstem*, and in 1969, incorporated it into *Dagbreek en Sondagnuus* which now became *Dagbreek en Landstem*. In 1968, Jooste managed to effect a collaboration between APB (1962) and Voortrekkerpers, and together they launched the Pretoria daily *Hoofstad* in April 1968. The editor of the conservative church organ *Die*

Kerkbode, Dr A Treurnicht, was appointed the first editor. By the end of the 1960s the circulation battle between *Die Beeld* and *Dagbreek en Landstem* had driven APB (1962) and Naspers to look for a compromise. They decided to merge the two papers into a new Sunday called *Rapport*, which came out in November 1970 under the editorship of T Wepener. *Rapport* was and is jointly owned by APB (1962) and Naspers.

In April 1971, Jooste consolidated the northern voice even further by merging APB (1962) with Voortrekkerpers to form Perskorporasie van Suid Afrika Beperk (Perskor). It is worth noting that Dagbreek Trust now came to be the controlling body of *Die Transvaler* as well as of *Die Vaderland* and *Hoofstad*. In November 1972 *Hoofstad* gained a sister paper, *Oggendblad*, which immediately took an anti-English line under H Pakendorf, its first editor. By the early 1970s Jooste had managed to consolidate northern control over every major paper issued in the Transvaal, effectively establishing an unchallenged voice for petty-bourgeois conservatism in the region, under the banner of the 'authentic' Afrikaner voice.

By the early 1970s the reforms needed to ensure continued capital accumulation for big capital were meeting with stiff resistance in the North. In 1974, Naspers made its second major effort to establish a 'verligte' pro-capitalist voice in the Transvaal, and it launched *Beeld* as a Johannesburg daily under the editorship of the highly regarded Schalk Pienaar. It was perceived as a direct challenge to Perskor, and indeed, that is just what it was. Perskor board members and Cabinet ministers Hendrik Schoeman and Dr Connie Mulder were outraged and they actively undermined *Beeld* in political circles. Indeed, Afrikaner politicians have always taken strong views on their partisan press, and Prime Minister Verwoerd had called for a boycott of *Die Beeld* in 1965. Politics in the 1970s were more clandestine and dirtier. In 1977, for instance, Mulder allocated ninety-eight percent of the Department of Information's publishing budget to Perskor[15]. And it was in 1977 that Perskor began to submit falsely inflated sales figures to the Audit Bureau of Circulation (ABC). What these tactics signify is that Perskor was attempting at all costs to hold together the Afrikaner conservative consensus based upon images of 'Volk' and 'Vaderland' that had proved so successful in the days of the RDB and the 1948 victory.

This essentially petty-bourgeois effort could not succeed, for it had history and a very real Afrikaner class split ranged against it, as we shall see. Nevertheless, by the beginning of the 1980s, both Perskor and Naspers could be found claiming support for the NP, promoting different notions of Afrikanerdom, and locked in struggle for a fast disintegrating Afrikaner readership.

The Fight for the Heartland: 1982-1983

In 1973, soon after its incorporation by Perskor in 1971, an astute theologian, Dr W A de Klerk, was appointed editor of *Die Transvaler*. De Klerk was a 'Dopper', a version of Christian nationalism that can be crudely characterised as theologically and socially conservative but relatively liberal in political terms. It was de Klerk who had coined the 'verligte/verkrampte' terminology in 1966, and who seemed in the mid 1970s to know most clearly what were the issues that troubled Afrikaners. For de Klerk, as for other Afrikaner editors, some form of Afrikaner unity behind the NP seemed essential. When the first wave of 'verkramptes' led by Albert Hertzog left the NP in 1969 to form the Herstigte Nasionale Party, the press and later the Bond closed ranks and effectively expelled them from the mainstream of Afrikanerdom. By the time the second NP split began to loom in early 1982, neither the press nor the Bond were so sure any more, particularly since it had become apparent under P W Botha's premiership that Afrikaner business was the dominant grouping, dictating issues of policy and reform.

The imminent crisis called for strong leadership and the press was not slow to accept this responsibility. As we shall see, a highly contradictory press situation slowly began to resolve itself in this period, as the widening class division began to impose its logic across the feelings of identity and community that had for so long been the unifiers of Afrikanerdom.

The Demise of 'Rueful Candour'[16]

"Information is one thing. Systematic propaganda is something entirely different" — Koos Buitendag, managing director of Perskor.

On 27 February 1982, Dr A Treurnicht, then leader of the Transvaal NP, led twenty-one MP's in a vote of no-confidence in Premier Botha and effectively out of the NP altogether. From then on, de Klerk in his column 'Perspektief' (Perspective) in *Die Transvaler* led an extremely vituperative campaign against Treurnicht and his fledgling Conservative Party (CP). Even the solidly pro-Botha Ton Vosloo of Naspers' *Beeld* found something complimentary to say about the benighted Treurnicht, but not de Klerk, who consistently editorialised against him during 1982.

The CP was not the only target of de Klerk's polemical journalism. He tackled the FAK in April for suggesting that the Afrikaner press was misleading the 'volk' and he tackled the ATKV (Afrikaanse Taal en Kultuurvereniging) rightists for siding with the CP and for sowing dissent in Afrikaner ranks.

It is not difficult to see what was happening here. De Klerk, being a political 'liberal', had decided to back P W Botha and to try to consolidate Afrikanerdom around a verligte identity. The traditionally conservative northern cultural organisations were feeling a very strong pull towards the CP, who set out to champion the rights of Afrikaner workers and petty-bourgeoisie. In a strongly worded call for unity, de Klerk was attempting to swing these bodies behind Botha. In the process, he was alienating a lot of influential northerners who were either overt or covert CP supporters. De Klerk later confirmed this: "I was insulting the most important people ... who, coincidentally also happened to be members of the CP"[17]. The tone of 'rueful candour' that had characterised his political comment for so long had given way to a partisan, strident crusade.

It also became clear that not everyone at Perskor shared de Klerk's sentiments. In April *Beeld*'s Vosloo had attacked *Oggendblad* and *Hoofstad* for seeming to support Treurnicht, but *Oggendblad*'s Human was openly expressing reservations about the reformist President's Council proposals, and Vosloo kept up his attack from April through August. Indeed, two days before de Klerk's dismissal, Vosloo accused Perskor of shifting its political allegiances, drawing an angry riposte from Jooste himself.

This was not the only bone of contention between Naspers and Perskor in this period. At the end of April, Perskor's circulation fraud was exposed. From January 1977 to September 1980, Perskor had inflated its circulation figures in a curious way — it had re-allocated distribution sales to make it seem as if sales figures in the Pretoria region were higher than they actually were. The re-allocated figure for *Die Transvaler* was 110 358 and that for *Die Vaderland*, 29 829[18]. What was at issue was the perceived readership for Perskor in conservative Afrikanerdom's heartland. It was this heartland which was starting to desert Perskor's flagship *Die Transvaler*. Inflated figures notwithstanding, the ABC figures for January 2 show *Die Transvaler*'s circulation as little more than two-thirds that of *Beeld*. All Media and Products Survey (AMPS) readership figures paint an even more revealing picture. In 1981, the difference in readership in the Transvaal as a whole was less than one per cent between *Die Transvaler* and *Beeld*. In 1982, *Die Transvaler* was lagging by more than twenty-four per cent.

It was this heartland that was both the financial and political stake for Jooste. That Human and *Oggendblad* were courting the CP in this period is doubly significant, given the local response to *Die Transvaler*. It is no wonder that the furious Naspers sued Perskor for R12 million (later settled out of court). Perskor was found guilty of fraud in September 1983 and fined R20 000.

A further small threat to Perskor's dwindling constituency arrived in May in the form of the fortnightly *Die Patriot*. A paper under this name had first appeared a century ago in Paarl, and had now been revived under the editorship of Dr C Jooste explicitly as a voice for the CP.

As 1982 neared its end, the newspaper situation in the Transvaal was a distinctly unhappy one. *Beeld* was increasingly cornering the market with a combination of hard-nosed pragmatism and uncompromising support for the NP and its proposed reforms. As it had always done, Naspers was advocating reforms that were essential for the continued prosperity of the big capitalists, still largely based in the South. Perskor was increasingly speaking with a forked tongue, and the division was mercilessly exploited by *Beeld*. The two Pretoria papers were moving increasingly to the right, while *Die Transvaler* under de Klerk found itself stranded in the middle, tying the language of group politics and petty-bourgeois social conservatism to an advocacy of the liberalising reforms of P W Botha. In short, de Klerk had become an anachronism that Perskor — mindful of its constituency, which was fast moving rightwards — could no longer afford.

De Klerk's last three editorials for *Die Transvaler*, on 23, 24 and 25 August, all expressed support for the NP. The last editorial affirmed apocalyptically that *Die Transvaler* "staan al nege jaar lank aan die voorpunt van hervorming" (led the drive for reform for nine years). That nine years had run its course. In the editorial-less *Transvaler* of 31 August, the headline announced, inaccurately, "Dr de Klerk tree uit" (Dr de Klerk resigns). Without consulting his fellow directors on Dagbreek Trust, of whom de Klerk was one, Jooste had fired him.

Like everyone else, P W Botha, incidentally also on the board of Naspers, had taken Vosloo's repeated accusations to heart, and Jooste felt constrained, the very next day (1 September), to affirm Perskor's support for the NP in conversation with Botha. A front page news report in *Die Transvaler* expressed the hope that this would put paid to rumours about the changing political line of Perskor. The editorial of that edition expressed muted support for de Klerk. This was the only public indication of intense behind-the-scenes dissatisfaction — six senior editorial members of *Die Transvaler* had resigned in protest, and a further seven took leave to consider their futures. De Klerk himself blamed the CP and "crypto-CP members inside the National Party"[19] for spreading false rumours about him, amongst them, that he was "trying to butter-up to the Cape Establishment"[20]. As always, regional differences became a convenient way for expressing what was essentially a class conflict. In any case, if the northern constituency was moving rightwards, Jooste would not let de Klerk stop him from following them.

Slowly Towards the (Far) North

Despite Jooste's assurances, *Oggendblad*'s Human continued to disparage Botha's plans for reform, drawing a stinging attack from Botha towards the end of September. During this time, *Die Transvaler* continued to express support for the NP, as did the afternoon *Die Vaderland*. Something had to be done to restabilise the shaken *Transvaler*, side-line Human who had become something of an embarrassment to Perskor, and above all, to re-capture the northern market.

Jooste's strategy was a bold one. He dissolved *Hoofstad* and *Oggendblad*, which in any case were not making much money, and he moved *Die Transvaler* to become the afternoon paper for Pretoria and the Northern Transvaal. The last Johannesburg edition, on 19 February 1983, carried an editorial on the paper's 'new task'. " 'n Nuwe en breër nasionalisme moet gesmee word" (A new and broader nationalism must be forged). The thrust of this kind of talk is clear: to hold the fragmentation of Afrikanerdom by the tried and tested method of nationalist appeal, or perhaps even to assist the CP in articulating a new nationalism. However that may be, the Pretoria edition of *Die Transvaler* of 21 February contained an affirmation of support for the NP and for 'die Afrikaner se strewe in die breedste sin van die woord' (the Afrikaner's struggle in the broadest sense of the word). Indeed, in October 1983, *Die Transvaler* was still supporting the NP, but with 'more tact than fire', as Deborah Davies puts it[21]. This is in fairly marked contrast to the style adopted by *Die Vaderland* and its new editor, Pakendorf, who moved to Johannesburg when *Hoofstad* dissolved. The hitherto cautious *Vaderland* became more assertive, critical and subtle. *Die Transvaler*, by contrast, invited conservative Prof Boshoff to write a fortnightly guest column and adopted a conciliatory tone towards the CP.

The overall result, by October 1983, had been for Perskor to leave the Afrikaans morning market to Naspers and to *Beeld*, and to tailor two different constituencies for its afternoon papers. *Die Vaderland* had become more like the southern-born *Beeld* — better, in fact, since it has rarely descended to the 'passionate adulation'[22] practised by *Beeld*. *Die Transvaler* had faced firmly North and in the general direction of the CP. As one would expect, the small Perskor community papers serving the northern hinterland had become even more stridently conservative. *Noord Transvaler* (in Pietersburg) and *Middelburg Observer* had, by late 1983, been told they need not support the NP editorially any longer, and had been publishing CP advertisements. *Oggendblad*'s Human had become a publicity secretary for the CP.

Perskor had, by these strategies, rationalised its market appeal but could not have solved its problems of political allegiance. Jooste had astutely avoided direct competition with Naspers, and *Die Vaderland* became a more tolerable and less inflammatory anomaly than *Die Transvaler* had been under de Klerk. Nevertheless, for the first time since 1948, the Transvaal had a sizeable non-NP class alliance of Afrikaner farmers, workers and petty bourgeoisie organised to oppose a Nationalist government, and for the first time since then, a major Afrikaner publisher had moved into confrontation with the NP. The long-standing feud between North and South has certainly not been laid to rest.

Resumé: A Question of Class

Conventional wisdom to the contrary, movement and change in Afrikanerdom has always had a lot to do with the aspirations of class groupings, as this chapter has tried to show. The coalition of wine and fruit farmers with the financial capitalists in the South gave rise to a specific set of southern imperatives to do with the conditions favourable for capital accumulation. Up until 1948, these were best served by courting the agricultural capital and 'loose money' of the North within the framework of the rhetorically generated ideology of Christian nationalism. In this period, all the major Afrikaner papers were established to evoke popular consent for this ideology, especially amongst the Afrikaner workers and petty bourgeoisie of the North.

The northern coalition depended far more on an emergent petty-bourgeoisie who had, in the pre-1948 period at least, been the most active in formulating a pure Christian nationalism within the Broederbond, voiced through the papers of the North. As the northern petty-bourgeoisie and workers became stronger, so conservative interests were increasingly articulated through their media.

Christian nationalism could hold only so much diversity of interest, and it began to fragment in various ways from the 1960s onwards. Politically, this took the form of splits in the NP. In the media, it translated itself into an increasingly vicious escalation of conflict between Naspers and Perskor as they began to struggle in earnest for the soul of the 'real' Afrikaner.

Notes and References

1. I have made extensive use of the following sources of information: J de Villiers, *South African Community and its Newspapers — a Socio-Historical Study* unpublished PhD thesis, University of the Orange Free State (1976); L J Erasmus, *'n Volk Staan Op Uit Sy As: Verhaal van die Afrikaanse Pers (1962)*, Johannesburg: APB; D O'Meara, *Volkskapitalisme — Class, Capital and Ideology in the Development of Afrikaner Nationalism 1934-1948*; and E Potter, *The Press and Opposition — The Political Role of South African Newspapers*. My analytical framework owes a lot to that developed by Dan O'Meara.
2. Interview with Keyan Tomaselli.
3. H Adam and H Giliomee, *The Rise and Crisis of Afrikaner Power* p 147
4. *Ibid*
5. De Villiers, *op cit* p446
6. O'Meara, *op cit* p 78
7. *Ibid* p 101
8. Adam and Giliomee, *op cit* p147
9. O'Meara, *op cit* p 106

10. *Ibid* pp 122-3
11. *Ibid* pp 163-6
12. In the preface to Erasmus, *op cit*.
13. O'Meara, *op cit* p 243
14. *Ibid* p 250
15. *New York Times* (10 May 1978)
16. A phrase used by James McClurg in the *Sunday Express* (5 September 1983).
17. Interview with Neil Hooper in the *Sunday Times* (5 September 1982).
18. See the *Rand Daily Mail* (20 September 1983).
19. *Sunday Times, op cit*
20. *Ibid*
21. Deborah Davies in *Sunday Express* (9 October 1983).
22. *Ibid*

Acknowledgement

Thanks are due to Ruth Tomaselli for helping me to gather data for this chapter.

Chapter 5
Cacophony of Consent: The Press in the Struggle for Educational Reform

Johan Muller

On 18, 19 and 20 March 1982, 1 621 delegates attended a Volkskongres (VK) in the University of the Orange Free State's Callie Human Hall to generate Afrikanerdom's response to the Government-commissioned Human Sciences Research Council (HSRC) report entitled *Provision of Education in the RSA*. The Afrikaner community was representatively convened to give a community response to a document that was contentious and potentially divisive for education, and indeed, for Afrikanerdom as a whole.

The report came out amidst a media-orchestrated clamour about the 'crisis in education', and the causes and cures of the crisis were actively debated in the media. In this chapter I pose the question of what role the press plays in mediating a public debate on issues of educational policy. An answer to this question requires placing the educational crisis into a historical and analytical context of generalized 'crisis' in the South African State; seeing it as a regional instance of, and contribution to, the complex restructuring of South African society showing a socio-political community, the Afrikaners, being radically fractured by the restructuring; and showing how the press, despite highly visible differences of interpretation, help to construct consent for the contentious policy and a fragile reprieve for Afrikanerdom.

The State, Afrikaner Nationalism and 'Crisis'

In this section I will briefly examine the 'crisis' of capital accumulation, and the conjoint 'crisis' in Afrikanerdom. I will then attempt to place these in the analytical perspective of a generalized crisis of hegemony.

Three reservations should be borne in mind. In the first place, this account of the crisis in both Afrikanerdom and education is only one aspect of a crisis for the State as a whole. This is not an account of the wider issues of class struggle and contradiction in education or in the State at large, but of the particular form of the crisis structured by the contradictions within, and responses by Afrikanerdom.

Secondly, the notion of 'crisis' has been much misused in radical accounts of capitalism. "People doggedly persist in seeing the approach of the final struggle every time a new rule of the social game makes its appearance"[1]. The Gramscian analogy of trench warfare is apt. It is easy to imagine that the whole defensive system of the state has collapsed when only the outer perimeter of defences has been destroyed[2]. What seems an irreparable schism in the structure of the modern bourgeois state is most often a strategic crisis, setting for the State a task of reconstruction to which it has more often than not proved itself equal.

Finally, what comes to be seen as critical by society at large is very often the result of definitions put forward by people in power and publicized by the media. These definitions are 'constructs'[3], often emphasizing one part of a problem and keeping other parts out of public view. I do not want to suggest that objective crises 'out there' in the economy compel changes in society in any mechanical way. A construed 'crisis' is therefore always a crisis *for* some group or set of interests.

'Crisis' of Capital Accumulation, 1960s-1970s

The 1960s' economic boom accompanied the transition from labour-intensive to capital-intensive production in many sectors of the economy. This transition involved an increase in technological production, in many cases replacing the traditional industrial division of labour between skilled and unskilled labour with a division between semi-skilled and technical/supervisory labour[4]. Technical/supervisory labour rapidly became a major requirement for industry while a stratum of unskilled labour became redundant.

By the time the economy entered its next downswing in the mid-1970s, three critical areas could no longer be muffled by prosperity. These were vast and growing unemployment, a growing shortage of technical labour, and increased labour union organization. The educational implication was that the only kinds of jobs available were those for which workers were untrained. Market pressures in the 1970s exacerbated the technical skills shortage. The import market, based on the exchange value of gold and other minerals, had begun to reach its ceiling and the necessity for a strong capital goods sector became apparent. Adequate skilled labour was essential for this to happen. Consequently, training 'needs' began to be requested by capital from an educational system which, for blacks at least, was too unwieldy and backward to cope, structured as it was to produce a 'dependent', unskilled workforce[5].

In the recessionary period of the 1970s, discriminatory employment, unemployment and bad education evoked two not unexpected responses: intensifying labour and political struggles in the black communities, and also growing resistance in black schools. In the latter, the resistance was not only anti-apartheid in form, but at times anti-capitalist too[6]. Taken together, these tendencies posed a threat to orderly capital accumulation and stable government. A set of reforms was therefore demanded by the big capital sector of the market, though these would not necessarily be seen to be in the interests of other sectors of society. The State's task was to introduce the reforms whilst retaining the confidence of sufficient numbers of the electorate to stay in power. It is necessary to look briefly at the changing pattern of Afrikaner society to see why this is so.

Shifting Patterns of Alliance and the Structure of Afrikaner Society

It can justifiably be said that the Nederduitse Gereformeerde Kerk (NGK), the Broederbond and its offshoots, the Nationalist Party (NP) and the media co-ordinate the entire cultural and political life of the Afrikaner. The NP is primarily a grouping of two major provincial party organizations, the Cape and the Transvaal, each with its own historically specific social arrangement. Natal and the Orange Free State are largely peripheral. When the NP came into power in 1948, the Transvaal NP represented a class alliance of farmers, white workers (principally in mining, construction, steel and transport), a large group of the petty bourgeoisie and a small group of commercial and financial capitalists. The petty bourgeoisie were the numerically superior group of this alliance.

The Broederbond, founded in 1918, had become the 'moral-intellectual' leadership of this Transvaal alliance by the 1930s, submerging potential differences of interest into an immensely powerful politico-cultural identity clustered around a notion of 'volk' and its 'divine calling'. I will examine this process in more detail in the next section. A whole range of cultural and political organizations were co-ordinated by the Broederbond to give organizational form to this identity:

> ... the Broederbond is an elitist organisation, representing the vast majority of Nationalist Cabinet ministers and parliamentarians as well as leaders in the Church, education, and cultural movements, newspapers, labour, police, government services, universities ... It links these leaders from parliament to Church councils and local village communities in the smallest centres. They are tightly knit

together, each cell receiving regular directives, study materials and other instructions are intensively discussed, so forging the members into a cohesive, nation-wide unit. A common approach to issues and problems is created so that public opinion can be masterminded ...[7]

An ex-chairman of the Broederbond, Dr P Meyer, has said that "the four sectors of the pyramid (of Afrikanerdom) are the political, the cultural, the economic and the educational side, with our own Afrikaans Christian National philosophy of existence and of the world as the base"[8].

Even today, the NGK represents about sixty-three per cent of all Afrikaners[9], and every second dominee of the NGK is a member of the Broederbond. In 1977, 2 242 teachers, or more than twenty per cent, were members, making up the single largest group in the Broederbond. It should not be supposed that the Broederbond simply manipulated these organizations. Since Broederbonders were prominent in the leadership structures of most of them, they led rather than manipulated. As Serfontein says, 'one cannot dictate to oneself'[10].

A different pattern had established itself in the Cape NP by 1948. The grouping here was primarily of wealthy Cape farmers and financial capitalists, located mainly in Sanlam and later Rembrandt. The Cape NP was thus more unproblematically capitalist than the Transvaal NP from the outset. It's construal of the 'volk' was correspondingly different, and although it certainly had some influence in the Cape, the Broederbond was never the force there that it was in the Transvaal. By the late 1950s, Cape financial capital had become independent of agricultural capital[11], finding greater common ground with English mining and financial capital, as well as with Afrikaans capital in the Transvaal. It was for this emerging trans-provincial coalition of big capital that the abovementioned reforms were becoming imperative. The other partners to the Afrikaner alliance were, however, far from convinced of their advantages.

The NP began to rearrange itself into two opposing interest groups. On the one hand were the reformists for whom the reforms were essential. On the other hand was the conservative grouping of farmers, white workers and especially the State-employed petty-bourgeoisie for whom the old 1948 alliance that had swept the NP into power still offered the most obvious benefits. The 1948 alliance was epitomized by old-style apartheid, which the reforms, at least in the labour and educational domains, were set to dismantle.

The upshot for Afrikanerdom as a whole was that by 1970 the nature of the Afrikaner 'volk' and what constituted its interests was in open dispute. This dispute manifested itself at every level of organization. It could be seen at the cabinet, civil service and party political levels, influencing State policy, or more often than not paralysing it. But the dispute was waged most bitterly in the cultural domain, within the Broederbond and its cultural offshoots, the Church and, of course, the Afrikaner press. The latter traditionally owed it allegiance either to the Cape NP (Nasionale Pers) or the Transvaal NP (Perskor). The struggle was now being waged within each of these groups as well, in terms of whether to support the ascendant reformists or to back the traditional conservatives.

The HNP split to the right in 1969, the Information Scandal of 1978, and the 1982 Conservative Party split to the right, all reflected reactions to the gradual ascendancy of the reformist tendency within the NP, which, under P W Botha, has been transformed into a body with considerably less popular-democratic power than it had had before. Government executive power has been increasingly centralized in the office of the Prime Minister (now State President), who exercises his power more and more in the interests of English and Afrikaans capital than those of the class-composite 'volk'. From this base, the reformists have set up a restructuring strategy with implications for all the major domains in 'crisis'. The means for introducing the strategy in each domain has generally been that of the State commission, with commissions into labour legislation (Wiehahn), manpower planning (Riekert), political reform (the President's Council proposals), education (de Lange), mass media (Steyn) and state security (Rabie), to mention only the more prominent ones.

It must be emphasised that the struggle for reform has

by no means been won within the NP, for two important reasons. Organisationally, the NP and the civil service, in the Transvaal in particular, are still extensively manned by the conservative petty bourgeoisie. Party rank and file have strong conservative leanings. The politics of the conservatives are rooted in the 'volk'. Reformist arguments, appealing to reason and the 'national interest', have no real purchase on popular consciousness, especially when these arguments are increasingly clearly seen to be against conservative interests. The reformists have therefore to negotiate consent to reform on exceedingly precarious terrain, and the conservatives to resist it by all means at their disposal.

The Travails of 'Volkseenheid', 1948-1980[12]

In South Africa, the meaning of apartheid implies that there is no 'general interest' for all the people, and so a factor vital for general consent-building is missing from the South African hegemonic armoury. In this section I shall examine the various Afrikaner discourses that have attempted to cope with this fact, as well as with the 'crisis' of the 1970s during which time this vital absence could no longer be ignored.

The major binding factor of the fairly loose alliance of Afrikaner classes that came to power in 1948 was a common-sense ethos of Christian nationalism. The alliance had not been easily accomplished. The Broederbond had established a base amongst the petty bourgeoisie in the Transvaal by taking over the leadership of the Transvaalse Onderwysersvereeniging of the 1920s, but it found difficulty in persuading the depression-stricken Afrikaner workers that the 'Christian-national Afrikaner' had anything to do with them. O'Meara writes that this was because of the 'literary' or traditional rather than 'organic' position of the Broederbond in the early 1930s[13].

It was probably the NGK in the mid-1930s that first began to rein in the relationships between the 'individual', the 'volk', culture and the State, as it became involved in the problems of Afrikaner poverty (setting up soup kitchens), education, language and so on. This

'Kultuurpolitiek' (cultural politics), as the NGK called it, had two overriding aims: to bridge class divisions within Afrikanerdom and to emphasize the need for an economic mobilization of the 'volk'[14].

The rallying cry of 'volkseenheid' was increasingly being heard, and its principal slogan was launched by Professor du Plessis in his opening address to the first Ekonomiese Volkskongres (Economic People's Congress) in 1939 — 'volkskapitalisme'. The Broederbond saw this congress as the turning point in the development of Afrikaner nationalism[15], a development definitively nailed down in the second Ekonomiese Volkskongres of 1950.

Volkskapitalisme had an ostensibly anti-capitalist tenor, but was in effect the means for welding very disparate classes of Afrikaners to an economic mobilization under the banner of a 'new' national identity — the 'Christian-national Afrikaner'. The main accomplishment of the mobilization was to secure a base for commercial and industrial capitalist accumulation. The Sauer Commission of 1948 added the stamp of political legitimacy, and Christian nationalism as a political doctrine enshrined the commonsense within an ideology of domination:

> The party (NP) subscribes to the view that God determined that there will be a variety of races and people whose survival and natural growth must be respected as part of the external and divine plan. In South Africa God in his all-wise rule has placed the white race and the non-white race groups with deep racial and other differences. Every race and race group possesses its own character, talents, calling and distinction[16].

The diverse themes of Christian nationalism were expressed in anti-market, anti-individualist, State interventionist talk, which accompanied the creation of a huge bureaucracy staffed predominantly by petty-bourgeois Afrikaners who executed the discourse by means of the labour and influx control machinery of the 1950s and 1960s.

By the 1970s the picture looked very different indeed. The same machinery set up to ensure continued capital accumulation now became a block to capitalist expansion, for the reasons outlined earlier. The economic apartheid that was so heavily weighted in the hegemonic principle by the discourse of Afrikaner nationalism now had to be de-emphasized. English-speaking businessmen like Harry Oppenheimer had been telling the Government this all through the 1960s, but it was the unionising of black workers and the success of their struggles in the early 1970s that clinched the argument.

The reform strategy that was finally launched through the commissions set about welding the diverse voices of Afrikaner and English capital into a new official discourse. Appropriately called 'total strategy' by Prime Minister Botha in 1977[17], there was no doubt that its primary aim was to be "a guarantee for the system of free enterprise"[18]. The disursive elements appropriate to total strategy were transformed out of the libertarian complaints of English industrialists into what is known as Free Market Ideology[19]. Free Market Ideology South African-style argued for a partial uncoupling of the economic and political domains, for a diminution of State interference in the economy, for deracialization of labour and influx legislation, and for recognition of black trade unions. All this was situated within talk about 'individual economic freedom', growth, and prosperity for all.

The hope clearly was that Free Market Ideology would become a platform on which to build a properly-constituted 'general interest', or at least one incorporating the interests of urban blacks, neatly caught in Urry's formula of 'freedom, equality, property and Bentham'[20]. The Wiehahn Report summed up the new orthodoxy in the following way, "The RSA (Republic of South Africa) subscribes to the principles of a free market economy based on individual freedom in the market place"[21]. In terms of the hegemonic principle, this discourse of Free Market Ideology de-emphasizes economic apartheid, stressing rather the 'pure' ideology of capitalist relations, but leaving political apartheid intact.

We can discern at least three different Afrikaner reactions to Free Market Ideology. In the top echelons, economists, businessmen and certain politicians like Fanie Botha articulated a relatively undiluted version, with some talk of 'separate freedoms' and a nod towards what was 'best for the volk' thrown in for good measure. In the lower echelons, State employees, white labour organizations (pre-eminently the Mine Workers Union), together with many academics and conservative cultural leaders like Professor Boshoff, expressed resistance and hostility to market principles in general and the private sector in particular. As the conservative paper *Die Patriot* put it, "Laat ons eerlik wees, ons word deur die ekonomie voorskryf. Wins aan die materiele rykdom het die wins van geestelike rykdom vervang"[22]. This group considers that strong State intervention is the only way to conserve the cultural identity of the Afrikaner. Along with an evocative discourse of 'chaos'[23], this manner of talking has proved enormously attractive to non-bourgeois Afrikaners who have nothing to gain and everything to lose by the proposed reforms. Between these reformists and the conservatives lies a large group of confused Afrikaners. Situated in the middle, they are pulled this way and that by the competing rhetorics that are locked in struggle for popular Afrikaner support.

For reasons that have to do with the evolution of late capitalism, as well as with the historically specific absorption of technocrats, economists and military leaders into the ruling group by P W Botha[24], another patterning of Free Market Ideological discourse is important to note. Technological rationality[25] is an ethos that characterizes 'political' problems as 'technical' ones, and introduces a new agent to solve them, the technical 'expert'. In a climate of confusion, the 'expert' is an excellently neutral 'trans-class' arbiter[26] of political disputes. That he is inevitably reformist behind his 'neutrality' will become clear when considering the Volkskongres.

Any hegemonic principle gives rise to a babble of discourses. This babble becomes a cacophony when 'real interests' are at risk, as they invariably are in periods of reconstruction and reform. It is rather ironic that the very 'volkseenheid' that provided the basis for Afrikaner capital accumulation in the 1950s and 1960s should now have to be dismantled to ensure continued accumulation in the 1980s. The threat to the 'real interests' of some Afrikaners is, to be sure, almost mild — coming in the form of economic and social rights for urban blacks and political rights for Coloureds and Indians. Some commentators prefer to speak of co-optation rather than reform[27]. Nevertheless, the threat of that small compromise has been enough to shatter the dream of 'volkseenheid'.

Forms of Consent to Reform in South Africa

The form of hegemony — the ruler-ruled relation, the kind of consent accorded a political dispensation or 'who consents to what and how?'[28] — differs for different strata of South Africa's social formation. For the disenfranchised blacks, the form is minimal hegemony. Rule over them has been little more than legal and physical domination, with a neutralization of interest and gradual incorporation of the emerging black middle-class producing at best the passive consent necessary to rule a technically regulated work force. While it is the slow transformation of this ruler-ruled relation for a small segment of the black population that is the purpose of the reform tendency, it is of course not nearly enough for the majority. Nevertheless, the formidable machinery of repression keeps them in their place, irrespective of whether they are convinced of their place or not.

The important consent that has to be won for the proposed reforms is amongst the white population with the franchise, as well as amongst the co-opted Coloured and Asian communities and the emergent black middle class. Non-NP voters have to be persuaded of the inevitability of the state of affairs, even if they do not support it wholeheartedly. The form of acceptance required here is pragmatic consent to the 'general interest'. The discursive separation of State action and party politics is most important at this level. The 'productivity problem' and the 'war on the border', for example must be seen as problems for the 'country as a whole'. Loyalty towards a broad, undefined 'South Africanism' — shored up by countless unconnected gobbets of commonsense, like for instance, 'buy South African' and 'support for the Springboks' — is the bedrock of pragmatic consent.

The most active consent to be won for the reforms must, however, come from the Afrikaner and hopefully NP rank and file. Active consent as a popular democratic process works best in the kind of cohesive 'volksgees' atmosphere that prevailed in the Afrikaner community from the 1930s. As we have seen, Afrikaner popular democracy was forged by 'Volkskongreses', organized and coordinated by the Afrikaner churches, especially the NGK[29]. This is the context in which the Bloemfontein Volkskongres should be seen. Most recently, the 'voice of the volk' exercised via the provincial NP congresses has been muted. The traditional right of veto has been replaced by the capacity to 'advise' the Cabinet only. That a 'Volkskongres' was convened to discuss the De Lange Report by consulting the 'volk' emphasizes the extraordinary importance that Afrikaner society at large accorded to the educational reform proposals.

Afrikaner Identity and Ideological Discourse

I have so far tended to refer to ideology as if it was some ghost in the machine of discourse. In order to show what ideological discourse does (or did) for the Afrikaner community, I need to reflect back upon the definition of ideology developed in Chapter 1. Following Althusser and Laclau, ideology can be seen as a discursive formation which creates identity[30]. This means that people live out the structured relations of society and their place in them through a particular ideology. To put it another way, the abstract hegemonic principle is clothed in commonsense by an ideological discourse, and the identity of each person in the social hierarchy is experienced through that commonsense.

The most important identity within ideological discourse is one's own. When a crisis and consequent reform prompts a shift in the hegemonic principle, with a parallel shift in discourse, it always entails an adjustment of identity. So when a hegemonic shift leads to a clash of discourses within a community, this implies an identity crisis for that community.

By 1970, the closely-woven fabric of Afrikaner society was being unstitched in an attempt to disarticulate three interwoven Afrikaner sub-identities — a religious identity (Christian), a cultural identity (nationalism) and a political identity (voting habit) from the conglomerate notion of the 'Afrikaner'. This disarticulation is the direct parallel of the reformist strategy of uncoupling the political from the economic domain. Four examples taken at random show how the reformist tendency is busy disarticulating the conglomerate Afrikaner identity, while the conservative tendency is trying to preserve the old or to articulate it anew.

The first example is an open letter that one hundred and twenty-three NGK theologians published in the *Kerkbode*[31]. This letter rejects the very foundation of Government policy based on apartheid. In ideological terms, it represents a concerted disarticulation of the Afrikaner Christian identity from the political identity. On an SABC radio panel discussion[32] the conservatives within the NGK were plainly very critical about the letter. As Dr Potgieter said to *Rapport*, "This is not the manner in which our church works"[33].

The second example involves the 1982 Afrikaanse Taal en Kultuurvereniging (ATKV) congress. The ATKV is a major Afrikaner cultural organ, and the keynote speech, given by conservative Professor M Swart, was a clear attempt to re-weld the fragmenting conglomerate identity together. In a remarkable outburst, Dr G Viljoen, the reformist Minister of Education, took Swart to task for attempting to realign the political and cultural identities of the Afrikaner. It was to no avail. As new chairman Conradie said, "Ons wil graag kultuur as die groot sametrekker gebruik om eenheid te herstel"[34].

The third and fourth examples are disarticulatory speeches given by reformist academics to cultural organizations. Professor A Brink disarticulated political from cultural identity at a 1982 Skrywersgilde (Writers Guild) colloquium and Professor J Degenaar did the same at a liberal Afrikaans students' forum, Polstu: "... the Afrikaner's own misunderstanding of his role in the present order is his identification of Afrikaner culture with Afrikaner power"[35].

In all of these cases, the disarticulatory or re-articulatory work is a public bid for support, and in practically every case, the bid is contested. These are only hints of the intense struggles going on in Afrikanerdom at present. What is at issue in each case is a complex negotiation of Afrikaner identity.

The major public forum for negotiating matters of ideology is of course the media, as we pointed out in Chapter 2. "Media belong first and foremost to the region of ideology"[36]. This does not mean that they are simply biased[37]. Newspapers negotiate identity, and they do this by addressing a specific reading community: "The papers do not speak directly to readers, but rather through the group ... to which the readers belong ..."[38]. Newspapers position their readers into their appropriate slot in the social hierarchy[39]. Every newspaper seems to have its 'we' which, Ignatieff says, "is not so much spoken of as laid claim to"[40]. Especially in times of crisis, when the identity of 'we's' is the subject of conflict in the community at large, the newspapers have a crucial role in consolidating a particular 'we' from the "clamour of we's"[41].

The final question to consider is the one of ideological reunification. Given the ideological process of disconnecting, it is necessary for a new coherence to be articulated by the reformists if they are not to lose their battle altogether. It is fair to say that the reformist articulators of Afrikanerdom are as yet more adept at disarticulating the dysfunctional conglomerate than they are at articulating a new unity. There is currently much talk of showing 'responsibility to South Africa', but the vagueness and precariousness of the unificaton is still very vulnerable to a conservative rejoinder in terms of the old accord. Consent therefore will depend, in any specific site of reform, on the articulation of a unity of discourse appropriate to the reforms and to the hopes and fears of the constituency concerned.

It is in the light of the whole foregoing analysis of 'crisis' in Afrikanerdom that the Volkskongres (VK) at Bloemfontein should be seen. In particular, a close analysis of the discourses at the VK will reveal the strategies of the disarticulating/re-articulating reformists and the specific resistances of the conservatives, as well as the diverse operations of temporary breaching that are always constructed to keep the peace 'for now'.

Making the Volkskongres Mean

All concerned — government, opposition, press, broadcasting media, and private enterprise — will have to co-operate in conveying a true and authoritative (story) to the world. This does not mean that all have to speak with one voice. The art of diplomacy is to say the same thing in different ways, for the benefit of different audiences[42].

The VK, in all its historical triviality and instrumental innocence, represents a site at which the conflict-laden paths of Afrikanerdom crossed, and it provides a means for understanding how a community and the press react to a situation which highlights ideological discourse in 'crisis'.

Convened largely by the NGK, it represented more than twelve hundred academics, the business community in the form of the Afrikaanse Handelsinstituut and institutions from every conceivable sector of Afrikaner life. The VK set itself the task of presenting some kind of unified answer to the De Lange Report on educational reform. The intricate processes of lobbying and the specific outcomes of the VK have been detailed elsewhere[43]. What concerns us here is the specific process of identity negotiation that took place, and the role played by the press in that process.

'Us' and 'Them':
Media Management of Identity

Onderwysers en onderwysleiers kan onderling verskil, maar buitestaanders, ook politici, kan daarvan verseker wees dat verdeel-en-heerspogings, net soos in die verlede, in 'n gees van professionele solidariteit hanteer sal word[44].

In this section I will consider press accounts of the VK by looking at headlines, lead stories and editorials, and by considering the primary-secondary defining process in representations of the VK. The newspapers considered are: *Beeld, The Citizen, The Star, Rand Daily Mail, Die Transvaler, Die Vaderland, Rapport, Sunday Times* and

Sunday Express. There was no black press response to the VK, *Drum's* poster head 'Promises, Promises, Promises' eloquently summing up popular black feeling about the De Lange Report[45]. The division of accounts into lead-stories, backgrounders, inside page reports and editorials is a common-sense one, but follows similar distinctions made elsewhere[46] (See tables 1 and 2).

Table 1: Headlines in the Dailies

Lead-story/ Backgrounders	Inside-page Reports
Beeld 19/3	
	Onderwys nie net vir staat — volke moet elk 'n bydrae lewer (Translation: Education not only for the state — each ethnic group must contribute). Beter skoling bepleit (Translation: Plea for better schooling). Die karakter van onderwys uitgespel (Translation: The nature of education defined).
22/3 Nee vir een ministerie (No to one Ministry). Beheer moet in eie hande bly (Control must remain in own hands). 'n Moeilike pad vir onderwys (A difficult road for education).	Ouervereeniging op Kongres gekies (Parent association chosen at Congress) Wees vrugbaar en vermeerder (Be fruitful and multiply). Kennis het gewen (Knowledge triumphed).
Citizen 19/3 Right hijacks Volkskongres	Much at stake in time of change Whites should not be losers in education
20/3 Volkskongres 'No' to integrated education	Massive vote in favour One ministry for all races rejected

156

Integration no solution
Teachers must give Govt
clear indication

22/3
Stength shown at
Volkskongres
Extremists planned collapse
of 'volkskongres'
Attempts to hijack Congress
foiled

Star
19/3

Boshoff hits at integration
in education

20/3
Verligtes swamp education
22/3
The volk says 'no' to reform

Rand Daily Mail
19/3
Victory for the Right as
vote put off
20/3
De Lange's education plan
walks into a wall of daggers
22/3
Volkskongres puts its
right foot down

HSRC's findings rejected
by 'volk'

Transvaler
19/3
Politiek slaan uit by
onderwysers (Politics rears
its head amongst teachers)

Status quo kan nie
gehandhaaf word (Status
quo can't be maintained)
Besinning is nodig oor
differensiasie (Necessary to
reflect on differentiation)
Landwye onafhanklike
ouervereeniging na Kongres
gestig (Nationwide independent parent association founded
after Congress)

22/3
Leerkragte sê ja vir gelyke
standaarde (Educationists
agree to equal standards)

Mouton raps na politiek-
praters (Mouton scolds the
politics-talkers)

Vaderland
19/3

Konserwatiewes maak hul stem dik (Conservatives raise their voice)	Christelikheid opperflakkig (Christian-ness is superficial)
	Te min oorlegplegging (Too little consultation)
	Ouers se finansiele bydrae moet meer (Parents' financial contributions must increase)
20/3	
	Nasionale ouerraad 'n dringende saak (National parents' council an urgent matter)
	Verhoudinge onderwyser se taak (Relationships teacher's task)
	Afrikaans bedreig (Afrikaans threatened)
	Kind moet leer van SA se probleme (Child must learn of SA's problems)
	Blanke is nie 'n minderheid nie (Whites are not a minority)
22/3	
Kongresgangers vrees gelyke standaarde (Congress delegates fear equal standards)	

Table 2: Headlines in the Sunday Papers

Lead-story/ Backgrounders	Inside-page Reports
Rapport 21/3	
Regse aanslag op Kongres gefnuik (Rightist onslaught on Congress foiled)	Kaping van Kongres misluk toe (Hijack of Congress fails)
Sterk steun vir RGN (Strong support for HSRC)	HNP se spoke by Onderwys (HNP ghosts present at Education Congress)
Vroue sorg vir beroering (Women cause stir)	

Sunday Times
21/3
Hijack! Dr No's men run
away with the Congress
Sunday Express
21/3
Warning from PW from
Volkskongres — mixed
education plan rejected

Headlines give the first and often the only impression gained by the reading public. They have therefore to summarize the gist of the story in a few words. This simplifying tendency is not without problems. Consider for instance two headlines of *The Citizen*: "Right hijacks volkskongres" (19 March 1982). "Attempts to hijack congress foiled" (22 March 1982). The premature closure of Friday's headline is quite cheerfully countermanded by Monday's headline. *Beeld* too had difficulties of interpretation, but these were of a different order. A feature on 22 March 1982 is headed: 'n Moeilike pad vir onderwys' (a difficult path for education), while the editorial heading appears much more confidently optimistic: 'Kennis het gewen' (knowledge triumphed). As we shall see, editorials have the last work in defining the framework of public understanding, and therefore must create closure, or a consensus, on important issues.

The difference between the headlines of the different newspapers is very noticeable. Read laterally, the headlines on their own bespeak deep ambiguity about what was happening at the VK. (See table 3).

Table 3: Headline Differences

Citizen	*Sunday Times*
Attempts to hijack Congress foiled	Hijack! Dr No's men run away with Congress.
Rapport	*Rand Daily Mail*
Kaping van Kongres misluk (Hijack of Congress fails) Regse aanslag op Kongres gefnuik (Rightist onslaught on Congress foiled)	toe Volkskongres puts its right foot down

Rapport
Sterk steun vir RGN (Strong support for HSRC)

Rand Daily Mail
HSRC's findings rejected by 'volk'

Transvaler
Leerkragte se ja vir gelyke standaarde (Educationists agree to equal standards)

Vaderland
Kongresgangers vrees gelyke standaarde (Delegates fear equal standards)

As the headlines write it large so they write it simply and extremely: 'gefnuik' (foiled); 'sterk steun' (strong support); 'rejected'. These are all definitive actions and they by no means correspond with each other. In general, it was the English papers (*The Citizen* excepted) who saw the VK under right wing control, and the Afrikaans press that saw victory in another quarter. However, the surface differences of interpretation only masked a deeper definitional correspondence.

Table 4: Congressional Identities in the Headlines

Citizen
Right
Extremists

Volkskongres
Teachers

Star
Boshoff
Verkramptes

the Volk
Verligtes

Rand Daily Mail
Right

Volkskongres
'volk'

Transvaler
Politiek-praters
(Political talkers)

Leerkragte (Educationists)
Onderwysers (Teachers)
Mouton

Vaderland
Konserwatiewes
(Conservatives)

Kongresgangers
(Congress delegates)

Rapport
Regse aanslag
(Rightist onslaught)
HNP

Sunday Times
Dr No's men

Sunday Express

Volkskongres

Only two kinds of identities are mediated in the headlines. (See Table 4.) The first is a neutral identity for all the delegates, either expressed in the plural — kongresgangers, teachers, onderwysers, leerkragte; or in the corporate singular — volkskongres, the 'volk'. The second is the identification of one particular sub-group at the VK, the conservatives.

In all newspapers except *The Star* — which identifies 'verligtes' in a headline on a minor inside story — the corporate identity, expressed by fully half the identities mentioned in the headlines, is couched in political, often negative terms. English and Afrikaans press concur in this implicit judgement. 'Mouton' is metonymic for the 'volk' and Boschoff for the 'right', as is 'Dr No' (Treunicht). All other protagonists at the VK are buried in the headlines. *Beeld* features no headline identities at all. Out of twenty-five headlines, only five (twenty percent) of Afrikaner daily headlines feature congressional identities. In the English dailies, the position is quite the reverse: only one headline out of seven does not feature a congressional identity. Various linguistic forms in both English and Afrikaans papers govern the information that they present[47].

Table 5: *Citizen* — 'Strength Shown at Volkskongres'

	Agent	Effect	Affected
1. Sentence type	X	beats	Y
2. Transforms to non-transactive	X	shows strength	(omitted)
3. Transforms to passive	(omitted)	strength shown	(omitted)

Table 6: *Rand Daily Mail* — 'Victory for the Right ...'

	Agent	Effect	Affected
1. Sentence type	Right	beats	Y
2. Transforms to passive	Right	is victorious	(omitted)
3. Transforms to nominal	Right	victory	(omitted)

The examples in tables 5 and 6 show that by using passive and nominal linguistic forms, 'who' does 'what' to 'whom' is quite substantially obscured. It is interesting to note that neither the optimistic (generally Afrikaans, plus *The Citizen*) nor the pessimistic (generally English) newspapers had any identity description for the reformist fraction in their headlines, *The Star's* 'verligtes' excepted. This is despite the highly specific designation given the conservatives. As we shall see, the hegemonic work of the newspapers will create an alternative voice to that of the conservatives, and this voice will be aligned to the safety of the 'volk', a process only hinted at in the headlines. At this level of operation, a process of marginalisation is already occurring; the conservatives, despite their own rhetoric at the VK, have been pitted against the 'volk' in the headlines. The 'positioning'[48] activity of the press is particularly clear here.

The second impression presented to the reading public comes in the lead or feature story. As well as capitalizing on the positioning work started in the headlines, a further differentiation occurs here. The tendency to divide the VK up into political groups is developed further in the English newspapers, as illustrated in Table 7. With the exception of the *Sunday Express*, the English newspapers name a counter group to the conservatives, and this is always construed in political terms. These newspapers (*The Citizen* excepted) construed the VK as the site of a political fight between two factions, and for them, the verligte faction lost. In other words, their interpretation of what happened at the VK was a direct outcome of their identity-positioning activity.

Table 7: Congressional Identities in Lead and Feature Stories

Beeld
          die Afrikaner
          opvoedkundiges
          (educationists)

Citizen
right wingers	strong Afrikaner	leftist liberal
rightist radicals	conscience	Afrikaner
the conservatives		leftist action

The Star
conservative criticism
right-wingers
right-wing approach
right-wing support
right-wing clergymen

reformist
verlig-voice
verlig delegates
verlig reformists

Rand Daily Mail
right-wing
right-wingers
conservatives
ultra-conservatives
verkrampte

progressive

Transvaler
hoogs konserwatiewe toon opvoedkundiges
(highly conservative (educationists)
tone)
'n deel van die gehoor
(a part of the audience)
polities (political)

Vaderland
hoogs konserwatiewe trant (highly conservative tendency)
predikante
(ministers - clergy)
die konserwatiewes
(the conservatives)

Rapport
groupie ver-regses beroepsonderwys-
(small group of mense
far-rightists) (professional
nie onderwysers nie educationists)
(not teachers)
kapers (hijackers)
politieke praters
(political talkers)
die regses (rightists)

HNP
regse politieke aksie (rightist political action)
geen mense uit onderwys beroep (no-one from teaching profession)

Sunday Times
dominees   educationists
verkrampte   verligtes
right-wing
right-wing assault

Sunday Express
right-wing forces
right-wing campaign

A different positioning division was beginning to take shape in the Afrikaans press reports. This was not a right wing/left wing political division, but a division between 'politicians' on the one hand and 'educationists' on the other (see asterisks). The emergent division, made at the outset by Dr Viljoen in his opening address, [49] was reinforced throughout the VK by various primary definers like Professor Stone and especially Professor Mouton, who went on SABC TV news on Saturday, 20 March 1982, to narrate the orthodoxy: 'Political moves failed after educationally motivated arguments were put forward'. Thus depoliticisation of the reform position and of professional educational expertise was taken to its natural conclusion in the editorials of the Afrikaans press.

The identity tags in the Afrikaner editorials are largely apolitical. (See Table 8.) The educational/political division is in the process of being replaced by a division between educationally informed and educationally ill-informed persons. The 'volk' as an identity is partially eclipsed in this division, but the significant category remains the conservative one. The cumulative force of all the conservative group designations — identity descriptors like 'stofopskoppers', action descriptors like 'hijack' and adjectival descriptors like 'lawaaierige' — re-

Table 8: Congressional Identities and Attributes in the Afrikaner Press Editorials

Beeld

stofopskoppers (trouble makers)	die opvoedkundiges (educationists)
onkundiges (ignoramuses)	kennis (knowledge)
	groot segment van ons plurale bevolking (large part of our plural population)

Transvaler

lawaaierige minderheid (noisy minority)	gebalanseerde realisme (balanced realism)

Rapport

isolasie denke (isolationist thinking)	onderwys (teaching)
hart wat harder praat as die hoof (heart speaks louder than the head)	
politiek (politics)	

sult in a highly negative semantic field, where each descriptor becomes metonymic for the field and is used principally under the figure of rejection.

The final positioning move was to align the educationally-informed group to the 'volk' as a whole — or to the public at large, which includes the volk, as for example in 'groot segment van ons plurale bevolking'. The Afrikaans press performed its consent-commandeering function in text-book style. Of course, no-one can make assumptions about the success of the manoeuvre. This argument deals only with the productionist activity of the press, not with its powers of persuasion. Nevertheless, the pattern of reformist rearticulation at the VK has been taken, amplified and put into a common sense idiom by the newspapers in a way that makes it particularly difficult for the ordinary reader to challenge.

The case should not be overstated. What is being noted here is a tendency, a tentative beginning towards canvassing consent for educational reform which was taking place at a time when various paths open to Afrikanerdom's splinter groups were still unclear. On the same weekend that the VK was in session, Dr Treurnicht was inaugurating his new Conservative Party in Pretoria. No wonder then that the terms at issue were so politically volatile. Since then, Perskor has sacked editor Dr Wimpie de Klerk and was set to change course from the one tentatively put here. Other newspapers, like *Rapport*, have set about consolidating their position. For instance, two weeks after the VK, *Rapport* ran a feature written by primary definer Professor Pieter du Plessis, who they had already said "het 'n prominente rol gespeel in die fnuiking van die regse kaappoging"[50]. He sounded the same theme of technicist reform cast in common-sense terms: "Gelukkig dat referente 'n baie meer gebalanseerde en realistiese benadering tot probleme geopenbaar het"[51]. The words echo almost exactly those used by the *Transvaler's* editorialist two weeks earlier: "gebalanseerde realisme (het) in hoofsaak geseevier"[52]. In this way, primary definitions are repeated by the press and in turn by the definers themselves, and come in time to seem natural and inevitable.

It may seem surprising that the Afrikaans press works harder for reform than the English press, at least in the case of the VK. Part of the reason lies in the belief touted by the English press that Afrikanerdom and reform are intrinsically inimical. Another part of the answer, as we have just seen, lies in the political identity division the English press used in reporting the VK. Both of these interpretative frames led to news production that orientated the English press towards a different use of primary definers. (See Tables 9 and 10.)

Table 9: Primary Definers in Lead Stories

Definer	Used by
Professor W Mouton	Transvaler
	Beeld
	Rapport
Mr K Steyn	Beeld
Professor J de Lange	Sunday Express
	Beeld

Professor C Boshoff	Sunday Express
	Sunday Times
	Rand Daily Mail
	Star
	Citizen
Professor H Maree	Vaderland
	Citizen
Dr D Viljoen	Beeld
	Sunday Times
	Rand Daily Mail
Professor H Stone	Citizen
	Vaderland
	Rapport
	Star
Mr H Stoet	Citizen
Professor D du Plessis	Rapport

Table 10: Primary Definers Quoted in Lead Stories (No of Lines)

	Mouton	du Plessis	Steyn	Sloet	de Lange	Viljoen	Boshoff	Stone	Maree
Beeld	40	-	8	-	12	23	-	7	-
Citizen	-	-	-	8	-	-	9	-	26
Star	-	-	-	-	-	-	-	-	-
Rand Daily Mail	-	-	-	-	-	8	7	-	-
Transvaler	6	-	-	-	-	-	-	-	-
Vaderland	-	-	-	-	-	-	-	4	-
Rapport	13	5	-	-	-	-	-	-	-
Sunday Times	-	-	-	-	-	2	8	-	-
Sunday Express	-	-	-	-	-	-	-	-	-
TOTAL	59	5	8	8	12	33	24	11	26

The only primary definer not, broadly speaking, in the reformist camp is Professor C Boshoff (Table 9). He was used as a negative primary definer by all five English newspapers, though by none of the Afrikaner ones. It is apparent that the English newspapers saw a Broederbond plot at work. Although the English press used Dr Viljoen, Professor Stone and Professor de Lange as well, the somewhat artificial tables 9 and 10 do not reflect that Professor Boshoff is used as the major symbol by all of them for a highly simplified political power struggle which they saw as won by Professor Boshoff and his cohorts. *The Citizen* is the exception. While seeing the Broederbond at work, it also idiosyncratically enough saw 'leftwing' persons at the VK, thus taking up what it obviously saw as a 'moderate right' standpoint.

Not properly clear from the tables is the fact that Professor Mouton was used extensively by all the Afrikaner newspapers except *Die Vaderland*. Actually, *Vaderland* was extremely wary about using primary definers and indeed, about mentioning any congressional identities at all. Highly cautious in tone throughout, *Vaderland* was the only Afrikaans newspaper not to editorialise on the VK. It was perhaps unsure about how to 'read' the VK, or perhaps, who to back. The others all used Professor Mouton in various ways. For example, his clever manoeuvre in asking the congress at large by show of hands to indicate who had actually read the De Lange Report — apparently only thirty-five per cent had — seems to have cued the press into the educationally informed/educationally-ignorant identity division. Having set the framework for that construal, it was left to the reformist academics to consolidate the point.

In effect, the moral-intellectual leadership mantle was being removed from the shoulders of the cultural-religious leaders and placed on the shoulders of the educational 'experts'. As we can see, the Afrikaner press took the cue, amplified the descriptors, added a highly value-laden connotation — and the work of naturalizing reform via legitimising educational 'experts' was underway. One further effect is created by this manoeuvre. The conservative intellectuals are explicitly labelled as ignorant people with 'onhebbelike motiewe' [53]. Their intellectualness, in effect,is denied them. This left the field open to the new 'experts' to appropriate the designation.

Again, the case should not be overstated. The Afrikaner press will have been well aware that the Broederbond is not a party-specific organ, though it might have been so in the past. Indeed, Professor Mouton is a past chairman, and in all likelihood most of the reformists at the VK were Broederbonders. They would know that the same battles fought at the VK are being fought in different ways within the specific domain of the Broederbond itself — the same can be said for the NGK, the culture organizations, and the large and powerful Transvaalse Onderwysersvereeniging. There was no way that the language of the old accord could be summarily ditched, for consent is never won by shattering cultural sensibilities. The important process of consent construction lay in the identity negotiation process.

The Cacophony of Consent

The production of consensus, the construction of legitimacy — not so much the finished article itself but the whole process of argument, exchange, debate, consultation and speculation by which it emerges — is the third key aspect of the media's ideological effect[54].

Despite their diametrically different interpretations of the VK, the English and Afrikaans press — each in its own way — began to disarticulate the conservative 'voice' from the corporate identity of the 'volk'. The terms of debate at the VK, paying the necessary lip-service to the still dominant Christian nationalist discourse, automatically signalled political conservatism to the English journalists. Indeed, when Professor P Jooste attempted too abruptly to articulate an alternative discourse, he was greeted by a stony silence from the delegates and was applauded by both the *Rand Daily Mail* and *The Star*[55] as being a lone 'verligte' voice. It was clear that the interpretative frame of the English newspapers was set in a rather simplistic mould.

The situation facing the Afrikaner press was more complex and much more demanding. In the first place, the threatening hegemonic fracture had as yet unknown consequences for their respective reading communities, or even for their own editorial policy. Die *Vaderland*, as we have seen, evinced extreme caution, writing mostly in the impersonal third person. In varying degrees, the Afrikaner newspapers were active in reporting the debates, re-creating the process of debate and fostering the impression of earnest deliberation within the terms of Christian national discourse. At a deeper level, the newspapers were busy negotiating identity, and the terms of identity opposition were transmuted through at least three stages, denoting a fairly intense process of identity negotiation: Conservatives versus the volk, then politicians versus non-politicians, and then finally non-educationalists versus educationalists.

Through the babble of differences and disagreements reported by the press, and despite the rhetoric of the old accord, what is discernible in the news reports on the VK is an active negotiation and positioning of the various strata of Afrikaner society. This re-positioning reflects the real changes in society at large, and indeed helps define them. In addition, the academic reformists had begun to assume intellectual leadership for the Afrikaners, a long, tortuous and risky process towards the consolidation of which the press, for all the reasons discussed, is destined to play an increasingly pivotal role.

Notes and References

1. J Donzelot, *The Policing of Families*, p 8
2. A Sassoon, 'Hegemony and Political Intervention' in *Politics, Ideology and the State*, edited by S Hibbin, pp 16 and 31
3. The notion of a 'construct' can be understood as a *representation* of a complex social situation which is always ideological. That is, it forgrounds certain aspects and backgrounds others.
4. D O'Meara, ' "Muldergate" and the Politics of Afrikaner Nationalism' supplement to *Work in Progress* vol 22 (1982), pp 1-19
5. C B Collins, 'Black Schooling in South Africa' in *Africa Perspective* vol 17 (1980), pp 4-16
6. J Davies, 'Capital, State and Educational Reform in South Africa', unpublished paper delivered at AFSAAR Annual Conference, University of New South Wales, Sydney (1981), p 3
7. J H P Serfontein, *Apartheid, Change and the N G Kerk*, p 56
8. *Ibid* p 87
9. J H P Serfontein, *Brotherhood of Power: An Exposé of the Secret Afrikaner Broederbond*, p 1
10. J H P Serfontein, *Apartheid, Change and the N G Kerk*, p 88

11. D O'Meara, *Volkskapitalisme -- Class, Capital and Ideology in the Development of Afrikaner Nationalism*, p 250

12. *Volkseenheid* and *Volkskapitalisme* were national slogans for Afrikaners in the 1930s. The word *volk* technically means 'nation'. Broederbond intellectuals in the 1930s used it in the narrow sense of a group with a separate language or culture. *Volkskapitalisme* therefore means 'Afrikaner capitalism' and *Volkseenheid* means 'Afrikaner unity', as opposed to the 'South Africanism' that Hertzog was attempting to link to the concept of *volk* at that time. See O'Meara, **op cit** (1983), pp 72-3

13. O'Meara, *op cit* (1983), p 74

14. *Ibid* p 71

15. A N Pelzer, *Die Afrikaner Broederbond: Eerste Vyftig Jaar*, Cape Town: Tafelberg (1979), p 126

16. National Party, Sauer Commission *Report*, translated by M du Toit (March 1948), p 3

17. G Moss, 'Total Strategy' in *Work in Progress* vol 11 (1980), pp 1-11

18. *Paratus* (July 1979)

19. A W Stadler, 'Problems of Legitimacy: Economic Liberalism and State Reconstruction in South Africa', unpublished seminar paper, Johannesburg: Department of Political Studies, University of the Witwatersrand (1983), p 6

20. J Urry, *The Anatomy of Capitalist Societies*

21. South African Republic, *White Paper on the Report of the Commission of Enquiry into Labour Legislation* part 1 (1979), p 181

22. *Die Patriot*. Translation: "Let's be honest; we are being prescribed to by the economy. Material gains have replaced spiritual profit."

23. See for example, S B Greenberg, 'Legitimation and Control -- Ideological Struggles within the South African State', unpublished paper delivered at the conference on *South Africa and the Contemporary Study of Class, Race and Nationalism*, New York: (1982) p 53

24. *Ibid* p 37

25. J Habermas, *Towards a Rational Society*, London: Heineman (1971), pp 111-113

26. N Poulantzas, 'On Social Classes' in *New Left Review* no 78 (1973)

27. A Erwin and E Webster, 'Ideology and Capitalism in South Africa' in *Change, Reform and Economic Growth in South Africa*, edited by L Schlemmer and E Webster, pp 100-101

28. C Buci-Glucksman, 'Hegemony and Consent' in *Approaches to Gramsci*, edited by A S Sassoon, London: Writers and Readers (1982), p 118

29. J Kriel, 'NGK's "grasping for control" slammed' in *The Star* (7 April 1982)

30. E Laclau, *Politics and Ideology in Marxist Theory*, p 103

31. *Die Kerkbode* (8 June 1982)

32. SABC (16 June 1982)

33. *Rapport* (13 June 1982)

34. *Beeld* (19 June 1982). Translation: "We wish to use culture as the great unifier to restore unity."

35. *The Star* (13 September 1982)

36. I Connell, 'Monopoly Capitalism and the Media' in Hibbin *op cit* (1978)

36. I Connell, 'Television News and the Social Contract' in *Culture, Media, Language*, edited by S Hall, D Hobson, A Lowe and P Willis, London: Hutchinson (1980)

38. T Trew, ' "What the Papers Say": Linguistic Variation and Practice' in *Language and Control*, edited by R Fowler, B Hodge, G Kress and T Trew, London: Routledge and Kegan Paul (1979)

39. G Skirrow, 'Education and Television: Theory and Practice' in *Media, Politics and Culture: A Socialist View*, edited by C Gardner, London: MacMillan (1979), p 30

40. M Ignatieff, 'It's a Riot' in *London Review of Books* vol 3 no 15 (1981)

41. *Ibid*

42. Report of the Steyn Commission of Enquiry, quoted in *Work in Progress* no 23 (1982), p 2

43. J P Muller, 'How a Community Responds: de Lange and the Afrikaans Volkspers' in *Perspectives in Education* Special Issue (1982), pp 52-61

44. Editorial in *Mondstuk* (May 1982), p 2. Translation: Teachers and educational leaders may differ, but outsiders — politicians included — can be assured that divide-and-rule attempts will be handled in a spirit of professional solidarity, as in the past.

45. *Drum* (April 1982)

46. S Hall, C Critcher, A Jefferson, J Clarke and B Roberts, *Policing the Crisis: Mugging, the State and Law and Order*, London: MacMillan (1978), pp 116-117

47. *Transactive* verb forms represent a causal process in which one agency affects another. A *non-transactive* verb form represents events as non-causal processes with only one participant: the agent. The affected is deleted. *Passive* verbs involve a deletion of the agent as well as a transformation from a process to a state. When this happens, an action or struggle is coded as a final state and the dialectic of the event is lost. *Nominalisation* represents a process as an object, further losing the sense of process. See for example, Trew, *op cit*, especially p 110.

48. Skirrow *op cit* p 30

49. *Beeld* (19 March 1982)

50. *Rapport* (21 March 1982). Translation: ... played a prominent role in foiling the rightist hijack attempt.

51. *Rapport* (4 April 1982). Translation: Luckily those presenting papers showed a much more balanced and realistic approach to problems.

52. Translation: ... in the main, balanced realism triumphed.

53. Editorial in *Rapport* (21 March 1982)

54. S Hall, 'Culture, the Media and the "Ideological Effect"' in *Mass Communications and Society*, edited by J Curran, M Gurevitch and J Woolcott, London: Arnold / Open University Press (1977), p 342

55. *Rand Daily Mail* and *The Star* (20 March 1982)

Chapter 6
Ideology on the Beat: Labour and the English-Language Press

Simon Burton

The growth and development in the 1970s of an independent black trade union movement has forced the English-language press to make room in its pages for labour issues. There have been too many strikes, too many detentions of labour leaders, too many 'new dispensations' from the State for the capitalist press to ignore. The South African black working class had developed its organisational strengths to the point where its struggles for better living conditions, wages, and political representation can no longer be ignored by even the most blinkered and out of touch white South Africans[1].

In this chapter I shall attempt to develop a basis for continued research into the question of how labour issues have come to be represented by the English-language press in contemporary South Africa. As an aspect of the study of the media in South Africa, labour reporting, particularly, has been neglected[2]. This absence is due to the small number of progressive publications in which such analysis can be attempted, and to the fact that a critique of the mass media in South Africa is only now finding a place on the agenda of social criticism. Criticism of the representation of 'labour issues' in the capitalist press is implicit in the emergence of union newspapers and newsletters, journals and fact sheets which are designed to reach workers, providing information and a forum for debate around concrete problems faced by worker organisations.

In setting out to examine the representation of labour issues in the English-language press we are confronting the relationship between two crucially important aspects of society. The first is its economic basis. By this I mean the central place of work in society, its form of organisation and control, the social relationships that prevail as a result, and the struggles to improve, overthrow or perpetuate these arrangements. The second is the system of justifications, rationalisations and 'explanations' of why society is as it is[3]. Although often dealt with under the term ideology, these justifications are always grounded in social practices and society's institutions. The relationship between the economy and the social system of justifications is a dynamic one. This chapter will pose certain questions about this relationship and try to offer an analytical perspective which could be employed in the further study of the way it is represented in the press.

Unpacking the Issues

Even a cursory glance at present day 'labour news' as reported in the English-language press generates a powerful impression of mass trade union activity in South Africa. There has of course been a resurgence of black worker organisation in the seventies and early eighties[4] which continued to grow and consolidate in the recession-ridden mid 80s. This invokes two important questions about labour reporting. First, is the new focus on black unionism being handled in an historical and analytical way, or in a reflective and descriptive way? Second, is the new focus on black worker organisation being subtly transformed into a discourse of 'the new black politics of the 80s?' If so, what are the implications of this shift for the development of black unions, State responses and newspapers themselves?

The second question will be considered later in this chapter. The answer to the first is not easy. As the process of incorporation into the definition of 'newsworthiness' continues, labour action and the phenomenon of 'organised labour' will be addressed in different ways. However, one or two general comments can be made.

The issues which have been so much the basis of the resurgence of an organised black workforce are not new. Low wages, insecure jobs, racism, poor living conditions, inadequate protection from victimisation and retrenchment are conditions which have existed for a long time in South Africa. Working class struggles to improve these conditions form an integral part of our history. From the days of the Industrial and Commercial Workers' Union (ICU), in the early part of the century, black labour organisations have fought for a range of worker rights (to organise, hold meetings, and so on) and struggled to improve conditions.

The process of labour organisation is not, however, a smooth one. Trade union organisation and labour history can only be viewed as a series of ruptures, where phases of unionisation have built on previous victories and defeats. Eddie Webster, for example, has argued that each wave of labour unrest has been followed by repressive legislation, thereby preventing the maturation of temporary and embryonic union movements into permanent organisations[5]. It is only by linking these developments to broader political and social changes that one is able to develop a picture of the continuities and discontinuities in the labour movement.

If we are to understand and explain recent labour organisation (the growing number of strikes and growing union movement), we are at the same time developing an attitude towards South African history which is no longer based on *events*. Our understanding of labour history is as yet necessarily partial and much of it has still to be written; but a commitment to history is an antidote to the fractured and isolated view generated by labour news as a 'commodity'. David Morley has argued that:

> ... if we look at the news media, and their role in providing for the audience an account of developments in society which is largely restricted to reflecting the surface level of social relations —

presenting these as an accumulation of 'spectacular' events which they provide, precisely because of its *ahistorical* 'foregrounded' nature, is the crucial locus of ideology[6].

The ahistorical nature of most labour reporting leaves the average news reader with the impression that there is no historical context to the labour 'news'[7]. This phenomenon may be attributed in part to ignorance, newsroom practices, editorial policies and so on, some (or all) of which will change. The trend towards labour columns[8] such as Stephen Friedman's column in the now defunct *Rand Daily Mail*, is one way in which the event-orientated reporting may be supplemented by more in-depth reporting, assessment and discussion. Before pursuing this argument, it is useful to sketch out some of the characteristics of the development of black trade unionism.

Contemporary Labour History

The re-emergence of black worker organisation occurred in the wake of a series of massive strikes in the early 1970s. There are many reasons for this re-awakening[9], but a thorough analysis of the period is beyond the scope of this chapter. However, a number of factors can be identified as having played a crucial role in these events.

Against a background of rapid industrialisation in South Africa,[10] black workers were increasingly subject to declining living standards[11], unemployment and unsatisfactory bargaining arrangements in the form of liaison and works committees. The industrial expansion of the late 1960s also led to an increased number of blacks working in the cities. The early 1970s saw South Africa riding the crest of an economic boom which had the effect of transforming the economy into one identifiable as 'monopoly capitalism'[12]. This process is characterised by a fundamental restructuring of the division of labour, as the concentration and centralisation of capital taking place requires a new division of skills, and new skills themselves, to cope with the increasing mechanisation of industry[13].

The restructuring of the division of labour took the form of a gradual lowering of the job colour bar. Despite this, the early 1970s did not produce a dramatic reformulation of State policy towards black workers, because their strength had been considerably diminished during the 1960s. The rapid economic development and rising expectations of the 1970s, seen in the context of meagre wages and considerable hardship, led to the wave of strikes to which allusion has already been made.

Following Namibia in 1971, where over 20 000 workers closed mines and disrupted transport, commerce and agricultural production, South African society entered a new era of black worker organisation. The strikes continued throughout 1972 (stevedores in Cape Town, PUTCO drivers in Johannesburg) and eventually spread to Durban where an estimated 100 000 workers were involved in many strikes predominantly over the issue of wages[14]. These strikes did not result in major victories for black workers, but they did win wage increases, while most workers retained their jobs. The major advance, it has been argued, was in the development of worker consciousness based on the realisation that conditions could be improved through mass collective action[15].

At the time of the Durban strikes, a number of small workers advice offices and benefit funds sprang up[16]. In Durban itself this led to the formation of TUACC (Trade Union Advisory and Co-ordinating Council) in late 1973, which was to join up with the Council for Industrial Workers of the Witwatersrand (CIWW), itself formed out of the Industrial Aid Society (IAS), to become a national TUACC in 1978. From this trade union grouping was to come the powerful FOSATU (Federation of South African Trade Unions) in 1979, a federation committed to non-racial unionisation. The Urban Training Project (UTP) began in 1970 as an educational body under the auspices of officials from the African Affairs section of TUCSA when it closed its doors to black unions. Never a worker organisation as such, the UTP gradually became more involved in union work and grew into the Black Consultative Committee (BCC), also known as the Consultative Committee of Black Trade Unions (CCOBTU). In the Cape, the Western Province Workers Advice Bureau (WPWAB), formed in 1973, set out to advise workers, help them organise benefit funds and also set up factory committees. The WPWAB was to become the Western Province General Workers Union in 1978. The African Food and Canning Union (AFCU), a union formed originally in 1947, began to organise once again in this period in the Cape, and along with the WPGWU provided the backbone of non-racial union activities in this area. The other major trade union grouping was the Black Allied Workers Union (BAWU) which was closely linked to the Black Consciousness movement. We can trace nearly all the major black trade union organisations which exist at present back to those humble origins in the early 1970s. The growth in the numbers of workers organised has been phenomenal: between 1975 and 1980, membership rose from about 60 000 black workers unionised to nearly a quarter of a million[17].

The development of this union strength in the 1970s coincided with both open political challenges to the State (Soweto uprisings of 1976) and a period of diminished profitability. Robert Davies shows how the net inflow of foreign investment fell dramatically in the mid 1970s as a result of the world recession and the oil crisis[18]. The restructuring called for in the early part of the decade, to provide a workforce for an increasingly sophisticated economy, was to become a necessity in the latter half of the same decade under the pressures of political instability and economic crisis. It is in this context that the Wiehahn Commission made its recommendations in 1979. The most important recommendation, accepted by the Government, was the recognition of black trade unions, because the prohibition of "African unions would drive them underground and unite African workers not only against the authorities, but more important, against the system of free enterprise in South Africa"[19].

The Wiehahn Commission and the Industrial Conciliation Amendment Act No 94 of 1979, which followed the publication of the Commission's report, repealed many job reservation clauses, extended trade union rights to blacks, and set up a Manpower Commission and an Industrial Court to deal with grievances. The State strategy cannot be seen as anything but an attempt to control and discipline the emerging trade union movement, to bring it under the "protective and stabilising elements of the system"[20]. The legislation provided for the regulation of black trade unions and their legal recognition. However, a debate within the union movement as to whether or not registration would deprive the union of its autonomy continued into the early 1980s[21].

Since the late 1970s, the State has acted to restructure South African society in a number of ways. The Riekert Report dealing with permanently domiciled urban blacks, the Koornhof Bills dealing with the restructuring of pass laws and influx control, of local authorities and the new security legislation have all been based on an offensive strategy *vis-à-vis* growing black resistance and the needs of the economy.

The union movement in the 1980s, while existing in a different socio-political and economic climate, cannot be seen as a new phenomenon. The continuities and discontinuities are difficult to isolate but the trajectory of worker organisation can be understood more clearly if we link it to the broader issues of economic imperatives and State restructuring. The press invariably sees strikes and dismissals, union harassment and management strategies as atomistic 'occurrences'. It has not provided the background to worker demands, seeing them largely as attacks on a stable society, disruption of the economy and threats to the basically contented majority of workers.

The press has not provided a view of trade union organisation as a process, nor is it in a position to do so as long as it accepts the dominant ideas about worker organisation and reflects worker problems in an 'event'-orientated way. It cannot explain 'events', and contributes to the general view of worker action as 'irrational', in many cases, because the history and process of worker organisation is concealed within the structure of the news.

The Discourse of Labour Reporting

The above discussion brings us back to the second question, namely, the problem of shifts in the representation of black worker organisation. Labour reporting in the English-language press has been centrally concerned with strikes, stayaways, retrenchments and labour disputes of various kinds, selecting these from the field of working arrangements. This selection does not exhaust the issues of working arrangements, type of worker action and organisation, the process of mechanisation, unemployment or the structure of the economy, either regionally or in terms of the role of mining, agriculture and manufacturing. The emphasis given to disruptive action has therefore led to the generation of certain discursive effects. This may not be a conspiratorial process — no groups have a monopoly on the generation of meanings. Stuart Hall has sketched the basis for looking at the process of discourse construction. He is worth quoting at some length:

> To give an obvious example: suppose that every industrial dispute could be signified as a threat to the economic life of the country, and therefore against 'the national interest'. Then such significations would construct or define issues of economic and industrial conflict in terms which would consistently favour current economic strategies, supporting anything which maintains the continuity of production, while stigmatising anything which breaks the continuity of production, favouring the general interests of employers and shareholders who have nothing to gain from production being interrupted, lending credence to the specific policies of governments which seek to curtail the right to strike or to weaken the bargaining position and political power of the trade unions. (For purposes of the later argument, note that such significations depend on taking-for-granted what the national interest is. They are predicated on an assumption that we all live in a society where the bonds which bind labour and capital together are stronger, and more legitimate, than the grievances which divide us into labour versus capital. That is to say, part of the function of a signification of this kind is to construct a subject to which the discourse applies: e.g. to translate a discourse whose subject is 'workers versus employers' into a discourse whose subject is the collective 'we, the people')[22].

Although the loose classification 'black politics' does

not take us very far, I would suggest that the discourse, or set of significations, most close to the hearts of the editorial staff of the English-language press regarding black labour organisation and action is 'black politics'[23]. The argument goes like this — since 1976, the most powerful expression of black grievances and aspirations has been through the trade union movement. There is undeniably a 'political' component to trade union organisation, but this varies widely across the trade union movement, and it cannot be glibly asserted that this is the aim of worker organisations. Politics in the sense of the struggle for power is on the agenda, but it is not the whole agenda.

The newspapers, however, have conveniently found a new commodity: labour news. At the same time, they have trivialised and sensationalised an ongoing and historical phenomenon into 'the new black politics of the 70s and 80s'. Nevertheless, the English-language press continues to assert an 'objective' and 'balanced' reporting policy with which it justifies the media's role as a 'dip stick' of public opinion and rational presenter of current affairs.

These processes mesh with a number of crucial challenges facing the English-language press. The most important is the massive growth in black readership in the urban centres of South Africa[24].

The other important aspect in the struggle for readership is the jockeying in the circulation stakes[25]. With the growth of a black readership, the English-language press will have to reorientate itself in some way[26]. One possible option is to translate discrete events on the labour front into 'political' events. This suggests a transformation of a basic social fact (the labour-capital relation) into a feature of ethnic political conflict through the media. The roots of this transformation are the State and employer strategies for combating the growth and development of worker strength[27]. Conflicts of employers and employees have been interpreted as a political threat even when there is no political content to worker demands (for protective clothing, for example). The argument that all worker demands have a political content is patently nonsense. However, if the recognition of worker action as 'political' action permeates the social consciousness of ordinary citizens, how much easier is it for the State and employers to hit back, in order to destroy an embryonic 'political' threat.

It is my contention that the ideological grounds for treating worker action as political are systematically being propagated, through the press, by the State and by employers. The discourse of 'politics' in South Africa is so wide as to justify all sorts of repression of labour action. This in turn feeds a 'confrontationist' mentality which in time reinforces the view of worker action and organisation as political. The 'event'-orientated newspaper coverage which predominates in the English-language press (notwithstanding a commitment to labour as a 'basic issue') creates the handles which further the consolidation of popular beliefs into a coherent ideological set, which Gramsci has referred to as hegemony. Discrete 'events' are cemented together through ideological work into a rhetoric of 'threats to the nation', which underlies a simultaneous strategy of co-optation and a rhetoric of 'labour reform'[28].

There is no straightforward transformation process here. We cannot argue that the press is merely a tool of capital or of the State, nor that the press merely reflects the events in the 'real world'. Events are selected and this sets in motion a discourse upon which further ideological work can be performed. The representations of the 'real world' are in turn structured in the press. This of course must be analysed in the context of class rule, which is the constant that transforms and consolidates popular beliefs into a coherent recognisable image of the nation, culture, politics, trade unions and so on. The following section will return to some of these points.

Exploring the Reporter

There are two initial points that need to be made concerning labour reporting. The first is that labour reporting is not, in and of itself, ideological. The second is that labour reporting as a 'news beat' necessarily has implications which can be called 'ideological'.

On the first point, it is important to remember that the reporter is an individual with his or her own ideas, interests, expectations and values. This is not to deny the individual a position in society with class affiliations, status and privileges or lack of them[29]. However, we cannot assume with some crude and reductionist accounts of the media, that the reporter passively reproduces the dominant ideas on a particular subject or news beat. The reporter always makes choices in terms of the consensual discourse based on the interlocking of his/her information, position, prospects, experience and so on. All too often the reporter is seen as reproducing 'policy' laid down by the newspaper, but there are a range of factors which stand between the reporter and editorial policy. Toni Griffiths makes this point clear when he suggests that, in the British context:

> Many of the industrial correspondents are intelligent and sensitive journalists whose integrity is not in doubt and whose personal efforts to present events in a straightforward and unbiased way may come to grief in the context of the leader, the feature, the 'colour column' and the selection of items actually printed[30].

The extent to which the reporter is affected by these constraints is of course an empirical and historical question. In the current South African situation, however, the labour reporter is subject not only to newspaper construction, but also to the way in which black labour issues are viewed by the 'consumers of news', the State, the media institutions, advertisers and other journalists. These constraints do not mean that the labour reporter is merely a structural entity or a robot in the organisation. In fact, it would appear that the labour reporter is increasingly perceived by editorial staff to be an important new acquisition on leading English-language newspapers[31]. The swiftness with which the English-language press has armed itself with labour reporters is a clear indication of this. The *Rand Daily Mail*, *The Star*, *The Argus*, the *Cape Times* and the *Eastern Province Herald* all started a labour beat in the late 1970s. This restructuring of the newsroom has important implications for the individual reporter, and may throw up a series of contradictions (between the business correspondent and the labour reporter, for example) which make the specific characteristics, both social and individual, of the reporter all the more crucial. As one labour reporter has put it:

> The fact that a newspaper represents particular interests does not mean that there are no gaps in the newsroom through which one can actually get other voices across, and reflect other interests. The newsroom is just a bed of contradictions. The contradictions allow one to get one's stories in[32].

There are a range of problems faced by the reporter, and by the labour reporter in particular. At issue here is not only newsroom control or editorial policy, but the personal pressures derived from holding a particular position in society. The broad class/cultural position from which reporters are drawn is a crucial determinant of the relationship which comes to be established between the media institution, in this case the newspaper, and the individual. The English-language press is overwhelmingly 'white', and black reporters are treated as specialists in black affairs, usually community affairs, providing an insider's view of the kinds of conditions that prevail in South Africa. This means that they rarely get to do the labour beat. We need to ask whether labour issues are too sensitive to be dealt with by black reporters, or whether black reporters are not subject to the generalised system of control exercised over white reporters. It is more than probable that their schooling, general knowledge, language proficiency, cultural 'valuables', political opinions — in other words, their 'common sense' — all tend to contribute to a different discourse.

We have in South Africa a situation where a reporter is likely to come under State scrutiny for taking up labour issues. Without any editorial pressure, the reporter may be forced to practice self-censorship in his or her journalistic endeavours[33]. This is a very different matter from the protection of the professional image manufactured and fortified by the newspaper itself, but is, in the last analysis, rooted in the image of the labour issue as something dangerous and threatening to the foundations of stability[34]. In other words, the individual reporter is constrained by forces outside of the media institution itself, whilst also being in a position to take up an oppositional role within it. The space occupied by the reporter within the institution is not theoretical, but can be carved out according to the *modus operandi* of the reporter and the level of supervision she/he is subjected to. An anonymous journalist has argued that: "The conservatism of our editorial executives makes our task more difficult, but they do not prevent it"[35]. How are we then to understand the contervailing forces of autonomy and control?

Who Makes the News?

A great deal of controversy surrounds the role of the journalist. Is the news made by the journalists, the sources, or the structures of the newspaper?[36] It seems quite clear that there are no simple answers. In the context of a growing reliance on labour reporters it is necessary to return to the point made at the beginning of this section, that not all labour reporting is necessarily ideological, and to place this assertion on a more solid theoretical footing. Goran Therborn has argued that:

> The historical materialist conception of ideology, it would seem, involves the not very far-fetched assumption that human beings tend to have some capacity for discriminating between enunciation of the existence or possibility of something, or of its goodness according to given criteria, and the actual existence/occurrence of what is enunciated. In other words, ordinary human beings are capable of judging, at least in certain circumstances whether a statement that the sun is shining, or that there is no unemployment, is true[37].

Therborn's argument is important in that it specifies a role for discrimination which underlies the process of change that all ideologies must go through. Ideologies, as beliefs in what is good or right, are always in the process of being formed, adapted and destroyed. This process takes place in and only in the context of individuals and institutions — in the context of 'affirmations and sanctions'. The journalistic practices of reporters within institutions, their production of news, is always subject to a wide range of affirmations and sanctions. Some of these sanctions suggested by one reporter may be: "Stories rejected by the news editor, spiked by the copytaster, rewritten by a night news editor, chopped to pieces by a down table sub, placed in an inconspicuous position by the chief sub, and so on."

These real sanctions may be the result of a profitability crisis, deteriorating press relations with the State, editorial policy on newsworthiness or individual conflicts within the newsroom, amongst others. To conceive of ideology in a crude sense is a mistake if we are committed to developing an understanding of how an alternative or oppositional view about something comes to be articulated. The necessity of subjecting particular ideologies to analysis has itself been a thorny problem which has not yet been satisfactorily resolved[38]. Attempts to resolve this problem have pushed contemporary writers in the direction of seeing all ideologies as concrete practices or social practices which continuously rework the way in which we view the world. John Urry has characterised a social practice as ideological in the following way: "The first condition for the designation of a particular social practice as ideological is that there must be a concealment which is derived from the system of concepts embodied within the practice"[39].

This concealment always takes place in the consciousness of real people and cannot be reduced to an abstract operation that always occurs in society. To argue that ideology is rooted in material conditions of existence does not refute the argument so succintly stated by Richard Johnson that: "Against the slides of 'material' and 'way of life' we would want to insist in a thoroughly orthodox manner on the distinctively 'mental' character of culture/ideology, their broad equivalence to Marx's general term 'consciousness' "[40].

Literature on the media abounds with analyses of the effects of concealment[41]. This approach has been clearly articulated by Urry, who draws up the basis of the production of ideological effects through the way in which concepts rooted in a social practice:

(i) do not permit explanation in terms of wider scale social and historical changes: there is an inappropriate *isolation of practices*;

(ii) produce an *eternalisation* of the practice, and a failure to see it as historically bounded and hence that it may be transcended;

(iii) obscure the social relations which underlie existent relations between material objects, hence, where such objects are seen to have powers which stem not from the social but from *their natural characteristics*;

(iv) hide the *conflicts of interest* between the differently located subjects within the practice[42].

This is not to suggest that there is a simple true/false dichotomy at work in the social practices that produce ideological effects. The various actors on the stage of society, be they classes, bureaucrats, whites or men and women, conduct their struggles within various degrees of concealment, for the changes and adaptations in social practices, historically, are not only determined by ideology.

The second point then, made at the beginning of this section, that all labour reporting has ideological effects, cannot be separated from the first. However, the problem of analysing these ideological effects can only be briefly sketched here and remains to be substantiated empirically rather than theoretically or intuitively.

It has already been stressed that the reporter has to rely to a large extent on the relationship she/he has with other journalists and media workers for the production of news. One's stories may be subjected to all kinds of maltreatment commonly analysed under the rubric of gatekeeping theory. This is a difficult framework on which to base a critique of the press, for it does not go to the heart of the production of beliefs and values through the news. The production of ideological effects, through concealment, eternalisation, isolation of practices and so on, can only be studied in terms of the social groups who are going to benefit from such concealment. Studies of the effects of the media are incomplete if they do not take into account the individual and his or her relationship with the institution, and if they base their analyses solely on the institutional practices that come to be solidified in different newspapers (or what the editors of this book have termed consensual signifying practices).

The theories of control in the newsroom cannot explain

the role of the newspapers; how certain 'events' come to be reported rather than others, or the division of the world into discrete areas for coverage. As we know, not all English-language newspapers in South Africa take the same approach to labour issues. The *Rand Daily Mail* gave and the *Cape Times* has given the labour reporter much more room than other newspapers. The *Cape Times* (and the *Mail* which was closed down in 1985) not only reports on strikes, dismissals, wages demands and so on, but also provides in-depth features on the labour movement as a whole; its background crises and possible directions. This relative freedom to report and interpret labour issues is difficult to explain. The relationship between editorial staff, the reporter, the newspaper's policy and broader social context would have to be researched. However, the point is that considerations other than that of institutional bias, for example, need to be analysed. Stuart Hall has argued that:

> The media then, do not simply 'create' the news; nor do they simply transmit the ideology of the ruling class in a conspiratorial fashion. Indeed, we have suggested that, in a critical sense, the media are frequently not the 'primary definers' of news events at all; but their structured relationship to power has the *effect* of making them play a crucial but secondary role in reproducing the definitions of those who have privileged access, as right, to the media as 'accredited sources'. From this point of view, in the moment of news production, the media stand in a position of *structured subordination* to the primary definers (Emphasis added)[43].

This passage reflects the intention to move beyond the institutionality of the media and to probe the mechanisms of the selection of news and its transformation through language, layout and editing of events into newsworthiness. That is, it is seeking to develop an understanding of the effects of media institutions on some 'reality' appropriated from and then returned to the 'public'.

I have briefly outlined the necessity to see both the media institution, with its own professional practice, labour process and so on, and the individual reporter as related.

It is necessary to view this relationship as a creative one, in which the basis of ideological reproduction is always a question of affirmations and sanctions. Hall *et al* in their analysis, identify an important issue, which is the structural location of the media in general in the power relations characterising capitalist society. However, their analysis is still somewhat reductionist because it does not allow for the articulation of ideologies (that which exists, that which is 'good') in the media institution itself; that is, the possibility that a constant attempt to confront the definition of newsworthiness may be partially, or wholly, successful.

The critique of purely structural explanations of the media is well advanced. We can no longer see the institution as merely a set of roles embedded in a consensus framework of society at large. Nor can we see the media as acting only to distort the basic reality of capitalism — an "economic system built on a profound division between those who own and control capital and those who do not"[44]. Instead, we must identify the context of media institutions, their particular interests and their linkage with capital in general, as well as the specific practices within the institution and the possible role for reporters with different views of industrial action[45]. Only in this way will we be in a position to identify the ideological effects of the English-language press.

The Press, the State and the Reporter in South Africa

What of the context in which these institutions are steeped? In the South African case, it is quite clearly one of capitalist domination[46]. One does not have to look very far to see the extent to which the newspapers themselves are embroiled in so-called 'industrial disputes'. The strike by black journalists at the *Cape Herald* in October 1980 brought home the nature of the press in South Africa[47].

More disturbing, however, is the relationship between the press and the State. After the closure of the *Post* and *Sunday Post* through their lapse in registration, the Minister of Justice, Mr H J Coetzee, is reported to have suggested that these papers "aimed at creating a revolutionary climate in South Africa"[48]. The 1977 bannings of the *World* and *Weekend World* and the Union of Black Journalists, as well as the banning of MWASA officials in 1981, are the more overt forms of State action against the press. The more covert State intervention is well known: the range of laws affecting the press means that its ability to report on certain aspects of South African society is highly circumscribed.

There are, then, two important effects that the State has on reporting, particularly on labour reporting. First, the newspapers themselves are anxious to remain in the clear, in which case censorship within the newsroom becomes important. Secondly, the individual reporter is personally placed at risk and either practices self-censorship or publishes in the knowledge that he/she may not have the support of the editorial staff should the police take an interest in the story[49].

The harassment of reporters is of course of major concern to those supporting a 'free press'. The more fundamental problem perhaps is the fact that editorial staff are operating within a particular conception of the State in general[50]. The State is often seen as standing above particular interests, and is seldom conceptualised as an institution which embodies particular interests, of the capitalist class, for example. This translates itself into the image of the State as the representative and defender of the 'national interest' and of 'law and order'[51].

It follows then that the repressive arms of the State — police, army and courts, are ensuring the public safety when intervening in industrial action. The reporters' stories, if they are too 'fair', may attract the attention of these defenders of the 'national interest'. It is conceivable that a reporter witnessing police action on striking workers may be hard pressed to justify a story which is critical of such action. The relationship between newspapers and police must remain reasonably good so that 'news' can be made. This relationship between the newspaper and police reproduces images of the latter which a labour reporter may find difficult to counteract. In this sense, then, the State becomes a 'primary definer' of news — reproducing its own image and exercising control over the reporters.

The parameters of the State and the media institutions,

I would argue, do not exhaustively define the role of the reporter. That is, they only create a system of affirmations and sanctions within which the reporter is relatively 'free'. This is the basis of the contradiction outlined earlier. The reporter can make a space for the articulation of an alternative ideology by using 'their paradigm', as one reporter put it. The 'oppositional' stance that a reporter may have (for example, some sympathy with striking workers) may nevertheless be transformed into a page five, four-line story, tucked beneath some advertising. This is the real limit on his or her autonomy.

The labour reporter has to develop more than just an oppositional consciousness to ensure that the ideological effect of that consciousness is realised. The organisational pressures thus become crucial. If a sub-editor fobs off a trade union story with "we have already had a blacks-crying-in-the-rain story this week", well, so much for that. What is necessary is to re-define the newsworthiness of events 'out there'. To this problem there are no easy answers. Its basis lies in the media itself. News is 'events' and unless one is in a position to re-define events, the likelihood of redefining newsworthiness is limited[52].

In capitalist society, 'events' are the saleable commodities of newspapers. Labour issues, too, become commodities insofar as they are saleable. However, in the current situation, the commodity is not yet firmly priced. Arthur Grobbelar, the TUSCA General Secretary, when asked about labour reporting, answered: "I think the problem areas are basically that most of the people that seem to report on labour matters have little knowledge of labour and industrial acts. I think that is the fundamental problem"[53]. Editors are faced with a situation in which 'labour unrest' is occurring all the time[54] and yet know very little about who is involved and why. The labour reporter can justify a re-definition of newsworthiness on the basis of this ignorance. This may of course lead to other problems, such as reporters being lumped with certain unions and rejected by others.

The reporter must turn 'labour' into an ongoing and important feature of society, which of course it is. This requires that the labour reporter "establish a distinctive media culture with its own set of values and orientations which is superimposed upon, and thus comes to modify the definitions articulated by the state"[55] and also upon other primary definers — the employers. The employers know very well that more wages means less profits. It is certainly in the interests of employers to play down the workers' demands in the press and to blame militant leaders, on the grounds that they are unrepresentative of the workforce, and so on[56].

A similar view of the newspapers themselves has been expressed by the State (for example by the Steyn Commission). Employers, or capital, have a specific matrix of interests which may be threatened by coverage of industrial action in the workplace, and which may inspire a 'no-comment' attitude to the press when such 'events' take place. This, however, is not always the case, as we cannot characterise employers in any hard and fast way. The problem is that of conflicting perceptions of industrial disputes. In a context where industrial disputes are perceived to be 'unnatural', coming to terms with them may be a painful process for management. However, since the 1970s, the interests of a stable and controllable workforce have no longer been left in the hands of the State only. The growth of interest in industrial relations and in the 'workers', in the wake of pressures exerted by the workforce, is a development that parallels the rise of labour reporting as a feature of the English-language press. More and more the press coverage of industrial disputes is handled by personnel managers, labour relations officers and the like. As one industrial relations manager has put it: "A lack of effective communication — simply understanding what it is all about — is probably the single most important cause for workers' unrest"[57]. And furthermore, that: "Employers should strive for a labour relations structure or system which is aimed at conflict avoidance rather than conflict resolution"[58].

The labour reporter has to take into account these new accents and approaches to the whole question of publicity. A favoured method of employers is to reveal all, but under an 'off-the-record' provision. On the other hand, the reporter may be treated to lavish lunches and company perks of various kinds which are intended to co-opt him or her, so that a favourable image of the employer will go into the press. The images manufactured by employers of their company as a 'happy family' of 'equal partners', and so on, will increasingly replace the conspiracy model and the 'irresponsible workers led by agitators' syndrome. The reporter has to be able to cut through to the real grievances, which may be a dissatisfaction with broader issues (detentions, for example), and be able to develop a relationship with employers which does not simply open a channel for the public articulation of employer interests. Real motives and interests may be well concealed and the images of a certain 'event' constructed by management should be combated through a thorough knowledge of the situation. This has implications for the relationship between the newspaper editorial staff and the employers whose views are considered important by that newspaper management. It would be interesting to discover how true, in the South African case, Francis Beckett's comments are, when he suggests that: "These, then, are the two major pressures on editors; the pressure to please his proprietor, and the pressure not to offend big business from which his newspaper's lifeblood, its advertising revenue, comes. There are no other pressures so strong as these"[59].

How strong are the employers as definers of news? In the case of labour issues, editorial staff may be placed under pressure to play down the 'events'. Moreover, in this situation, the image generated by the way in which the views of the workers and employers are presented may be distinctly ideological — in the interests of employers generally, including the employers of newspaper workers.

The possible lines of interference and distortion are manifold, and labour reporters find themselves in an exceedingly difficult position, being subject both to institutional pressures and to the images of the field (labour, trade unions) 'fed' to the reporter and editorial executive by interested parties.

In this section I have tried to show that we cannot hope to analyse the function of the reporter, particularly the labour reporter, in abstract terms. These individuals find themselves in a cross-current of changing labour relations, which has important implications for the way the world is divided up into discrete areas of news coverage; together with changing editorial policy on the part of the English-language press which has important implications for social practices within the newsroom. These remarks need to be fleshed out with empirical research (primarily the analysis of newspaper coverage compared to in-depth studies of certain labour issues), and ought to be seen as tentative.

Finally, the power to define the news, and to define the issues, does rest to a certain extent with reporters. An interest in labour affairs brings with it suspicion and difficulty which other reporters do not have to deal with. The field is defined — it is 'politics', it is 'subversion', it is not in the 'national interest'. Employers, the State, newspaper management and editorial staff often provide rhetoric or 'brick walls' and do not give up their constructed images easily. It is necessary to understand their basis, their interests and their theories (of trade unionism for example) thoroughly if the labour reporter is to combat the 'solidification' of definitions of newsworthiness; the gross imbalance in reporting management's news and workers' news; and the discourse of management (which 'means' the economy) and the workers (which 'means' politics).

Conclusion

It has been demonstrated that working class issues cannot be relegated to a back seat in South Africa. The development of black worker organisation has been slow and is marked by ruptures which must be explained if we are to locate the present strength of the worker movement in an overall understanding of South African society. The economy is not just business affairs, but is the bread and butter of the vast majority of South Africans. We cannot pretend that we live in an equal and democratic society, and if we are to have any basis for understanding where the worker movement is going, we must take cognisance of whence it has come. This is not a major feature of the media's 'explanation' of the development of South African society. The news does not set out to conceal the origins, significance and strength of worker movements, but does implicitly offer us explanations by default. The current rhetoric of reform, expressed by the State and reproduced in the press, has not taken into consideration the aspirations of the vast majority of South African people.

The structural location of the media in a society where the dominant groups view it as natural for economic arrangements to be organised in a particular way, makes the task of de-mystifying the real roots of worker issues a difficult one. It has been suggested that this is possible, if we begin to differentiate the various factors that go into 'making the news'. The individual reporter can be effective in combating particular views and 'explanations', but not without re-orientating the focus on labour issues from 'events' to process. The media institution is not a tool in the hands of the dominant groups and classes, although it is not autonomous either. Ideas about society are not static but are based on particular interests which are themselves changing, albeit slowly. These ideologies or images can be changed, and the role of the media in this process of change is a crucial one.

Notes and References

1. The Black Municipal Workers' strike in Johannesburg in 1980 is one example. Ten thousand City Council workers downed tools and left the city with a major service crisis. See the *South African Labour Bulletin* (hereafter referred to as *SALB*) vol 6 no 7 (1981).

2. Although criticisms of labour reporting have been voiced by management and labour leaders alike, these have been framed in the context of 'biased reporting'.

3. See for example, Stuart Hall's argument that "the first great cultural function of the modern media (is) the provision and selective construction of social knowledge" in the paper 'Culture, the Media and the "Ideological Effect"' in *Mass Communications and Society*, edited by J Curran, M Gurevitch and J Woolacott, p 341

4. For a recent assessment of this resurgence see P Bonner, 'Trade Unions Since Wiehahn' in *SALB* vol 8 no 4 (1983).

5. E Webster, *Essays in South African Labour History*, Johannesburg; Ravan Press (1978), p 111

6. D Morley, 'Industrial Conflict and the Mass Media' in *The Sociological Review* vol 24 no 2 (1976), p 264

7. For a useful (and accessible) background on South African labour history see: R Friedman, 'The Political Implications of Industrial Unrest in South Africa' in *Africa Perspective* no 18 (1981), p 5; N Haysom, 'The Right to Strike in South African Law' in *SALB* vol 5 no 1 (1979); E Webster, *op cit*; S Miller, 'Trade Unions in South Africa 1970-1980: a Directory and Statistics' in *SALDRU Working Paper* no 45 (1982); D Lewis, 'The South African State and African Trade Unions, 1947-1953' in *Africa Perspective* no 18 (1981); and D Hemson, 'Trade Unionism and the Struggle for Liberation in South Africa' in *Capital and Class* no 6 (1978).

8. The *Cape Times* created a labour 'scene' regular feature in 1983.

9. See Institute for Industrial Education, *The Durban Strikes — 1973*, (1974) for a full account of the Durban strikes.

10. See Comment: 'The State and Change in Industrial Relations' in *SALB* vol 4 no 5 (1978). See also P Bonner and E Webster, 'Background to Wiehahn' in *SALB* vol 5 no 2 (1979).

11. K Luckhardt and B Wall, *Working for Freedom: Black Trade Union Developments in South Africa throughout the 1970's*, Geneva: World Council of Churches (1981), p 21. These authors argue that prices rose forty per cent from 1958 to 1971, and forty per cent again between 1971 and 1973.

12. R Davies, 'Capital re-structuring and the modification of the Racial Division of Labour in South Africa' in *Journal of Southern African Studies* vol 15 no 2 (1979), p 182

13. *Ibid* p 182. Much of what follows is based on Davies' insight.

14. See 'Background' in *SALB* vol 5 no 2 (1979).

15. Hemson, *op cit* p 21

16. See Friedman, *op cit*; Miller, *op cit*; and Luckhardt and Wall, *op cit* for details of the developments set out below.

17. See Miller, *op cit* p XXV, for the details of union membership.

18. Davies, *op cit* p 188

19. 'The Wiehahn Commission: A Summary' in *SALB* vol 5 no 2, p 22

20. Quoted in *SALB* vol 5 no 2, p 59

21. See for example, *SALB* vol 7 no 3; and *SALB* vol 7 nos 1 and 2

22. S Hall, 'The Rediscovery of "Ideology": Return of the Repressed in Media Studies' in *Culture, Society and the Media*, edited by M Gurevitch *et al*, p 69

23. Interviews with editors of two leading morning dailies.

24. The *Cape Times* is reputed to have approximately fifty-five per cent black readership. Consider too, the *Rand Daily Mail's* 'Black Edition', and other supplements (to the *Natal Witness* for example).

25. For example, the new *Star* Saturday morning edition and the *Rand Daily Mail's* reduction of price, and introduction of *Business Day* were introduced to fight this encroachment.

26. This suggestion is, of course, subject to regional differences.

27. See Miller, *op cit* for an overview of the harsh labour legislation that has existed in South Africa for decades.

28. See *Addressing the Nation* vol 2's Chapter entitled 'Square Vision in Colour: How TV2/3 Negotiates Consent' for an elaboration of co-optive strategies.

29. South African journalists share the characteristics identified by Philo who suggests that "the background of most journalists in broadcasting and the world in which they live mean that they share a common culture with the most powerful groups and interests in our society". See G Philo and P Beharrel, *Really Bad News*, London: Readers and Writers, in association with Glasgow Media Group (1982), p 13.

30. T Griffiths, 'The Production of Trade Union News' in *Trade Unions and the Media*, edited by P Beharrel and G Philo, London: Macmillan (1977)

31. For example, the editor of one of the Eastern Cape English-language newspapers made it clear that the labour reporter was of secondary importance to the political correspondent only. This, of course, reflects the regional importance of black labour issues in the wake of the 1979/1980/1982 strikes in the area.

32. See Chapter 2 in this volume.

33. According to one labour reporter this is the most important implication of either State or editorial pressure.

34. Although it is difficult to know how many reporters there are employed in South Africa, (some people report on labour issues, but effectively cover another beat) it is clear that most labour reporters regularly on the beat have had police express interest in their activities. At least four people writing on labour issues have been detained.

35. *Work in Progress* vol 12 (1980), p 33

36. For a brief but useful overview, see J W C Johnstone, 'Who controls the News?' in *American Journal of Sociology* vol 87 no 5 (1982); also chapter 2 in this volume.

37. G Therborn, *The Ideology of Power and the Power of Ideology*, pp 33-34

38. C Sumner, *Reading Ideologies*

39. J Urry, *The Anatomy of Capitalist Societies* p 63

40. R Johnstone, 'Histories of Culture/Theories of Ideology:

Notes on an Impasse' in *Ideology and Cultural Production*, edited by M Barrett *et al*, p 59

41. Morley, *op cit* pp 264-265

42. This is a shortened version of Urry's list, (*op cit* p 59) selected for its applicability in the South African context.

43. S Hall *et al*, *Policing the Crisis: Mugging, the State and Law and Order*

44. Philo and Beharrel, *op cit* (1982), p 128

45. Instead of a view that sees industrial action as "random, meaningless acts which break out in an otherwise peaceful and ordered society". See Philo and Beharrel, *op cit* (1982), p 5.

46.
> It is more accurate to see the journalists and editors and the mass media generally as one part of a society which takes private ownership, social hierarchies and profit for granted as the natural way of organising economic production and social relationships. (Philo and Beharrel, *op cit* (1982), p 128)

47. See *SALB* vol 6 no 6 (1981) for details of the MWASA strike.

48. *Argus* (22 January 1981)

49. See footnote 34 above.

50. See for example, N Poulantzas, *State, Power and Socialism*, especially chapter 2.

51. Morley, *op cit* p 251

52.
> ... If we are to think of distortion in the media, it is not in terms of this or that individual piece of misrepresentation. Rather the process of news production involves the systematic organization of information around narrow and particular ways of understanding the social and industrial world. (G Philo, P Beharrel and J Hewitt, 'Strategies and Policies' in Philo and Beharrel, *op cit* (1977), p 137)

53. Interview with Arthur Grobelaar in *SALB* (1983).

54. In 1981 for instance there were approximately 340 strikes involving about 90 000 workers.

55. Morley, *op cit* p 266

56. See *Ibid* for a more detailed analysis of this point.

57. F Ferreira, 'Labour's new Face: Crisis Management in Industry' in *Leadership SA* vol 1 no 1 (1982), p 31

58. *Ibid* p 31

59. F Beckett, 'Press and Prejudice', in Philo and Beharrel, *op cit* (1977), p 48

Chapter 7

On the Social Construction of Urban Problems: The Press and Black Housing, 1925-1979[1]

Jeffery McCarthy and Michelle Friedman

Yet still this dormitory world of low new huts
In ranked battalions, uniform by blocks,
Quilts the tilting hugeness of the veld.
House patterns, A, B, C, D, E
In turn insist their order to our eyes

Lionel Abrahams — 'Soweto Funeral'

The way news media react on a daily basis to social problems, isolating them as naively given social 'events', was mentioned in chapter 2 of this book. In a longer-term historical context, however, the fluctuating level of concern with apparently dramatic, focussed and short-term 'events' can reveal trends that are suggestive of the material role of the media within specific social formations.

The authors' own interest in black housing as a media issue stems only indirectly from a concern with the media itself and more directly from a concern with social science research into the problem of urban development in South

Africa[2]. It should become evident in the course of this chapter, however, that we regard it as very difficult to separate the analysis of housing in the media from the analysis of housing as a social problem, and vice versa. Indeed, it is to be argued that both types of analysis tend to interlock at the point of understanding how and why a given 'urban problem' is defined and redefined in the course of social struggle.

For the (black) majority of South Africans, it might be argued, housing has been a matter of continuing significance sustained in the realm of everyday experience over decades. The pitch at which it is sustained, if we are to accept the message of the likes of Abrahams' poem, is that of a monotonous and insistent drone. With more than ten persons occupying the average township house, this is hardly surprising. Social scientists may have been a little less perceptive than the poets in their interpretation of the existential role of the dilapidated built environment assigned to blacks in South Africa. But from the snippets of already published research, it emerges that housing may well be the most important aspect of self-defined 'satisfaction' or 'dissatisfaction' amongst urban black South Africans[3].

If it is accepted that black housing has long been regarded as a salient aspect of everyday experience by the majority of South Africans, a question arises as to how and why it was suddenly seized upon by the commercial media as a 'topic' meriting concern at certain points in time. As we shall demonstrate shortly, black housing only became an 'issue' in the commercial print media at certain times in South Africa. *Why* did the media 'discover' black housing during these periods; and did certain media detect the issue in a different temporal sequence because of their different positions within the political/ideological spectrum? Against what background was the 'discovery' of black housing made by different sectors of the media and in what context was it discussed once it emerged as an issue? This chapter investigates these questions whilst seeking to contribute towards the more explicitly theoretical debates on ideology and the media represented in this volume.

Housing and Ideology in Capitalist Societies

Chapter 2 argues that the neo-Marxist concept of ideology can be usefully applied to an understanding of the media in capitalist societies. A parallel argument can be advanced with respect to housing. The radical literature on housing in capitalist societies is a rich and growing one that utilises many of the Althusserian and Gramscian concepts developed elsewhere in this volume[4]. It would be inappropriate to attempt an exhaustive review of this literature here, but we can distil certain aspects of the debate that have special relevance for our analysis. Three particularly important concepts within the Marxist literature on housing are outlined below. These concepts provide the basis for a theoretical model of housing and the State in semi-peripheral capitalist societies: a model that may serve as an 'ideal type' — an organising framework — against which the empirical materials at our disposal may be contrasted and compared.

The first concept that needs to be clarified here is the meaning and significance of housing itself. Clearly, housing cannot be seen as a thing itself, devoid of any connection to social relations. Rather it must be regarded as having an existence in relation to a range of (often contradictory) material interests. It is these interests which define housing, and give it socially communicable meaning. Following Harvey, they might be identified as follows:

(i) A fraction of capital seeking the appropriation of rent either directly (as landlords, property companies, and so on) or indirectly (as financial intermediaries or others who invest in property simply for a rate of return);

(ii) A fraction of capital seeking interest and profit by building new elements in the built environment (the construction interests);

(iii) Capital 'in general', which looks upon the built environment as an outlet for surplus capital and as a bundle of use values for enhancing the production and accumulation of capital; and

(iv) Labour, which uses the built environment as a means of consumption and as a means for its own reproduction[5].

Harvey goes on to argue that conflicts between these interests must emerge because groups (i) and (ii), for example, define the built environment in terms that are consistent with the exchange value needs of capital accumulation whereas (iv) defines the built environment largely in use value terms. This notion that exchange value and use value priorities are in conflict may seem foreign to those trained in the ideology of neoclassical economics. Here housing use values are usually regarded as originating out of the 'demands' of 'sovereign consumers': consumers who ostensibly bring forth into social existence a highly compliant set of co-ordinate producers[6]. For Marxists, however, the realisation of profits through production exists in a much more problematic relation to the process of acquiring use values. With specific regard to housing, these contradictions are manifest in a host of individually and collectively stated dissatisfactions on the part of user groups: in rent strikes, in civic association militance over poor neighbourhood conditions and/or unwanted developments in their areas; and in city-wide or even nation-wide protests over conditions in urban areas[7]. This is a pattern which becomes intensified, as we shall see, when the State is a major supplier of housing.

The second concept to be developed here is another dealt with by Harvey: that is, in the conflict that arises over housing between the interests identified above, the contradiction between capital in general and labour is central *although it is a conflict that is often mystified in the realm of (socially construed and created) everyday 'reality*[8]. There are several components to the complex problem of mystification in housing struggles, but two may be isolated here because of their particular relevance for the 'black housing issue' in South Africa at the present time. The components are those of *home-ownership* and *rent*. These are very closely related in the sphere of social struggle, as Harvey observes:

> The struggle which labour wages in the living place against the appropriation of rent is a struggle

against the monopoly power of private property. Labour's fight against the principle of private property cannot be easily confined to the housing arena and the vexed question of the relation between rent and wages ... easily slides into that of capital and labour. For this reason, the capitalist class as a whole cannot afford to ignore it because they have an interest in keeping sacrosanct the principle of private property. A well-developed struggle between tenants and landlords ... calls the whole principle into question. Extended individualised homeownership is, therefore, seen as advantageous to the capitalist class because it promotes: the allegiance of at least a segment of the working class to the principle of private property; an ethic of possessive individualism and a fragmentation of the working class into housing classes of homeowners and tenants[9].

Home-ownership not only assists in legitimising 'the principle of private property' and in promoting internecine struggles within labour. It also contributes towards a mode of 'responsible' behaviour that capital is especially interested in promoting during periods of crisis and overt challenge to the legitimacy of the prevailing social order:

The majority of owner-occupiers do not own their housing outright. They make interest payments on a mortgage. This puts finance capital in a hegemonic position with respect to the functioning of the housing market: a position of which it is in no way loath to make use. In reality, the apparent entrance of workers into the petty form of property ownership in housing is, to a large degree, its exact opposite: the entry of money capital into a controlling position within the consumption fund. Finance capital not only controls the disposition and rate of new investment in housing, but also controls labour, as well, through chronic debt encumbrance. A worker mortgaged up to the hilt is, for the most part, a pillar of social stability, and schemes to promote homeownership within the working class have long recognised this basic fact. And, in return, the worker may build up, very slowly, some equity in the property[10].

With more specific reference to rent, it must be recognised that the cost of housing is an important component of the cost of the reproduction of labour power. To the extent that labour links this cost to its wage demands, and hence to conflicts with capital in general, both inflated rents and housing costs can become practical obstructions to the general progress of capitalist accumulation:

> In the interests of keeping the costs of reproduction of labour power at a minimum, the capitalist class as a whole may seek collective means to intervene in the processes of investment and appropriation in the built environment. In much the same way that the proletariat frequently sided with the rising industrial bourgeoisie against the landed interest in the early years of capitalism, so we often find capital in general siding with labour in the advanced capitalist societies against excessive appropriation of rent and rising costs of new development. This coalition is not forged altruistically but arises organically out of the relation between the wage rate and the costs of reproduction of labour power[11].

The point that must be noticed, however, both with regard to home-ownership and rent, is how capital in general can apparently alleviate some of the crises of everyday life for labour with respect to housing, and at the same time drag it further into a state of dependence within the prevailing order. Therein lies the power of mystification and fetishism under capitalism. To the alienated worker a deeper level of co-option into capitalist relations of production *apparently* provides the ability to establish 'final control' — even if it is only with regard to five hundred square metres on the earth's surface. In addition, to the debt-encumbered home-owner or tenant, the occasional indignant forays of industrial capital into the realm of criticising land speculation, excessive rentals, mortgage interest rates, or 'bureaucratic inefficiency' in management of Government housing estates all *seem* to indicate that the problem resides in an identifiable and circumscribed enemy *outside* any possible fundamental contradiction between capital and labour. It is for this reason that Harvey argues tellingly that "the overt forms of conflict around the built environment depend upon the outcome of a deeper, and often hidden, ideological struggle for the consciousness of those doing the struggling". The role of the mass media in the general pattern of conflict over the built environment, therefore, can hardly be regarded as incidental. For insofar as the mass media both select and interpret what is 'salient' in conflict over the built environment; and insofar as they then diffuse this 'salient' interpretation into the consciousness of 'those doing the struggling', they are obviously an important intervening variable or 'filter' in the development of patterns of conflict around the built environment[12].

The third and final point to be made in this section, and one which Harvey unfortunately overlooks, is that the *State* plays a key role in a great deal of the conflict described above. The Marxist theory of the State is fraught with controversy, and there is relatively little literature linking it to problems of conflict over the built environment[13]. Perhaps the most convincing analysis proceeds along the lines that increased levels of interdependence in the forces of production, with corresponding privatisation of the relations of production in capitalist societies, enforce growing State intervention and the proliferation of a wide range of urban planning and urban administration activities. Land use regulation, urban highway administration, urban renewal projects, and the like, can all be interpreted in this way[14]. In addition, the contradiction referred to above and also that which exists between Harvey's categories (i) and (ii) on the one hand, and categories (iii) and (iv) on the other, leads to State housing programmes and other forms of direct control over the reproduction of labour power[15]. Such measures, in turn, lead to what Castells terms "the politicisation of everyday life" and the rise of "urban social movements" involved in squatting, rent strikes, campaigns against traffic hazards, pollution, etc[16].

There are some sophisticated empirical studies that have demonstrated the salience of Castells' analysis, even at the level of national political alignments[17]. Nevertheless, it should be recognised that Castells and most of his cohorts firstly adopt a Poulantzian 'structuralist' position on the State and, secondly, assume the (historically specific) conditions of advanced capitalism[18]. It is, at the very least, arguable as to whether these assumptions apply in the South African case. Some thoughts on the question have been offered by Wilkinson, but they are, by his own admission, of a highly exploratory nature[19].

We are not arguing here that Castells' thesis on the politicisation of everyday life and the attendant rise of urban social movements has little relevance for the South African urban scene. On the contrary, Stadler and Lodge's studies of squatter movements, bus boycotts and resistance to urban renewal indicate that urban social movements have been an important element, for some time, in the general pattern of resistance to State control over the reproduction of labour power within South African cities[20]. All that is being suggested is that Castells's analysis may require modification in terms of the historically specific realities of a given social formation[21]. In the South African case, for example, State involvement in managing the sphere of reproduction has arguably arisen less in response to an internal contradiction between the forces and relations of production than it has in response to the need to ensure a cheap and docile source of labour within the cities. From the 1923 Natives Urban Areas Act to the 1982 Disorderly Movement and Settlement Bill (withdrawn), it may be argued, State policy towards blacks in South African cities has had two things in common: an attempt to limit the black presence in cities to the minimum required for capitalist accumulation, thus externalising much of the cost of reproducing labour power onto the precapitalist reserve economy, and an attempt to limit the economic and political cost to capital of housing those 'labour units' who *are* allowed into cities to an absolute minimum[22]. In this regard, however, South Africa is perhaps not entirely unique and may share certain features with other more peripheral capitalist societies characterised by complex articulations between the capitalist and precapitalist components of their social formations[23].

Indeed, to argue that urban policy in South Africa has

uniquely and invariably been concerned with minimising the costs of the reproduction of labour power could lead towards the errors of methodological principle of which Castells stands accused: namely, those of ahistorical and economistic tendencies in theory construction. However, it may be possible to arrive at a structured sense of the historical in urban policy formulation, and also at a sense of conjunction of economic and political forces, through an elaboration of a scheme derived by Borja for the analysis of urban social movements in Spain[24]. Briefly, our reading of Borja suggests that State responses to the contradictions of urbanisation under peripheral capitalism may be divided into three overlapping historical phases:

t1 an *urbanisation of raw accumulation* where the infra-structural preconditions for production and surplus appropriation within cities become the principal object of the State's and capital's concerns;

t2 a subsequent *urbanisation of social control* where the State's interest is forced to switch to problems of reproduction in a 'saturated and underequipped' reproductive sphere that is seen 'merely as an object of public order'; and

t3 an *urbanisation of ideological* and *physical intervention* where the sphere of reproduction is once again paramount in the priorities of the State, but where that sphere increasingly becomes 'an object of plunder (for the rent-seeking and construction interests) and of ideology (for capital in general's promotion of a property owning petty bourgeoisie)' (see figure 1).

What is being suggested in this periodisation is that the urbanisation that is produced by capitalist accumulation in the initial phase (t1) is one that operates principally in terms of the rapid appropriation of labour power from the precapitalist rural hinterland in order to install the roads, railways, factories and other physical requirements of urban production. Neglect of the urban reproductive sphere and the sheer rate of exploitation in this period, however, can generate considerable labour militancy and community agitation over urban conditions. In addition, the inability to control the 'pull' and 'push' forces of rural-urban migration that originate out of the articulations of the capitalist and precapitalist economies lead to an enforced State concern with land use order in the city in general and the sphere of reproduction in particular. Thus, whereas the t1 phase is characterised by 'neglect by oversight' of the sphere of reproduction, the emerging t2 phase is characterised by 'neglect by control'. This concern for control is heightened by the co-ordination or efficiency problems that increasingly emerge out of an urbanism that on the one hand requires interdependence in production and consumption but which on the other hand is based upon the relation of anarchical *private* decision making. Thus, as Borja observes of the t2 phase:

> The reality, or the least the legitimacy, of the centralisation process is denied in terms of a traditional 'ruralist' concept of society and the fear that is aroused by large industrial working class concentrations ... The result is a *laissez-faire* urban policy turning the cities into chaotic encampments, saturated and underequipped. *The city is seen by the state merely as an object of public order*[25].

This conception shores up the city's parasitic structural relation to the precapitalist hinterland by limiting migration to only 'useful labour units'. It also ideologically justifies the rudimentary living conditions for labour in the city on the grounds that 'the future lies elsewhere'. Urban policy in this period, therefore, tends to consist of a welter of 'thou shalt not' legislation applicable in particular to the urban reproductive sphere.

The political progress of community activism over living conditions and the related struggles of the urban labour movement, however, together with increasing recognition by the bourgeoisie of a collapse in the precapitalist hinterland's ability to act as a self-supporting reservoir of labour power for the expanding centres of urban production, forces the conclusion upon the State that a whole new urban policy is required. Instead of 'benign neglect' of physical conditions and the simple use of police powers of urban regulation, the recognition now dawns that the urban reproductive sphere can become the terrain for dual forms of 'secondary exploitation'[26]. In the first instance, the urban reproductive sphere is seen as a potential avenue for the expansion of the increasingly powerful construction and financial interests, provided that this does not lead to a marked increase in the cost of reproduction of labour power. In this t3 period, then, there is emphasis upon State-assisted suburban housing estates — particularly when these help to iron out underaccumulation crises in the national economy. In other words, housing construction is periodically used by the State as a 'Keynesian regulator' so that expenditure on 'publicly assisted' housing is temporally cyclical and concentrated near the end of downswings in the business cycle.

The second form of exploitation that is evident during this period is fundamentally ideological. Thus, for example, despite a common emphasis throughout the period (t3) on home-ownership for the more solvent sections of labour, when the accumulation climate is such that the State is either unwilling or unable to meet demands for centrally supplied housing estates it tends to fall back upon an ideology of 'self help'. This 'willed' ideology attempts, in part, to shift the 'moral' or ideological obligation for providing housing onto labour itself. Furthermore, part of the actual economic *costs* of reproducing labour power are displaced onto labour itself by requiring work in the evenings and the weekends in order to secure some form of access to housing[27]. If this strategy seems in partial contradiction to a parallel emphasis upon State-provided, -owned and -regulated housing for labour at certain times, what it indicates is that the State itself is caught upon the horns of a complex dilemma — a dilemma, it must be emphasized, that is not so much of its own internal making as it is of the fundamentally contradictory social processes over which it must attempt to preside[28].

The South African Case

At this juncture it is opportune to remark upon the relevance of Borja's framework to the specific sequence of urban policy and urban protest that has been evident in South Africa. The t1 phase in South Africa, we would argue, corresponds approximately to the period prior to 1925. For purposes of illustration, whereas after 1925 provincial expenditure on hospitals and public health in South Africa was 140 per cent of the amount spent on roads, bridges and public works, before 1925 provincial expenditure on hospitals and public health was only 65 per cent of that applicable to roads, bridges and public works[29]. The State's relative neglect of the reproductive sphere in comparison to productive infrastructure during this period is also implicitly manifest in contemporary literature on the social and economic history of the Witwatersrand. Charles van Onselen's white working class of the early twentieth century, for example, was not being proletarianised whilst building schools, hospitals or worker housing. They were constructing the *Main Reef Road*[30].

Anti-urban postures adopted by the State during the t1 phase, as indicated earlier, compliment neglect of the urban sphere of reproduction. In the South African case this anti-urbanism was most obvious in the so-called Stallard Doctrine that led to the 1923 (Natives) Urban Areas Act. The racial selectivity of this Act raises issues about the specific characteristics of colonial capitalism that are too complex to enter into here[31]. Nevertheless, it can be noted that, in general, labour's resistance to the State's anti-urbanism, its neglect of the sphere of urban reproduction and the high rate of exploitation at the point of production was reflected in increasing labour militancy and community activism during the 1920s. In the period 1918 to 1922, for example, strike activity reached an all time high in South Africa, precipitating a crisis of major proportions. The switch to a new set of State strategies towards urbanisation during the t2 phase seems to have been partly precipitated by this crisis.

In South Africa the t2 period of limiting legislation applicable to the sphere of urban reproduction (corresponding to the period 1925 to 1945) saw, for example, the introduction of the first town planning ordinances and the promulgation of the Slums Act[32]. These measures helped to rationalise many of the internal contradictions and anarchical features of capitalist land use made evident during the t1 phase. In particular, powers of land-use zoning and eminent domain allowed local and provincial authorities to facilitate the geographical expansion of industrial and commercial capital within cities, and some of the more obvious 'failures' in the operation of the private market mechanism for residential land were corrected. However, State *investment* in the sphere of reproduction was still minimal. The consequence was escalating costs of land and housing in relation to general consumer prices: a turn of events that was exacerbated by the scarcity rents that are the concomitant of State intervention into the process of urbanisation, urban land allocation and urban development[33].

By the 1940s, however, labour had begun to remobilise and direct itself against such contradictions. Squatter movements increasingly challenged the costs of restrictive control over urbanisation and the sphere of urban reproduction[34], and pressures were being exerted (mainly by white labour) for public housing schemes and housing guarantees and subsidies from the State[35].

In the sphere of production labour militancy also increased, with strike activity reaching a new peak immediately after the Second World War. In the meantime, capital in general appears to have discovered that one way in which surplus value can be appropriated from labour, even when losses are sustained *vis-à-vis* labour at the point of production, is to extend itself into the sphere of reproduction. Thus, in the 1940s we find the sudden emergence of real estate agencies and building societies and the rapid growth of the construction sector of capital. Indeed, official statistics show that during the period 1943 to 1952 the construction sector grew at the truly remarkable rate of twice that applicable to the industrial sector[36].

These developments, of course, were symptomatic of the shift to the t3 phase of State responses to the contradictions of capitalist urbanism. As South Africa entered the 1950s the State placed increasing emphasis upon public support for corporately supplied housing estates and the demolition of inner city 'slums'. This, in turn, facilitated the appropriation of surplus (in the form of rent) in those sections of the urban land market that were particularly attractive from the point of view of the speculative real estate/construction interests. In South Africa, however, all of this was mixed up, both in terms of the

State's logic and in the minds of the common people, with the policy of Group Areas. It is a pity, therefore, that in examining the history of the destruction of the likes of District Six, Cato Manor or Sophiatown, commentators are inclined to focus exclusively upon the racial/symbolic dimension of the problem rather than its context within the historical pattern of capitalist accumulation upon urban terrain[37]. A similar problem occurs in the analysis of those urban social movements that emerged in response to the rising transportation costs that are the necessary concomitant of the suburbanisation and exurbanisation of labour's housing[38].

Having accomplished the transition to the t3 phase, in the face of much resistance from residents in the neighbourhoods to be 'redeveloped', South Africa became caught within a 'consumption sector' problematic that was difficult for the State to resolve[39]. In creating public housing estates (mainly for black workers) so as to minimise the costs of reproduction of labour power whilst allowing landed capital and the construction interests some space (mainly in white areas) to continue to appropriate rents, the State inadvertently succeeded in politicising the living place assigned to blacks. Soon, the costs of housing and other problems associated with 'township life' were observed to be the direct consequence of State priorities in the reproduction of black labour power. The State attempted to insulate itself from attacks in this regard by devolving limited powers of administration, revenue raising and expenditure to authorities run by local black elites (the so-called 'Community Councils'). However, these bodies were rapidly appreciated by the black working classes for what they were. Thus, for example, rent boycotts were instigated and these heightened the legitimation crisis of the State.

It was at this stage that pressure began to build up amongst the forward-looking intellectuals of the black petty bourgeoisie and the South African bourgeoisie in general for the *commodification* of black housing: pressures that have now been realised in a new State housing policy[40]. At the same time the State appears to have appreciated that in order to recover a modicum of legitimacy for the status quo-orientated black petty bourgeois classes it would have to develop a more convincing and extensive system of 'local control' over the townships. It is within this context that the part of the constitutional proposals (of the National Party) that deals with urban blacks (such as Regional Sources Councils) should be appreciated. However, this strategy is unlikely to be without its own contradictions. Because the State still feels relatively insulated from pressures by the black working class for enhanced conditions of urban reproduction, and because it is increasingly manifesting itself as a truly *capitalist* state, it is unlikely to provide the material resources necessary to sustain even moderate legitimacy for the system of local control that it now envisages. Instead, it will have to try to hide behind a capitalist variant of the philosophy of 'self-help': a philosophy, in fact, that it is increasingly turning to as it peers worriedly behind the veil of massive black urbanisation[41].

Black Housing and the Media in South Africa

Against the background of our discussions of housing and ideology in capitalist societies in general, and South Africa in particular, it is possible to proceed to an analysis of *media* impressions of the black housing issue in South Africa. Our intentions in this regard are to work more inductively than deductively towards theory. That is to say, by going first to 'the facts' of media content rather than first to theories of the media. An appropriate point to begin is with a macro-level perspective on black housing as an element within the Johannesburg *Star*'s representation of urban issues for the period 1925 to 1979. From here it will be possible to narrow to a more focused and refined comparative analysis of media interpretations of black housing during the 1970s — a period of apparently critical importance in changing media interpretations of the black housing issue.

The Star and South Africa's 'Urban Issues', 1927-1979

In order to develop an assessment of *The Star*'s perspective on 'urban issues' in general a content analysis was conducted on a six per cent stratified random sample of all editions of that newspaper for the period 1925 to 1979[42]. That is, a sample of approximately 1 200 was drawn from a universe of 20 000 editions, the study period and universe being chosen simply according to limitations on source material, and the sample size being dictated essentially by the constraints of field research time available.

Such a data base provides a relatively coarse sieve with which to sift the fine nuances of ideology in the media, of course. Nevertheless, accepting the principles of probability sampling, longer-term trends identified on the basis of such a sample can be regarded with a high degree of statistical confidence[43]. Having identified an initial total of some twelve hundred *Star* articles on urban issues for the period 1925 to 1979, then, the next logical step was to derive salient and statistically valid trends out of this total: trends that could be used as a basis for making inferences about changing media definitions of urban issues in South Africa.

The use of the phrase '*salient* and statistically valid trends' immediately gives rise to the question of which theoretical constructs should be employed in the selection of appropriate categories of urban issues for historical and graphical analysis. It may be noted in this regard that category selection in the case of *The Star* material has been motivated largely by a desire to examine the local relevance of the adaptation of Borja's conception of how the various tensions and contradictions, described earlier, tend to unfold around the urbanisation process in peripheral capitalist societies (see figure 1).

Before attempting to exemplify this framework with material from *The Star*, however, it is worth emphasising that no commercial news medium is likely to act simply as a passive 'mirror' of the everyday ramifications of the three stages of urban policy. The commercial media, after all, have their own independent economic and political dynamics which are separate from those of urbanisation. These dynamics, in turn, impinge upon the media's conception of which aspects of urban reality are 'noteworthy' at any point in time. To theorise rigorously the logic underlying the development of *The Star* in this regard is beyond our competence[44]. On the basis of our historical reading of that newspaper, however, it would seem that Bozzoli is justified in inferring a shift of editorial policy by about 1930 — a shift away from a relatively explicit concern with the opinions and interests of the mining bourgeoisie and towards a more broadly based white South African 'news market'. It is difficult to say, on the basis of evidence available to us, whether Bozzoli is correct in regarding this shift as the result of an emergent South African 'consumerism': a consumerism that is an apparent concomitant of the ascendance of manufacturing *vis-à-vis* mining within the general structure of capitalist accumulation[45]. One point is clear to us at this stage, however, and that is that the more popularised news base of *The Star* which emerged by 1930 is likely, if anything, simply to *underline* any shift of emphasis in media content that could have arisen through its 'mirroring' of changing urban conditions. Production-orientated infrastructural urban issues, it might be argued, have less popular news appeal than issues pertaining to the apparently more 'public' reproductive sphere. With this in mind it is now possible to turn our attention to the statistical distribution of *Star* articles for the study period.

From figure 2 it is immediately evident that the frequency of articles addressing problems of productive infrastructure in cities has indeed declined over the study period as a whole. In the period 1925 to 1979, urban issues in general were extraordinarily well represented in *The Star*, but the proportion devoted to productive infrastructure was also clearly exceptionally high. The degree of concern with productive infrastructure in relation to reproductive issues remained high into the early 1930s, in fact, but this pattern had changed sharply by the early 1940s, when a reproductive focus associated with a period of urbanisation of social control came into effect. Thus by the late 1940s, the frequency of reporting on reproductive issues reached a maximum, the specific focus of concern being the proliferation of squatter camps, shanty towns and 'slums' that were beginning to penetrate and encircle the country's major cities[46]. In the early 1950s, when State policy switched from viewing the city as an object of public order to that of ideological and physical intervention, the ratio of articles dealing with productive infrastructure in relation to reproductive problems reached an all time low. This was the time of protracted conflict over the demolition of working class shantytowns and the promotion of sprawling, suburban, State-administered 'housing estates'[47]. It is worth noting too that, with the exception of the early 1960s — when the State made a desperate, last-ditch attempt to shift the burden of so-called 'development concern' onto the disintegrating precapitalist hinterland[48], and when the supposedly 'opposition' *Star* also dropped its concern with reporting on the urban condition to an all time low — despite the ever increasing reality of the urban condition for the mass of South Africans — the lion's share of concern with urban reproductive issues in *The Star* for the period as a whole was in fact *black* urbanisation and the *black* presence in cities. Indeed, approximately eighty per cent of *The Star*'s articles dealing with urban reproductive sphere were related to the so-called 'problem of urban blacks'[49].

Having established that reproductive issues increased relative to concern with productive infrastructure in *The Star* over the period as a whole (albeit in a complex manner), and having clarified that the bulk of reproductive issues centred upon the black presence in cities, it may now be advantageous to examine temporal variations in *The Star* of 'concern' for the black urban presence. From figure 3 it is evident that — apart from the late 1920s when the Stallard Doctrine's emphasis upon 'locations' for urban blacks probably led to media interest in the notion of 'administered townships' — in most of the earlier period of study (the 1930s and 1940s) *The Star* was predominantly preoccupied with 'unplanned settlement' issues pertaining to urban blacks. This would correspond to the period of State response labelled as the 'urbanisation of social control'. From the early 1950s onward, however, attention shifted to the question of planned, administered townships and home-ownership for blacks — the latter issue becoming especially pronounced in *The Star* in the late 1970s. Again, this would correspond to a period of State response that we have labelled as the 'urbanisation of ideological and physical intervention'.

But what of the *causes* of these stages? Were they simply 'structurally produced' by some 'capitalist logic', or were they partly forged in class struggle? It will be recalled from earlier theoretical discussion that the unfolding of the stages we have described should be impelled, in part, by the struggles of the urban masses both in the workplace and living place. These struggles are not entirely divorced, of course:

> The split between the place of work and the place of residence means that the struggle of labour to control the social conditions of its own existence splits into two seemingly independent struggles. The first, located in the work place, is over the conditions of work and the wage rate which provides the purchasing power for consumption goods. The second, fought in the place of residence, is against secondary forms of exploitation and appropriation represented by merchant capital, landed property and the like. This is a fight over the costs and conditions of existence in the living place. When focusing on the second kind of struggle, we must therefore recognise ... that the dichotomy between *living* and *working* is itself an artificial division which the capitalist system imposes[50].

The question therefore arises in a South African context as to the correlation of historically changing emphasis upon work-place and living place struggles with *reporting* on the latter; in particular, with *The Star's* awareness of the black housing issue. From figure 4 it is evident that, in historical terms, the balance of labour's protest activities (at least as interpreted by *The Star*) shifted from an early focus upon home issues to a subsequent (1930s and early 1940s) focus upon workplace issues. In the late 1940s and in the 1950s, however, labour's protest again began to converge on conditions in the living place; and then shifted once more in the 1960s

and early 1970s to workplace issues. It could be
hypothesised in this regard that the shifting balance of
interest might have parallelled popular experiences of,
and reactions to, varying patterns of exploitation. The
rate of exploitation at work in the 1930s, for example,
was high, whereas during the 1950s and 1960s it was
principally the reproductive sphere which, in Borja's fe-
licitous phrase, became "the object of plunder and of ideology"[51]. A rigorous analysis of such questions must await
further research of an economic nature[52]. Slightly more
enlightening, however, is figure 5, in which reports of
protest centering on the black reproductive sphere are
graphed against general reports on the urban black condition. Although the correlation is by no means perfect
(Pearson's r=0.49, and on the graph the two exceptions of
the early 1940s and early 1960s are notable); it can be
seen that when reporting on black community or living
place protest activity is high, so is reporting on the black
urban condition in general. Perhaps *The Star*'s coverage
of the black urban condition, then, is principally the result of an *enforced* awareness brought about by militant
action 'from below' so to speak. This provocative hypoth-
esis is subject to more detailed scrutiny for the decade of
the 1970s in the section to follow.

The *Financial Mail*, the *Weekend World* and the Black Housing Issue, 1970-1979

In order to penetrate more deeply into the circumstances conditioning media coverage of black housing it is
necessary to extend the range of media consulted and to
expand the sample size, so as to have a relatively fine
sieve with which to sift content during a short period. In
so doing, it may be possible to identify similarities and
differences in the treatment of the black housing problem
within the media which suggest a good deal about both
the role of black townships in the context of ongoing
social struggles in South Africa, and the media's attempts
at the definition of that role.

The particular empirical strategy adopted here was to
conduct a content analysis of a fifty per cent stratified
random sample of editions of the *Financial Mail* and the

Weekend World for the period 1970 to 1979[53]. It is recognised, of course, that neither of these weeklies escapes from the dual constraints of authoritarian oversight by the Government and the exigencies of profit and mass circulation imposed by their role as 'businesses'[54]. There are certain advantages, however, in being able to demonstrate similarities between a *laissez-faire*-orientated businessman's weekly such as the *Financial Mail* and a more left-leaning urban black weekly such as the *Weekend World* (since banned). For instance, the identification of certain commonalities in the treatment of black housing might serve to undermine the widespread notions that the *Financial Mail* and the *Weekend World* are or were somehow autonomously 'liberal' and 'radical' respectively in their treatment of social problems. By the same token it must be recognised that each weekly does in fact occupy a different 'ideological subregion' in South Africa, with the *Mail*'s staff being largely integrated into the bourgeoisie proper, and the *World*'s staff being more closely allied to an aspirant black petty bourgeoisie (or new middle class) that is forced by the particular circumstances of neocolonial domination in South Africa to rub shoulders with the urban proletariat.

As far as results are concerned, the content analyses revealed first of all that both weeklies were very much more concerned with black housing as an issue during and after 1976 than they were before 1976 (figures 6 and 7). It is true, of course, that there are differences between the *Financial Mail* and the *Weekend World*: in proportional (as opposed to absolute) terms the *World* was more concerned with black housing prior to 1976 and the *Mail* was more concerned with this issue during and after 1976 (figure 7). These important aspects of media response will be examined shortly. The empirical regularity that is of immediate concern, however, is the common intensification of interest in black housing during and after 1976 (figure 6).

The reasons for the empirical realities identified here can only be indirectly inferred, unfortunately, and not directly assessed with further empirical tests. Yet we should venture to hypothesise that the increased concern on the part of both weeklies, beginning in 1976, was a reflection of a new editorial concern with 'environmental' and 'community' conditions applicable to urban blacks: a concern occasioned by the 1976 uprisings centered in Soweto. Such an editorial response would be entirely consistent with petty-bourgeois and bourgeois responses to violent outbursts by the proletariat in other capitalist societies. Walker, for example, has commented on the 'discovery' of 'social disorganisation' in 'the slum' in nineteenth-century North America in the following manner:

> In the process of escaping to the Suburbs the American bourgeoisie has created ... like the British bourgeoisie — a 'vast terra incognita', as Gareth Stedman-Jones has described it, which they dubbed 'the slum'. Thereafter, whenever the dominant classes heard rumblings from below, they had to re-enter this strange land to discover its secrets and evils — from bad housing to bad politics — to be expunged[55].

Stedman-Jones and Walker, respectively, provide penetrating analyses of the way in which the ideology of 'community self-improvement' was harnessed by the bourgeoisie and petty bourgeoisie: an ideology that served both to mystify the sources of class oppression, and to alleviate some of the objective causes of dissatisfaction (and hence class action) amongst the urban poor in nineteenth-century Europe and America[56]. It is interesting to note, however, how the *Financial Mail*, in a special edition on the Urban Foundation (a liberal 'self-improvement' organisation for urban blacks sponsored by the likes of Harry Oppenheimer and Anton Rupert), drew some perceptive historical and cross cultural parallels in the reactions of American big business to the Watts and Harlem riots of the 1960s.

> The aftermath of the shockwaves of the urban (read: black) riots in the US in the second half of the sixties brought it forcibly home to big business there, firstly, that government was incapable of dealing with the crises on its own, and then that social responsibility was indeed 'the business of business' — otherwise there might not be enough business in the longer run ... South African busi-

ness won't be permitted to luxuriate in continuing to lag behind, or in catching up at leisure; there is a penalty to be paid for having delayed reacting to our first 'Watts' — Sharpeville — until after Soweto. It is having to deal today with problems infinitely more pressing than those that confronted US business in 1965[57].

It is no secret of either the *Financial Mail* or the Urban Foundation, of course, that the 'social responsibility' of big business in South Africa was and still is identified as being in the area of the rapid creation of a black petty bourgeoisie, and the promotion of the philosophy and practice of 'self-help' in areas such as housing and the provision of community facilities[58]. It might be argued, therefore, that the spate of articles during and after 1976 reflects this new political consciousness brought about by the 1976 'rumblings from below'.

Exemplifying this trend was a lead article in the 9 July 1976 edition of the *Financial Mail*. The article implied, on the one hand, that the housing problems of Sowetans could be attributed largely to 'bureaucratic insensitivity' on the part of township administrators. On the other hand, it urged that the solution to the problem lay in the direction of the extension of freehold ownership rights to urban blacks, and greater degrees of 'local control' in township government and administration. The article in question opened in the following manner:

> The inhabitants of Soweto have all the amenities that make for a healthy community life (West Rand Bantu Affairs Administration Chairman, Manie Mulder, in the recently published brochure *Soweto Kaleidoscope*).
>
> They also have riots. What they don't have is any permanent stake in an urban area. And if they don't get that soon there's risk of more riots[59].

Without departing from its basic philosophy of 'free enterprise', then, the *Financial Mail* could simultaneously appear as the champion of 'the black cause' and the apparent opponent of 'insensitive bureaucrats'; and at the same time it could advocate a deeper and more subtle level of ideological dependence amongst urban blacks via home-ownership and the 'municipalisation' of the townships. The *Financial Mail*'s support for home-ownership will be examined in greater depth shortly. It might be noted, with respect to the *Mail*'s support for greater degrees of local governmental control by blacks, however, that their philosophy of 'run your own slum' has parallels with the bourgeois response to problems of political legitimacy in America following outbursts of proletarian violence in the 1960s in areas such as Watts and Harlem. The political commentator Altshuler, for example, urged it upon the status quo in America that:

> the central issues (with respect to community control) ... are social peace and legitimacy, not abstract justice or efficiency. (Community control has several advantages) ... But most important, it would give blacks a tangible stake in the American political system. By giving them systems they considered their own, it would — hopefully — enhance the legitimacy of the whole system in their eyes[60].

In addition to concern for political legitimacy, one other factor might account for the heightened interest in black housing amongst all sectors of the commercial press in the period 1976 to 1979. During this period, and in 1977 and 1978 in particular, the State was gearing up for a major assault on the recession which had begun in 1975. By June 1978 the 'liquidity problem' in the national economy was beginning to show signs of easing for the first time in several years and all indications were that, with the appropriate stimulus from central government, new private investment opportunities might emerge via 'spinoff effects' from the activities of large scale construction companies[61]. The policy context, therefore, was ripe for discussions of the need for State expenditure on items such as highway construction and low income housing projects: projects to allow Government to 'spend its way out of the recession'. In a publication such as the *Financial Mail*, therefore, the interest in black housing may not have been entirely provoked by a concern with black living conditions *per se*, but a macro-economist's concern with those forms of State intervention that might improve the national investment climate. Some indication of the relevance of this point is provided in the way in which the *Financial Mail* reacted to news of new black housing projects in its 5 May 1978 edition: "Understandably in the present economic climate, Finance Minister Owen Horwood's welcome R250m boost to black housing has received a great deal of publicity. As a confidence booster so it should."

Evidence of the *Financial Mail*'s not entirely philanthropic interest in black housing was again manifest on 20 July 1979, when a lead article on urban development and services upgrading in Soweto discussed the marketing implications of the electrification of that suburb at length:

> If the violent upheavals that shook Soweto and shocked the world three years ago thrust the million or more people in the township onto the centre of the political stage, businessmen in recent years have been waking up to the fact that they are a large potential market. (An expert in the marketing field) said that nearly 70 per cent of Soweto's residents aspired to replacing their coal stoves with electric stoves, and he estimated the market for electrical appliances and other electrical goods at R150m at 1978 prices.

The arguments advanced thus far, of course, do little to explain the marked *differences* between the *Weekend World* and the *Financial Mail* in the treatment of the black housing issue. In this regard it might be noted that we are severely hampered by not being allowed to quote directly from the *Weekend World* in support of any of the points made in this chapter. Such are the constraints upon critical research in authoritarian society. Readers who can gain access to back issues of the *Weekend World* either abroad or by permission (in South Africa) may wish to follow up on articles whose page and date references we indicate.

We would argue that the difference in the relative level of interest shown by the *World* and the *Mail* on either side of the June 1976 time divide can be attributed, in part, to the fact that the staff of the former weekly would have been much more likely to have personally experienced some of the frustrations of housing conditions in the black townships. In addition, the *World*'s earlier concern might also be explained by the fact that its staff would have been more likely to encounter and experience similar frustrations amongst the black proletariat on a more or less daily basis. The more bourgeois, and white, reporters of the *Financial Mail*, on the other hand, will have been more closely integrated into different kinds of social networks: networks of individuals who take fright at black housing conditions only when they are seen to be potentially disturbing to variables like 'the investment climate', 'the threat of socialism', etc. (Illustrative of the *World*'s perspective is a page 2 article on housing conditions in Soweto in the 17 November 1974 edition.)

The speculations above concerning differences between the *Financial Mail's* and the *Weekend World*'s treatment of black housing are borne out, in part, by the relationships identified in figures 8 and 9. What is evident when one considers the two major 'sub issues' surrounding black housing — those of rent and home-ownership, — is that the *Financial Mail* demonstrates relatively increased concern with home-ownership after 1976, whereas the *Weekend World* manifests a strong and *consistent* interest in questions of rent.

The *Financial Mail* has been an implicit supporter of home-ownership rights for urban blacks for some time, of course, but it really only pursued the issue with any vigour after 1976, presumably because it perceived that home-ownership was then particularly desirable to fulfil the socially conservatising functions identified by Harvey earlier[62]. The staff of the *Weekend World*, on the other hand, perhaps because of their highly ambiguous and strained position as a petty bourgeoisie without private property rights, had been reporting rather energetically on the home-ownership issue for some time (see, for example, the page 6 editorial on 8 November 1970 and the page 6 editorial on 6 February 1972 of the *World*). This was a trend that was merely augmented after 1976, when the *Weekend World* presumably felt that it now had the example of proletarian violence to add to the case it was building for the black petty bourgeois cause (see figure 8). (An example of such an article is on page 4 of *The World*, 10 April 1977.)

The position of both the *Financial Mail* and the *Week-*

end World, however, is perhaps epitomised in the way in which the former weekly cited with approval the position of the executive director of the Urban Foundation, Mr Justice Jan Steyn, on the question of 'what is to be done' after the Soweto uprising:
> No society or people can survive without doing reasonable justice to other people ... The focus of concern of the Urban Foundation during the initial period should constitute the general area and conditions of housing. That is to say the normalisation of land tenure for urban blacks[63].

What is remarkable here, of course, is the assumption, first, that 'social survival', as defined by the Urban Foundation, could be best achieved by the application of some norm of 'justice' to black *housing* (note, not primarily national wealth distribution and wages); and, second, that such 'justice' is defined in the bourgeois terms of how deeply a group is embedded in capitalist relations of production (i.e. 'normalised' land tenure is assumed to be *capitalist* land tenure which, in turn, is considered to be 'justice'.)

Perhaps the most interesting results of all are contained in figure 9. It is clear that in the case of both weeklies, time period exerts a significant effect. Pre-1976 reporting on black housing rentals in both the *Financial Mail* and the *Weekend World* is considerably lower than the post-1976 level of reporting on the same topic. Interestingly enough, the rate of intensification of reporting on black housing after 1976 is much the same for both weeklies (i.e. for both the *World* and *Mail* pre-1976 levels of reporting compare to post-1976 levels in the ratio of approximately 1:3). However, what this obscures is the *base* against which the post-1976 intensification of reporting on rents occurred. In absolute terms the *Weekend World* was and continued to be much more concerned with rents than the *Financial Mail* (see figure 9). This difference, we assume, can partly be attributed to the *World*'s staff's greater degree of ideological and physical proximity to the urban proletariat for whom rents and rent strikes are central concerns related to the broader struggle with capital in general and the State. In addition, insofar as Government control over black housing has been instrumental in the politicisation of everyday life in the black townships, the *World*'s concern with rent issues reflects in part a deepening legitimation crisis for the State that is popularly expressed in 'urban social movements' such as rent strikes, bus boycotts and protests over the costs of upgrading physical infrastructure in the townships[64]. (See, for example, articles on page 2 of the 28 January 1970 edition of *World*; page 1 of 28 April 1977 edition of *World*; and page 1 article and page 2 editorial of the 13 November 1977 edition of *Weekend Post*.)

It is perhaps, the *World*'s greater sensitivity to such manifestations of the State's legitimation crisis that led to its being banned, whilst the danger of banning for a weekly such as the *Financial Mail* seems remote indeed. In the meantime the only media that demonstrate much interest in rent strikes, bus boycotts, issues of the legitimacy of the 'community councils', and the emergence of radicalised civic associations like Port Elizabeth's PEBCO or Durban's JORAC are the non-commercial media, scattered and erratic as they are. However, even these tend to get banned as soon as they begin to demystify bourgeois ideology with any degree of clarity[65].

Conclusion and Postscript

This chapter has examined a configuration of relationships between the dynamics of capitalist accumulation under peripheral capitalism, the process of urbanisation, the progress of class struggles at points of production and reproduction, and media interpretations and representations of these. It should, however, be noted that the chapter was written four years prior to this concluding postscript. We believe that there are many aspects of the analysis that have stood the test of time, but some of the basic concepts seem to us now to be insufficient in relation to our original research problem — viz a critical analysis of the ways in which urban problems become defined and redefined in the course of social struggle in South Africa.

The main problem that occurs to us in 1986 is the rather mechanistic way in which we projected standard Marxist concepts onto the subtleties of the South African urban scene. We should qualify ourselves here by saying that it is not merely our methodology that we now see as simplistic. Despite the current ascendency of qualitative historical methodologies in the humanities and social sciences, we remain convinced that quantitative methods can be profitably integrated with social theory in unravelling the social role of the media in South Africa. At the very least, we feel that a greater degree of methodological diversity in approaches to ideology would be a healthy development in critical media studies. A more serious problem with our work in retrospect, is the almost exclusive reliance upon European Marxist concepts to interrogate specifically South African urban problems.

As the French Marxist anthropologist, Jean Copans, remarked in a recent paper, the problem of class in an African context poses a distinct set of problems for Marxist analysis which have not yet been adequately addressed[66]. Others might argue that Marxist theory itself, modified into an indigenous context or otherwise, should be seen as *part* of a theory of the ideology of urban and regional issues, but that it by no means can lay claim to exclusive dominance[67].

These qualifications aside, we hope that the chapter may stimulate further thought amongst students of urban affairs on the way in which they receive their research agendum.

It is remarkable how often urban economists, geographers, planners, communications scientists or sociologists are given to assume that 'socially relevant' research on urban problems derives from sensitivity to those ostensible barometers of public opinion, the media. With predictable monotony, papers appearing in the professional journals, or academic proposals submitted to the official dispensers of research funding largesse, open with the remark that their research topic is currently a popular topic of media or 'public' (i.e. State) debate. For many, this is *prima facie* evidence that the research in question 'matters'. To some extent this media/academic research relationship is reciprocal, of course. Academic research is generated in response to media fanfare on a topic. The results of the same research are then fed back into the media as 'news'. Such are the incestuous relationships within the ideological State apparatus[68].

In urban geography and planning in South Africa, for example, the entire agendum of publication and research appears to have been adjusted in the wake of 1976, and even more intense crises in the 1980s. To have successfully grasped the rules of the common sense world and to have become a man or woman of one's time, so to speak, now means that research and teaching must focus in part upon black housing, the so-called 'informal sector' markets of the townships, and an array of related *terra incognita* of times past[69]. This is a situation that is not entirely without opportunity for the critical intellectual, of course. But a real danger arises from the possibility that that academic community may, once more, be caught up within a momentum of the social construction of urban problems, the complex nature of which is seldom the subject of scrutiny or critical self-reflection. We now find, in urban geography and planning, for instance, erstwhile liberal intellectuals marching hand-in-glove with progressive elements of the State and capital in a veritable orgy of work on 'informal sector solutions to black housing problems'. These 'solutions', however, are inevitably slanted towards the principles of home-ownership, 'self help' and 'local control', the profoundly ideological nature of which has been alluded to in this chapter.

Thus, to conclude, we would argue that an important contribution of a possible convergence of critical media studies and research into urban problems would be in the advantage to the latter of a deeper understanding of the subtlety of the social struggles shaping their own research agendas. The task of sustaining a critical posture towards research into urban problems will not be an easy one, however. In this regard it may be appropriate to echo the reflections of sometime theoretical geographer, now Director of the Nordic Institute for Planning, Gunnar Olsson, on the pitfalls of the atheoretic, 'socially relevant' research agenda that overtook his field in the 1970s:

> There is again a choir of hollow voices echoing (the) ... warning that 'if we, as geographers, fail to perform in policy relevant terms, we will cease to be

called on to perform at all'. The key verb here, however, is not 'to perform' but 'to be called on'. Perhaps the mistake was not in performing, but in listening too obediently to those timely sirens who did the calling. Perhaps our responsibility as independent intellectuals is not to stand with hat in hand, but to be jesters, sometimes performing when called on and sometimes refusing altogether. But at whose mercy is the jester, who cuts too closely to the truth he is supposed to suggest but never tell?[70].

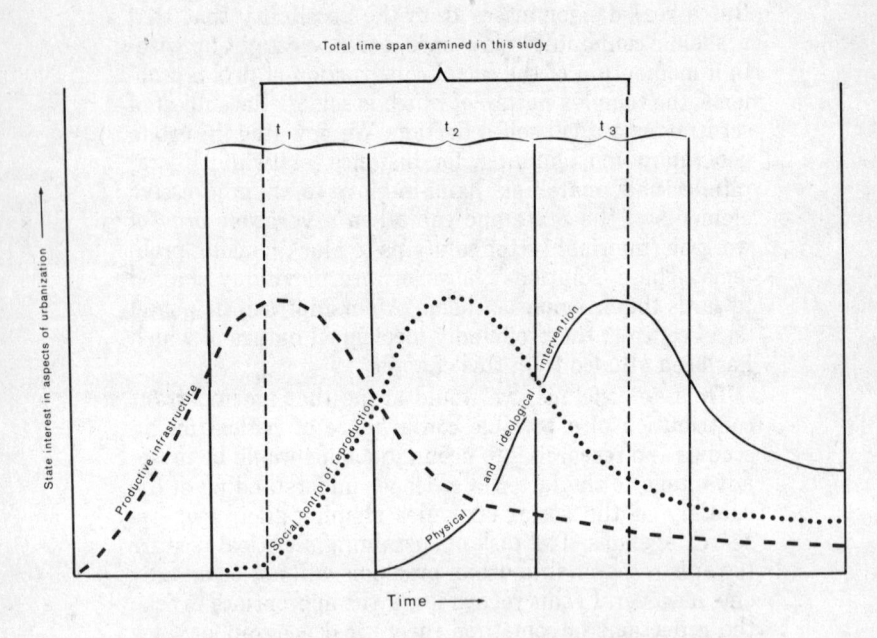

Figure 1: Simplified Model of State Responses to the Historically Changing Contradictions of Urbanisation under Peripheral Capitalism.

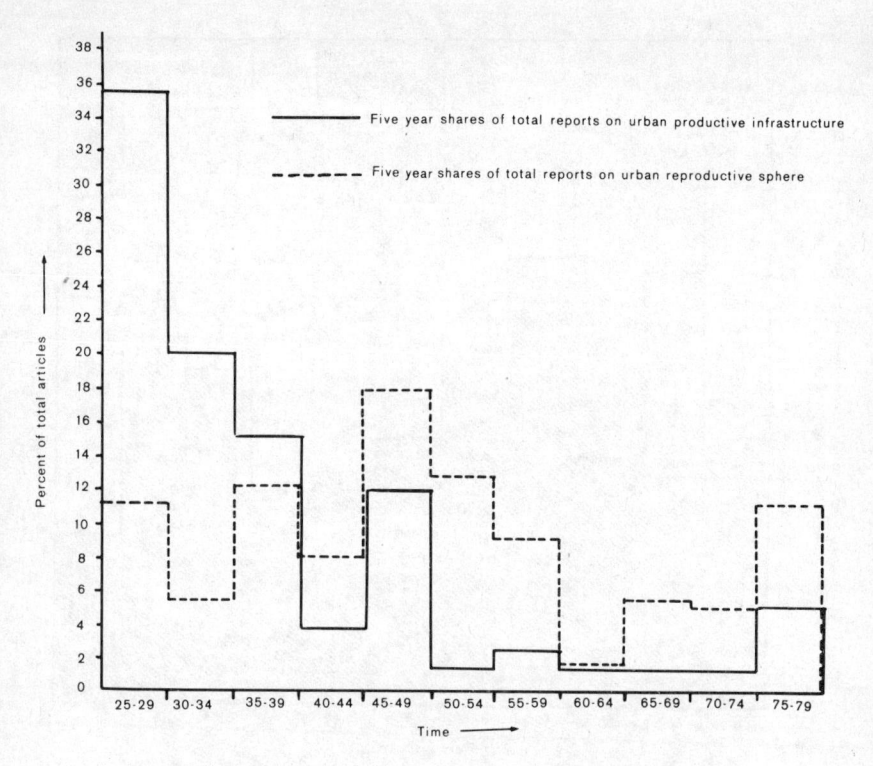

Figure 2: Relative Frequency over Time of *Star* Articles Addressing Urban Productive Infrastructure and the Urban Reproductive Sphere.

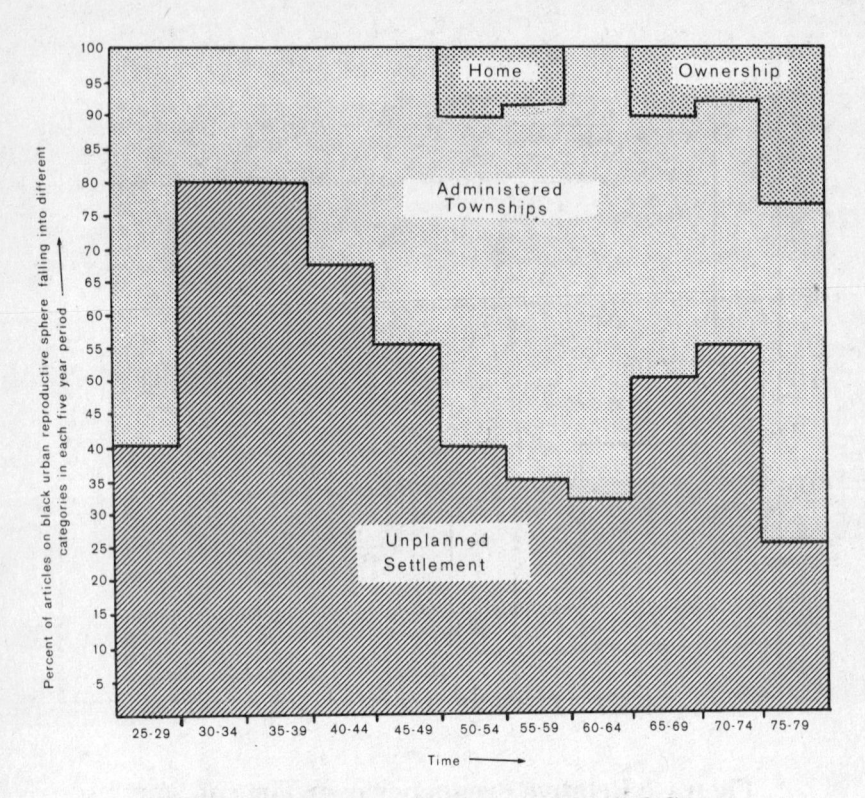

Figure 3: The Changing Composition of *Star* Interest in the Issue of the Black Urban Reproductive Sphere.

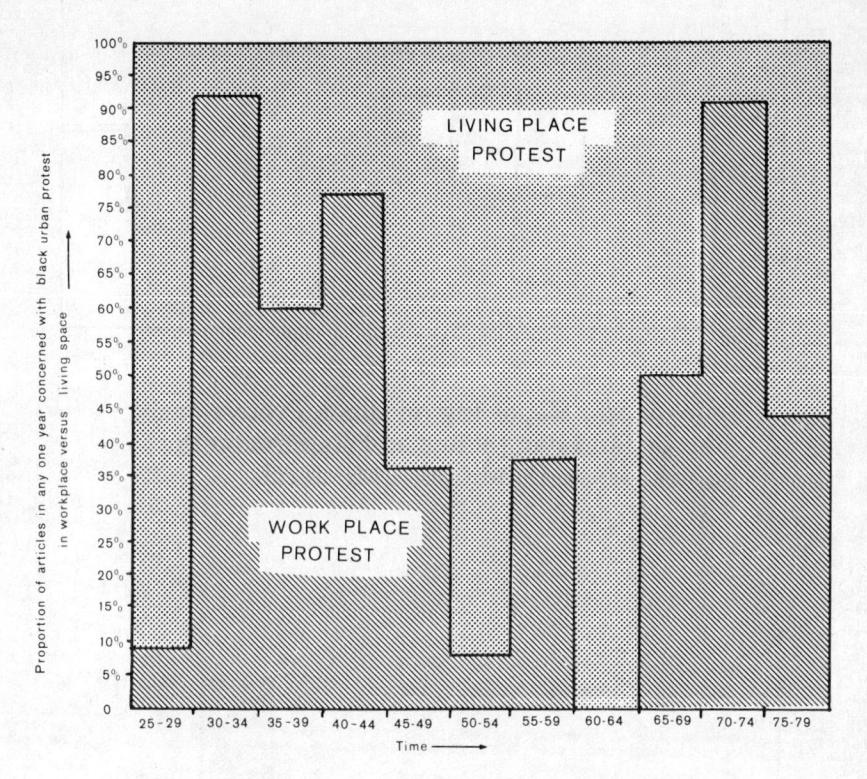

Figure 4: The Historically Changing Balance of Labour's Protest Activity as Identified by *The Star*.

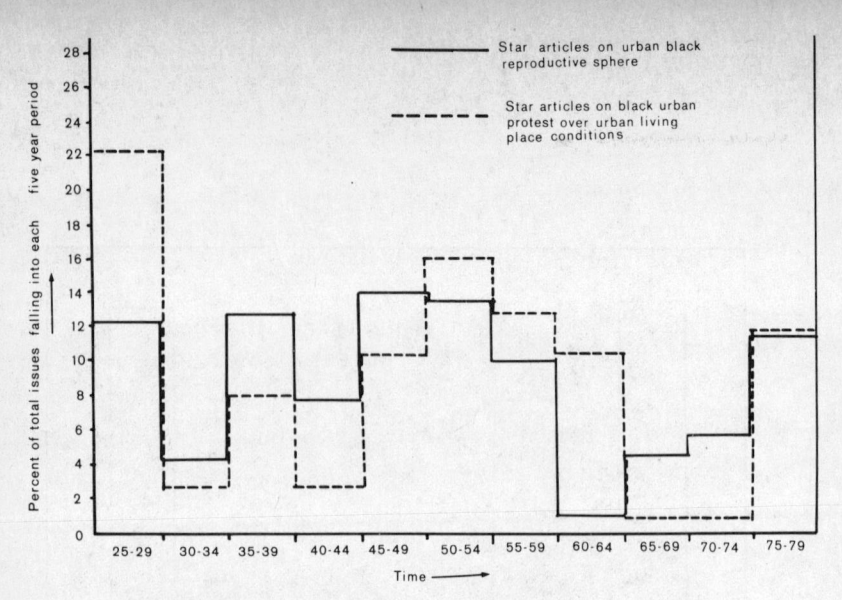

Figure 5: *Star* Reporting on Black Protest over the Urban Living Place and Reports on the Black Urban Conditions in General.

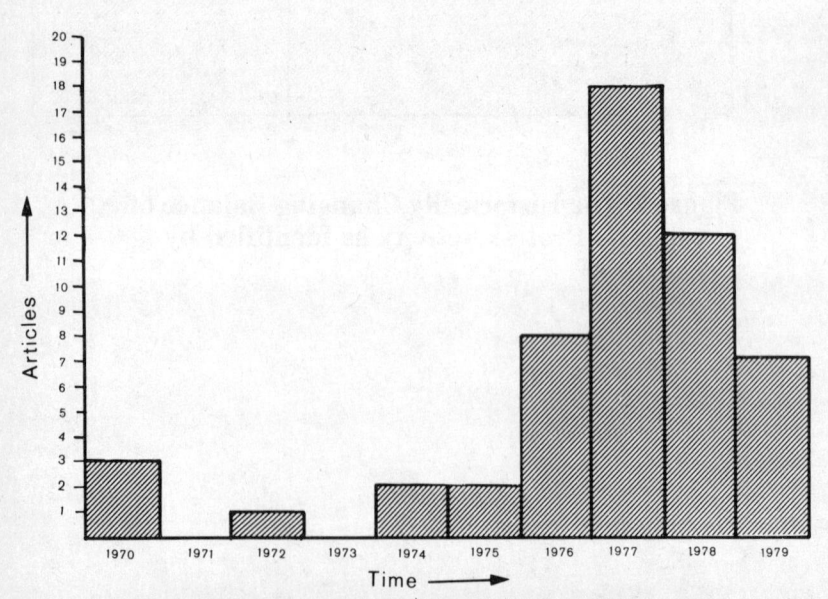

Figure 6: Fluctuation over Time in *Financial Mail* and *Weekend World* Reporting on the Housing Condition of Urban Blacks (Excluding Home Ownership and Rent Issues).

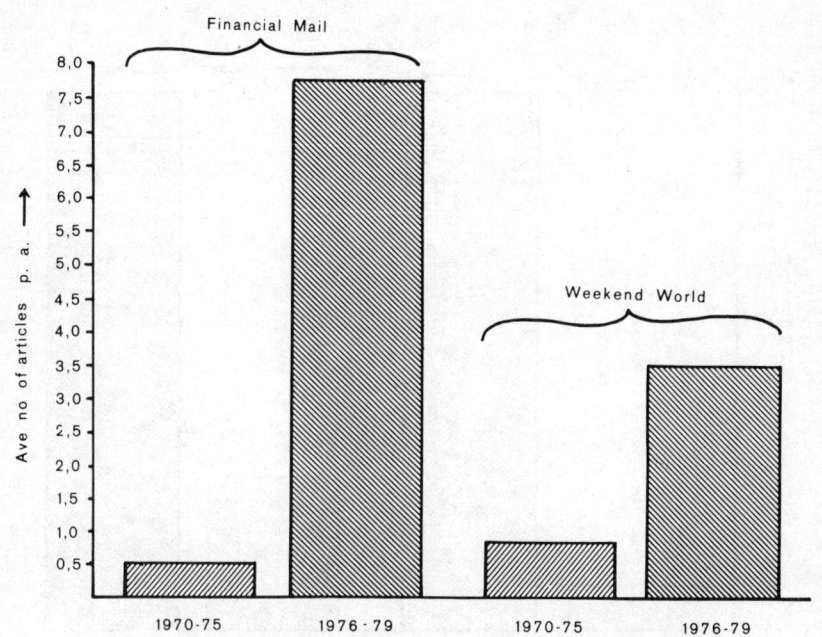

Figure 7: Rates of Reporting on the Housing Condition of Urban Blacks (Excluding Home Ownership and Rent Issues) by Media Channel and Time Period.

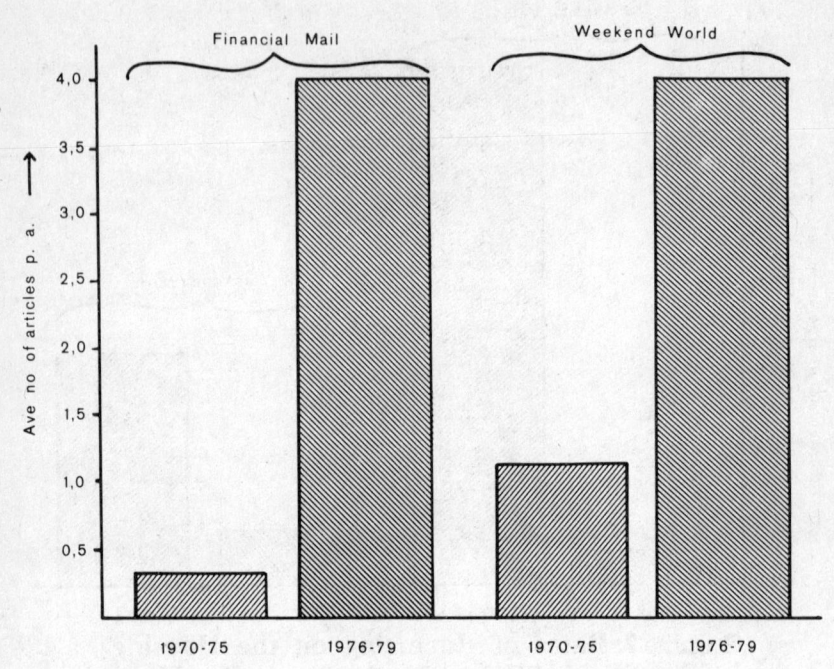

Figure 8: Rates of Reporting on Home Ownership for Blacks by Media Channel and Time Period.

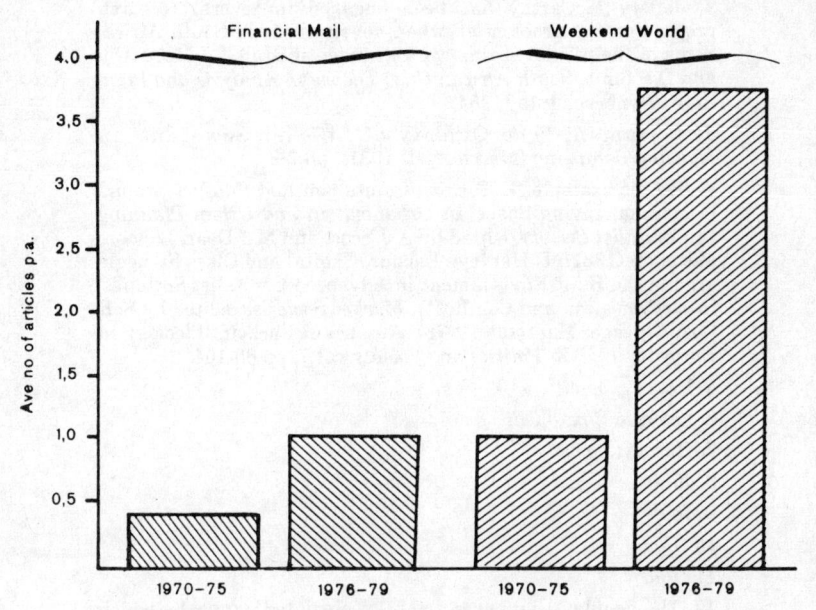

Figure 9: Rates of Reporting on Rents Applicable to Black Housing by Media Channel and Time Period.

Notes and References

1. This chapter is a considerably revised and extended version of an earlier work. See J J McCarthy and M Friedman, 'Black Housing, Ideology and the Media in South Africa 1970-1979' in *Critical Arts* vol 2 no 2 (1981), pp 51-56.

The authors wish to acknowledge the financial assistance of Rhodes University in gaining access to empirical material.

2. Jeffery McCarthy has been engaged in several research projects on the problem of urban development in South Africa. Some of the results of this work are identified in J J McCarthy and D P Smit, *South African City: Theory in Analysis and Planning*, Wynberg: Juta (1984).

3. P Human, 'The Quality of Life for Sowetans' in *Housing/Behuising* (March/April 1981), pp 2-9

4. See for example, K R Cox, 'Capitalism and Conflict around Communal Living Space' in *Urbanisation and Urban Planning in Capitalist Society*, edited by A J Scott and M J Dear, London: Methuen (1981); D Harvey, 'Labour, Capital and Class Struggle around the Built Environment in Advanced Capitalist Societies' in *Urbanisation and Conflict in Market Societies*, edited by K R Cox, Chicago: Maaroufa (1978). Also see R Rackoff, 'Ideology in Everyday Life' in *Politics and Society* vol 7, pp 85-104

5. Harvey, *op cit*

6. See also Cox, *op cit*

7. Harvey, *op cit*

8. *Ibid*

9. *Ibid*

10. *Ibid*

11. *Ibid*

12. The doubly — and even triply — mediated nature by which the 'housing crisis' is reported is discussed in K Tomaselli, 'A Journalist's Introduction to the Concept of Ideology' in *Sociology of News*, Grahamstown: Department of Journalism and Media Studies (1984).

13. See, however, M Castells, *The Urban Question: A Marxist Approach*, Cambridge, Mass: MIT Press (1977); and A J Scott, *The Urban Land Nexus and the State*, London: Pion (1980).

14. C F Scott, *op cit*

15. See Harvey, *op cit*; and D Massey and A Catalano, *Capital and Land: Land Ownership by Capital in Great Britain*, London: Edward Arnold (1978).

16. M Castells, *City, Class and Power*, London: MacMillan (1978).

17. See P Dunleavy, 'The Urban Basis of Political Alignments' in

British Journal of Political Science vol 9 (1979), pp 403-43. Also see J Kemeny, 'Homeownership and Privatisation' in *International Journal of Urban and Regional Research* vol 4 no 3 (1980), pp 372-38.

18. Refer to J Lojkine, 'Contribution to a Marxist Theory of Capitalist Urbanisation' in *Urban Sociology: Critical Essays*, edited by C Pickvance, New York: St Martin's Press (1980); J Olives, 'The Struggle against Urban Renewal in "Cite d'Aliart" (Paris)' in Pickvance, *op cit*, for Castells' cohorts. For the Poulantzian theory of the state under capitalism see for example, N Poulantzas, *Political Power and Social Classes*, London: New Left Books (1973).

19. P Wilkinson, 'The Politics of Housing in South Africa: A Framework for Analysis' in *Work in Progress* (17 April 1981), pp 61-9

20. A W Stadler, 'Birds in the Cornfields: Squatter Movements in Johannesburg, 1944-1977' in *Labour, Townships and Protest*, edited by B Bozzoli, Johannesburg: Ravan Press (1979); T Lodge, 'The Destruction of Sophiatown' in *Journal of Modern African Studies* vol 19 no 1 (1981), pp 107-32

21. For critiques of Castells in this vein see for example, S S Duncan, 'Housing Policy, the Methodology of Levels and Urban Research: The Case of Castells' in *International Journal of Urban and Regional Research* vol 5 no 2 (1981), pp 231-54; N H Buck, 'The Analysis of State Intervention in Nineteen Century Cities: The Case of Municipal Labour Policy in East London, 1886-1914' in Dear and Scott (eds), *op cit*.

22. For an argument along these lines, see H Wolpe, 'Capitalism and Cheap Labour Power in South Africa: From Segregation to Apartheid' in *The Articulation of Modes of Production*, edited by H Wolpe.

23. On the articulation of modes of production, see C Meillasoux, in Wolpe, *op cit*; A Foster-Carter, 'Can we Articulate Articulation?' in *The New Economic Anthropology*, edited by J Clanmere, New York: St Martin's Press (1978).

24. J Borja, 'Urban Movements in Spain' in *Captive Cities*, edited by M Harloe, New York: John Wiley (1977)

25. *Ibid*

26. *Ibid*

27. On the ideology of self-help see for example, R Burgess, 'Petty Commodity Housing or Dweller Control? A Critique of John Turner's Views on Housing Policy' in *World Development* vol 6 no 9/10 (1978), pp 1105-1133.

28. For an excellent exposition of the 'horns of a dilemma' thesis on the South African State, see J S Saul and S Gelb, *The Crisis in South Africa*, New York: Monthly Review Press, (1981).

29. Statistics here are derived from South Africa, *Union Statis-*

tics for Fifty Years, Pretoria: Bureau of Census and Statistics (1960).

30. C Van Onselen, *New Babylon, New Nineveh: Studies in the Social and Economic History of the Witwatersrand 1886-1914*, Johannesburg: Ravan Press (1982).

31. See, however, S B Greenberg, *Race and State in Capitalist Development: South Africa in Comparative Perspective*, Johannesburg: Ravan Press (1980).

32. See, for example, F G Price and J W M Cameron, *The Evolution and Application of Town Planning Legislation in South Africa* Technical Report RT/45/81, Pretoria: NITRR, (1982).

33. For an explanation of, and data applicable to, these developments see J J McCarthy, 'The Political Economy of Urban Land Use: Towards a Revised Theoretical Framework' in *South African Geographical Journal* vol 65 No 1 (1983), pp 25-48.

34. Stadler, *op cit*

35. G H Pirie, 'Sleepers Beside Tracks: Housing in South Africa's State Railway Corporation, 1910-1980' in *South African Geographical Journal* vol 64 no 2 (1982), pp 144-54

36. South Africa, *op cit* (1960)

37. Lodge, *op cit*, provides a case in point of such a slant towards the racial/symbolic in his discussion of the destruction of Sophiatown.

38. The papers by Tom Lodge and Alf Stadler in *Working Papers in South African Studies* vol 2, edited by P Bonner, provide useful discussions of bus boycotts around Johannesburg. However, it is not clear how characteristic these case studies of Alexandra might be of the *general* pattern of bus boycotts that emerged in the 1950s in South Africa.

39. For outstanding presentations of the consumption sector problematic in relation to the British case see P Dunleavy, *Urban Political Analysis*, London: MacMillan (1980); and an article by Michael Harloe in *City, Class and Capital*, edited by M Harloe and E Lebas, London: Arnold (1981). Very little has been written on the subject in relation to the South African case, although it is touched upon in McCarthy, *op cit* (1983).

40. On the new State housing policy see for example, A S Mabin and S Parnell, 'The State, Capital and the Housing Question: New Directions for South African Cities?' in *South African Geographical Journal* vol 65 no 2 (1983).

41. The cynicism of the South African State's interpretation of the self-help philosophy is well illustrated in an article by David Dewar and Vanessa Watson in a critical article on Khayelitsha in the *Argus* (30 June 1983), p 20.

42. Twenty-one issues of *The Star* were randomly selected from each year in the study period as a whole. Randomness thus occurs within strata selected according to time period.

43. In the discussion to follow, five-year time periods are chosen as the unit of analysis (i.e. 105 issues of *The Star*). In addition, trends are usually established over three or more five-year time periods. Thus, any given trend reflects a pattern within approximately three hundred issues of *The Star* or approximately five hundred news articles. It follows that the possibility that such a trend could be due simply to chance is very remote.

44. Before such a theorisation could be confidently embarked upon, much more data would be required, for example, on the staffing, circulation and overall news content of the paper at different time periods.

45. B Bozzoli, *The Political Nature of a Ruling Class: Capital and Ideology in South Africa 1890-1933*, London: Routledge and Kegan Paul (1981).

46. The historical geography of the South African city is poorly documented. However, a useful sketch of the typical morphology of South African cities at this time is provided in R J Davies, *Of Cities and Societies: A Geographer's Perspective*, Cape Town: University of Cape Town Inaugural Lecture Series (1976). In addition Stadler, *op cit*, provides a very useful glimpse into political struggles centering around the State's attempt to impose an 'urbanisation of social control' solution at this time.

47. An Illuminating case study of conflict over the demolition of such inner city shantytowns is provided by Lodge, *op cit*. Some data on the economic implications of the shift from such inner city shantytowns to State-supervised suburban housing estates is provided in G Maasdorp and A S B Humphreys, *From Shantytown to Township*, Johannesburg: Juta and Company (1975).

48. For a discussion and bourgeois critique of State policy in this period see in particular P Smit and J J Booysens, *1977: Urbanisation in the Homelands*, Pretoria: Institute for Plural Studies, University of Pretoria (1977); also P Morris, *A History of Black Housing in South Africa*, Johannesburg: South Africa Foundation (1981).

49. As will be argued later in the paper, this interest in the black presence does not necessarily reflect *The Star*'s populist editorial stance. Much of *The Star*'s concern with black urbanisation was a reaction to the perceived threat that this urbanisation posed to the interests of its (largely white) readership. The overview in chapter 3 of this volume of the position held by the English language press within the political economy makes a similar point with regard not only to newspaper items concerned with urban blacks, but also their rural counterparts.

50. Harvey, *op cit*

51. Borja, *op cit*

52. The authors are currently collecting data that will permit us to explore and examine such problems. It should not be imagined, however, that we envisage a one-to-one relationship between the rate of exploitation and worker discontent. As Kevin

Cox has pointed out to us in a personal communication, there is not a direct relationship between the rate of exploitation and labour's ability to secure use values, labour's sense of alienation at work, etc.

53. The sample was stratified according to time period (year and month) and media channel (*World* versus *Mail*) and samples were drawn randomly from within strata. A fifty per cent sample was drawn. Notice that the *Weekend World* was banned in 1977 and replaced by *Sunday Post*, which was also banned in 1980. Back copies are only available in the State Copyright Libraries and no quoting is permitted from any issue.

54. L Switzer and D Switzer, *The Black Press in South Africa and Lesotho*; K G Tomaselli and R E Tomaselli, 'The South African Mass Media and the Dissemination of Apartheid Ideology' in *The Sociology of News*, Grahamstown: First Year Reader, Department of Journalism and Media Studies, Rhodes University (1981).

55. R A Walker, 'The Transformation of Urban Structure in the Nineteenth Century and the Beginnings of Suburbanisation' in Cox (ed), *op cit*.

56. G Stedman-Jones, *Outcast London: A Study in the Relationship between Classes in Victorian Society*, Harmondsworth: Penguin (1971).

57. *Special Report* on the Urban Foundation, supplement to *Financial Mail* (16 February 1979), p 4

58. Statements of such views are contained in the *Special Report* referred to in note 57 above, and in numerous editorials of the *Financial Mail* and the occasional publications of the Urban Foundation.

59. *Financial Mail* (9 July 1976), p 101

60. A A Altshuler, *Community Control: The Demand for Participation in Large American Cities*, New York: Pegasus (1970)

61. The liquidity situation is reflected in the fact that the bank rate (5,5%)had risen consistently from the beginning of 1974 until mid 1978 (9,0%). Interest rates are, of course, an indication of the relative scarcity of capital for deployment in the accumulation process.

62. Harvey, *op cit*

63. Mr Justice Jan Steyn, quoted in *Financial Mail* (22 July 1977), p 316. Note that this is a different individual from Mr Justice M T Steyn of the Steyn Commission of Inquiry into the press in South Africa.

64. On the politicisation of everyday life see Castells, *op cit*.

65. For a discussion of the non-commercial black press in South Africa see Switzer and Switzer, *op cit*, and volume three of *Addressing the Nation — The Limits of Dissent: Resistance, Community and the Press in South Africa*. The authors of the present

paper have found that student newspapers such as *SASPU National* are also consistent sources of information on the matters referred to. It is noteworthy, however, that any sign of radical penetration of the issues is rewarded by banning.

66. J Copans, 'The African Working Classes: Proletaranisation, Informal Sector, Wage Labour and the Reproduction of Class Structure', paper presented to Association for Sociology in Southern Africa, University of Cape Town (July 1985).

67. For a specifically feminist critique of Marxist concepts in urban studies see M Friedmann and A Wilkes, 'Androcentric Knowledge and Human Geography: Examined?' in *South African Geographical Journal* vol 68 no 1 (forthcoming).

68. In a different context, this has already been remarked upon in relation to the English press' sporadic, academically triggered interest in homeland news (chapter 3).

69. For a review of recent trends in this regard see, for example, K S O Beavon, 'Black Townships in South Africa: *terra incognita* for urban geographers' in *South African Geographical Journal*, vol 64 no 1 (1982), pp 30-40; also K S O Beavon and C M Rogerson, 'Trekking On: Recent Trends in the Human Geography of Southern Africa' in *Progress in Human Geography* vol 5 No 2 (1981), pp 159-189.

70. G Olsson, 'On the Mythology of the Negative Exponential or on Power as a Game of Ontological Transformations' in *Geografiska Annaler* vol 60B no 2 (1978), pp 115-130

Selected Bibliography

Part 1. Ideology, Culture and Hegemony

Althusser, L.: 'Ideology and Ideological State Apparatuses' in *Lenin and Philosophy and Other Essays*. London: New Left Books, 1971.

Althusser, L.: *For Marx*. London: Allan Lane, 1971.

Barrett, M., **Corrigan**, P., **Kuhn**, A., and **Wolff**, J. (Editors): *Ideology and Cultural Production*. London: Croom Helm, 1979. Particulary useful are the chapters by R **Johnson**: 'Histories of Culture/Theories of Ideology'; and T E **Perkins**: 'Rethinking Stereotypes'.

Brake, M.: *The Sociology of Youth Cultures and Youth Subcultures*. London: Routledge and Kegan Paul, 1980.

Cohen, S.: *Folk Devils and Moral Panics: The Creation of the Mods and Rockers*. London: MacGibbon and Kee, 1972.

Femia, J.: 'Hegemony and Consciousness in the Thought of Antonio Gramsci' in *Political Studies* vol 23 no 1, 1975.

Frith, S.: *The Sociology of Rock*. London: Constable, 1978.

Geras, N.: 'Althusser's Marxism: An Account and Assessment' in *New Left Review* no 71, 1972.

Hall, S. and **Jefferson**, A.: *Resistance through Ritual*. London: Hutchinson, 1976.

Hall, S., **Critcher**, C., **Jefferson**, A., **Clark**, J., and **Rob-**

erts, B. (Editors): *Policing the Crisis: Mugging, the State and Law and Order*. London: Macmillan, 1978.

Harnecker, M.: *The Elementary Concepts of Historical Materialism*, translated by E Sadler and W Suchtung. Sydney: University of Sydney, 1971.

Hawkes, T.: *Structuralism and Semiotics*. London: Methuen, 1979.

Hoare, Q., and **Nowell-Smith**, G.: 'The Study of Philosophy' in *Selections from the Prison Notebooks*, by A **Gramsci**, edited by G Nowell-Smith. London: Lawrence and Wishart, 1971.

Johnson, R.: 'Three Problematics: Elements of a Theory of Working Class Culture' in *Working Class Culture*, edited by J **Clarke**, C **Critcher** and R **Johnson**. London: Hutchinson, 1979.

Laclau, E.: *Politics and Ideology in Marxist Theory*. London: Verso, 1977.

Mandel, E.: *Introduction to Marxism*. London: Ink Links, 1977.

Miliband, R.: *The State in Capitalist Society*. London: Quartet Books 1973.

Poulantzas, N.: *State, Power and Socialism*. London: Verso, 1978.

Sassoon, A. S.: 'Hegemony and Political Intervention' in *Politics, Ideology and the State*, edited by S **Hibbin**. London: Lawrence and Wishart, 1978.

Sumner, C.: *Reading Ideologies*. New York: Academic Press, 1979.

Therborn, G.: *The Ideology of Power and the Power of Ideology*. London: Verso, 1980.

Thompson, E. P.: *The Making of the English Working Class*. Harmondsworth: Penguin, 1968.

Urry, J.: *The Anatomy of Capitalist Societies*. London: Macmillan, 1981.

Williams, R.: *The Long Revolution*. London: Chatto and Windus, 1961.

Williams, R.: *Marxism and Literature*. London: Oxford University Press, 1977.

Part 2. Media Theory

Arheim, R.: 'The World of the Daytime Serial' in *Mass Communications* 2nd edition, edited by W **Schramm**. Chicago: University of Illinois Press, 1972.

Barnouw, E.: *A Tower in Babel: A History of Broadcasting in America to 1933*. London: Oxford University Press, 1966.

Barthes, R.: *Mythologies*. London: Jonathan Cape, 1972.

Barthes, R.: *S/Z*, translated by R Miller. London: Jonathan Cape, 1975.

Belsey, C.: *Critical Practice*. London/New York: Methuen, 1981.

Berger, J.: *Ways of Seeing*. London: BBC and Penguin, 1972.

Breed, W.: 'Social Control in the Newsroom' in *Social Forces* no 33, 1955, pp 326-335.

Briggs, A.: *The History of Broadcasting in the United Kingdom*, 3 vols. London: Oxford University Press, 1961.

Centre for Contemporary Cultural Studies: 'Television as a Medium and its Relation to Culture', stencilled Occasional Paper. Birmingham: CCCS, Birmingham University, 1972.

Connell, I.: 'Monopoly Capitalism and the Media' in *Politics, Ideology and the State*, edited by S **Hibbin**. London, Lawrence and Wishart, 1978.

Curran, J., **Gurevitch**, M., and **Woolacott**, J. (Editors): *Mass Communications and Society*. London: Arnold/Open University Press, 1977. Of special interest is the essay by S **Hall** entitled 'Culture, Media and the "Ideological Effect" '.

Curran, J., and **Seaton**, J.: *Power Without Responsibility: The Press and Broadcasting in Britain*. London: Fontana, 1981.

Dexter, L. A., and **White**, D. M. (Editors): *People, Society and Mass Communications*. Glencoe: Free Press, 1964. Of special interest are the chapters by W **Gieber**: 'News is What Newspapermen Make Of It'; and D M **White**: ' "The Gatekeeper": A Case Study — The Selection of News'.

Dimmick, T.: 'The Gatekeeper: An Uncertainty Theory' in *Journalism Monograph* no 37, 1974.

Eagleton, T.: *Criticisms and Ideology*. London: Verso, 1978.

Enzenburger, H. M.: 'Constituents of a Theory of the Mass Media' in *New Left Review* no 64, 1970.

Fiske, J., and **Hartley**, J.: *Reading Television*. London: Methuen, 1978.

Gans, H.: *Deciding What's News*. New York: Vintage, 1980.

Garnham, N.: *The Structures of Television*. London: British Film Institute, 1980.

Gerber, G., **Gross**, L. P., and **Melody**, W. H.: *Communications, Technology and Social Policy: Understanding the New Cultural Revolution*. New York: Wiley and Sons, 1973.

Gurevitch, M., **Bennett**, T., **Curran**, J., and **Woolacott**, J. (Editors): *Culture, Society and Media*. London/New York: Methuen, 1982. Of special interest is the essay by S **Hall** entitled 'The Rediscovery of Ideology: Return of the Repressed in Media Studies'.

Hale, J.: *Radio Power: Propaganda and International Broadcasting*. London: Paul Fleck, 1975.

Hall, S., **Hobson**, D., **Lowe**, A., and **Willis**, P. (Editors): *Culture, Media, Language*. London: Hutchinson, 1980. Of special interest are the essays by I **Connell**, 'Television News and the Social Contract'; S **Hall**, 'Encoding/Decoding'; S **Hall**, 'Cultural Studies and the Centre: Some Problematics and Problems'; M C **Heck**, 'The Ideological Dimension of Media Messages'; and D **Hobson**, 'Housewives and the Mass Media'.

Hartley, J.: *Understanding News*. London: Pluto, 1980.

Head, S. W.: *Broadcasting in America*, 3rd edition. New York: Houghton Mifflin, 1976.

Hood, S.: *On Television*. London: Pluto, 1980.

Johnstone, J. W. C.: 'Who Controls News?' in *American Journal of Sociology* vol 87 no 5, 1982.

Katz, E., and **Wedell**, G.: *Broadcasting in the Third*

World. Cambridge, Mass.: Harvard University Press, 1977.

Lichy, L., and **Topping**, L.: *American Broadcasting: A Sourcebook on the History of Radio and Television*. New York: Hastings House, 1975.

Mattelart, A., and **Siegelaub**, S.: *Communications and Class Struggle. Volume 1: Capitalism, Imperialism*. Bagnolet, France, IMMRC, 1979.

McDonald, O.: 'Is Objectivity Possible?' in *Ethics and the Press*, edited by S C **Merril** and R D **Barney**. New York: Hastings, 1975.

McGillem, C. D., and **McLaughlan**, W. P.: *Hermes Bound*. West Lafayette: Purdue University, 1978.

Modleski, T.: 'The Search for Tomorrow in Today's Soap Operas' in *Film Quarterly* vol 33, 1979.

Molden, U.: *Telecommunications and Black Americans: A Survey of Ownership, Participation and Control*. Centre for Development Technology, Missouri University Press, 1975.

Morely, D.: 'Industrial Conflict and the Mass Media' in *The Sociological Review* vol 24 no 2, 1976.

Newcomb, H. (Editor): *Television: The Critical View*. New York: Oxford University Press 1976.

Open University: 'Mass Communications in a Cross-Cultural Context: The Case of the Third World' in *Mass Communications in Society*, block 5, unit 2. London: Open University Press, 1977.

Open University: 'Mass Communications: Media Organisations' in *Social Sciences: A Third level Course*. London: Open University Press 1977.

Overman, M.: *Understanding Telecommunications*. Guildford: Lutterworth, 1974.

Paulu, B.: *British Broadcasting*. Minneapolis: University of Minnesota Press, 1956.

Philo, G., and **Beharrel**, P. (Editors): *Trade Unions and the Media*. London: Macmillan, 1977. Of special interest are the essays by F **Beckett**, 'Press and Prejudice'; and G **Philo**, P **Beharrel** and J **Hewitt**, 'Strategies and Policies'.

Philo, G., and **Beharrel**, P. (Editors): *Really Bad News*. London: Writers and Readers, in association with the Glasgow Media Studies Group, 1982.

Skirrow, G.: 'Education and Television, Theory and Practice' in *Media, Politics and Culture: A Socialist View*, edited by C **Gardner**. London: Macmillan, 1979.

Smith, A.: *The Shadow in the Cave: The Broadcaster, His Audience and the State*. London: Allen and Unwin, 1973.

Smith, A.: *The Politics of Information: Problems of Policy in Modern Media*. London: Macmillan, 1978.

Smith, A.: *The Geopolitics of Information*. London: Faber and Faber, 1980.

Steadman, R.: *The Serials: Suspension and Drama by Installments*, 2nd edition. Oklahoma: University of Oklahoma Press, 1977.

Swift, K.: 'A Conflict Analysis of the Mass Media' in *Communications in Africa* vol 1 no 3, 1972.

Webster, B. R.: *Technology and Access to Communications Media*. Paris: UNESCO, 1975.

Williams, R.: *Television, Technology and Cultural Form*. London: Fontana, 1974.

Part 3. The South African Political Economy

Adam, H., and **Giliomee**, H.: *The Rise and Crisis of Afrikaner Power*. Cape Town: David Phillip, 1979.

Bonner, P. (Editor): *Working Papers in Southern African Studies* vol 2. Johannesburg: Ravan, 1981.

Bozzoli, B.: *The Political Nature of a Ruling Class: Capital and Ideology in South Africa, 1890-1933*. London: Routledge and Kegan Paul, 1981.

Bozzoli, B. (Editor):. *Town and Countryside in the Transvaal: Capitalist Penetration and Popular Response*. Johannesburg: Ravan, 1983. Of special interest are the essays by E **Kock**, ' "Without Visible Means of Subsistence": Slumyard Culture in Johannesburg'; and T Lodge, 'The Parents' School Boycott, 1955'.

Clarke, S.: 'Capital, "Fractions" of Capital and the State' in *Capital and Class* no 5, 1978.

Davenport, T. R. H.: *South Africa: A Modern History*. Johannesburg: Macmillan, 1977.

Davies, R. H.: *Capital, State and White Labour in South Africa, 1900-1960: A Historical Materialist Analysis of Class Formation and Class Relations*. Brighton: Harvester Press, 1979.

Davies, R. H.: 'Capital Restructuring and Modification of the Racial Division of Labour in South Africa, *Journal of Southern African Studies* vol 15 no 2, 1979.

Gerhart, G. M.: *Black Power in South Africa: The Evolution of an Ideology*. Berkeley: University of California Press, 1978.

Glass, H. G. L.: *Apartheid Gedagte: Apartheid Cultural Hegemony*. Ann Arbour, Michigan: University Microfilms International, 1982.

Leatt, J., **Kneife**, T, and **Nürnburger**, K.: *Contending Ideologies in South Africa*. Cape Town: David Philip, 1986.

Legassick, M.: 'Legislation, Ideology and Economy in Post-1948 South Africa' in *Journal of Southern African Studies* vol 1 no 1, 1974.

Lipton, M.: *Capitalism and Apartheid, South Africa 1910-1986*. Cape Town: David Philip, 1986.

Lodge, T.: 'Black Opposition — An Historical Perspective' in *Sash*, February 1979.

Moodie, T. D.: *The Rise of Afrikanerdom*. Los Angeles: University of California Press, 1980.

Moss, G.: 'Total Strategy' in *Work in Progress* vol 11, 1980.

O'Meara, D.: 'The Afrikaner Broederbond 1927-1948: Class Vanguard of Afrikaner Nationalism' in *Journal of Southern African Studies* vol 3 no 2, 1977.

O'Meara, D.: *Volkskapitalisme — Class, Capital and Ideology in the Development of Afrikaner Nationalism*. Johannesburg: Ravan, 1983.

South African Institute of Race Relations: *Surveys of Race Relations*. Johannesburg: SAIRR, various dates.

South African Research Services: *South African Review 1*. Johannesburg: Ravan Press, 1984.

South African Research Services: *South African Review 2*. Johannesburg: Ravan Press, 1985.

South African Research Services: *South African Review 3*. Johannesburg: Ravan Press, 1986.

Saul, J .S., and **Gelb**, S.: *The Crisis in South Africa: Class Defence, Class Revolution*. New York: Monthly Review Press, 1981.

Schlemmer, L., and **Webster**, E. (Editors): *Change, Reform and Economic Growth in South Africa*. Johannesburg: Ravan, 1978.

Serfontein, J. H. P.: *Brotherhood of Power: An Exposé of the Secret Afrikaner Broederbond*. London: Rex Collings, 1978.

Serfontein, J. H. P.: *Apartheid, Change, and the N G Kerk*. Johannesburg: Taurus, 1982.

Simpkins, C.: 'Measuring and Predicting Unemployment in South Africa' in *Structural Unemployment in South Africa*, by C **Simpkins** and D **Clarke**. Pietermaritzburg: University of Natal Press, 1978.

Webster, E.: *Essays in Southern African Labour History*. Johannesburg: Ravan, 1978.

Wilkins, I., and **Strydom**, H.: *The Super-Afrikaners: Inside the Broederbond*. Johannesburg: Jonathan Ball, 1978.

Wolpe, H.: 'Capitalism and Cheap Labour Power: From Segregation to Apartheid' in *Articulation of Modes of Production*, edited by H **Wolpe**. London: Routledge and Kegan Paul, 1980.

Part 4. Media Studies in South Africa

Adelman, S., **Howard**, J., **Stuart**, K., and **van Edgen**, A.: *The South African Press Council: A Critical View*. University of the Witwatersrand, Johannesburg: Centre for Applied Legal Studies, 1979.

Addison, G. N.: 'Drum Beat: An Examination of *Drum*' in *Speak*, July/August 1978.

Addison, G. N.: 'The Union of Black Journalists: A Brief Survey'. Unpublished Seminar Paper, Rhodes University, 1981.

Anderson, M.: *Music in the Mix*. Johannesburg: Ravan, 1981.

Barton, F.: *The Press in Africa — Persecution and Perseverance*. London: Macmillan, 1979.

Brown, T.: 'Free Press Fair Game for South Africa's Government' in *Journalism Quarterly*, Spring 1971, pp 120-127.

Chimutengwende, A.: *The Press and the Politics of Liberation*. London: Barbicon Books, 1978.

Corrigan, E. C.: 'South Africa Enters the Electronic Age: The Decision to Introduce Television' in *Africa Today* vol 21, 1974, pp 15-28.

Collett, H. O.: 'The Development of Broadcasting in the Union of South Africa' in *Transactions of the South African Institute of Electrical Engineers*, May 1951.

Collett, H. O., and **Stevens**, D. J.: 'VHF/FM Sound Broadcasts in the Republic of South Africa' in *EBU Review Part A: Technical* no 84, April 1964.

Couzens, T.: 'A Short History of *The World* and Other Black Newspapers, 1832-1960'. Extract from Ph.D. thesis, University of the Witwatersrand, Johannesburg, 1983.

Cutten, T. E. G.: *The History of the Press in South Africa*. Cape Town: NUSAS, 1935.

De Beer, A. S.: 'Afrikaans Press Enjoys Freedom Within Limits' in *South African Outlook* vol 110 no 1308, 1980.

De Klerk, W.: 'Newspapers Need to be More Patriotic' in *Issue*, Spring 1982.

De Villiers, J.: 'South African Community and its Newspapers — A Socio-Historical Study'. Ph.D. thesis, University of the Orange Free State, 1976.

De Villiers, S.: 'Die Uitbouing van Radiodienste vir die Bantoe' in *Hertzog — Annale van die Suid Afrikaanse Akademie vir Wetenskap en Kuns* vol 10, no 16, 1963.

Doherty, C.: 'The Wits-Koornhof Debate: Is There Really a Difference Between the English and the Afrikaans Presses?' in *Critical Arts* vol 2 no 2, 1981.

Dommisse, E.: 'The Changing Role of the Afrikaans Press' in *The Afrikaners*, edited by E S **Munger**. Cape Town: Tafelberg, 1979.

Drum/Ravan: *The Beat of* Drum, *the Magazine that Documented the Rise of Africa*. Johannesburg: Ravan, 1982.

Erasmus, L. J.: *'n Volk Staan Op Uit Sy As: Verhaal van Die Afrikaanse Pers (1962)*. Johannesburg: APB, no date.

Erasmus, P. F.: 'The Second Television Channel: The Challenge' in *Communicare* vol 2 no 2, 1980, pp 60-65.

Fine, A.: 'Allied Publishing: Round Two' in *south African Labour Bulletin* vol 6 no 6, 1981, pp 30-36.

Flather, K. F.: *The Way of an Editor*. Cape Town: Purnell, 1977.

French, T. M.: 'The *World* — A Content Analysis'. Unpublished paper, Rhodes University Library, 1977.

Friedgut, J.: 'The Non-European Press' in *Handbook of Race Relations in South Africa*, edited by E Hellman. London: Oxford University Press, 1949.

Fuchs, D.: 'Die Radio en die Gesproke Woord' in *Tydskrif vir die Geestewetenskappe* vol 9 (includes translation), 1969.

Giffard, C. A.: 'South African Attitudes Towards News Media' in *Journalism Quarterly*, Winter 1976, pp 653-660.

Giffard, C. A.: 'The Impact of Television on South African Newspapers' in *Journalism Quarterly*, Summer 1980.

Giffard, C. A.: 'Circulation Trends in South Africa' in *Journalism Quarterly*, Spring 1980.

Ginwala, I.: 'The Press in South Africa' in *Index on Censorship* vol 2 no 3, 1973, pp 27-39.

Hachten, W. A.: *Muffled Drums: The News Media in Africa*. Iowa: Iowa State University Press, 1979.

Hachten, W. A.: 'Black Journalists Under Apartheid' in *Index on Censorship* vol 8 no 3, 1979, pp 43-48.

Hachten, W. A.: 'Policies and Performance of South African Television' in *Journal of Communication* vol 29 no 3, 1979.

Harrison, R., and **Ekman**, P.: 'TV's Last Frontier: South Africa' in *Journal of Communications*, Spring 1976.

Head, S. W.: *Broadcasting in Africa*. Philadelphia: Temple University Press, 1974.

Hepple, A.: *Censorship and Press Control in South Africa*. Johannesburg: Hepple, 1960.

Hepple, A.: *Press Under Apartheid*. London: International Defence Aid Fund, 1974.

Hopkinson, A.: *In the Fiery Continent*. London: Gollancz, 1962.

Hybels, S. K.: *News and Editorial Bias in the South African Broadcasting Corporation*. Ann Arbour, Michigan: University Microfilms International, 1971.

Jack, A.: 'The Steyn Commissions: An Annotated Bibliography' in *Critical Arts* vol 2 no 3, 1981, pp 29-32.

Jooste, J. A.: 'Die Bydrae van die SAUK tot Kultuurontwikkeling in Suid Afrika' in *Hertzog — Annale van die Suid Afrikaanse Akademie vir Wetenskap en Kuns* vol 8 no 14, 1961.

Kunene, O.: 'The Role of the Black Journalist in South Africa Today' in *The Journalist*, July 1977.

Kurian, G. T.: *World Press Encyclopaedia* vol 2. See chapter on South Africa by J C Merrill, pp 793-806.

Lawyers for Human Rights: *Distrust in Democracy: Commentary on the Report of the Steyn Commission of Inquiry into the Mass Media*. Cape Town: Stewart, 1947.

Lodge, T.: 'Soviets and Surrogates: Black Nationalism and the Steyn Commission' in *Critical Arts* vol 2 no 3, 1981, pp 23-28.

Manoim, I.: 'Getting the Press to do its Own Dirty Work' in *Critical Arts* vol 2 no 3, 1982, pp iv-ix.

McCarthy, J., and **Friedmann**, M.: 'Black Housing, Ideology and the Media in South Africa, 1970-1979' in *Critical Arts* vol 2 no 2, pp 51-66.

McGregor, R. W. G.: *Who Owns who in the Newspaper Industry*. Cape Town: Purdy Press, 1982.

Media Studies Group: 'MWASA; Trying to Set Deadlines' in *South African Labour Bulletin* vol 6, no 6, 1981, pp 24-29.

Meyer, P.: *The Spiritual Crisis of the West*, a four part series. Johannesburg: South African Broadcasting Corporation, 1966.

Meyer, P.: *Report of the Commission of Inquiry into Matters Relating to Television*. Pretoria: Government Printer, 1971.

Mills, D. H.: 'Some Unusual Aspects of SABC's Second Television Channel'. Unpublished paper, SABC, Johannesburg, no date.

Mills, D. H.: 'Survey of Broadcasting in South Africa' in *Transactions of the South African Institute of Electronic Engineers*, March 1970.

Mills D. H.: 'The Introduction of Television to South Africa' in *Communications and Broadcasting*, Autumn 1976.

Muller, J. P.: 'How a Community Responds: De Lange and the Afrikaans Volkspers' in *Perspectives in Education*, special issue, 1982.

O'Meara, D.: ' "Muldergate" and the Politics of Afrikaner Nationalism' in *Work in Progress* no 22 (supplement), 1982.

Orlik, P.: 'The South African Broadcasting Corporation: an Historical Survey and Contemporary Analysis'. Unpublished Ph.D. thesis, Wayne State University, 1970.

Orlik, P. B.: 'South Africa: How Long Without TV?' in *Journal of Broadcasting* vol 24 no 2, 1970, pp 245-258.

Orlik, P. B.: 'Co-opting the Messenger: The Afrikaner Takeover of the SABC'. Unpublished seminar paper, Department of Journalism, Rhodes University, Grahamstown, 1979.

Philpott, T.: 'The Arrival of Television in South Africa: A four part series' in *The Listener*, 8, 15, 22, 29 July 1976.

Pienaar, S.: *Getuie van Groot Tye*. Cape Town: Tafelberg, 1979.

Pogrund, B.: 'The South African Press' in *Index on Censorship* vol 5 no 3, 1976, pp 10-16.

Pollak, R.: *Up Against Apartheid: The Role and the Plight of the Press in South Africa*. Carbondale: Southern Illinois University Press, 1981.

Potter, E.: *The Press as Opposition: The Political Role of South African Newspapers*. London: Chatto and Windus, 1975.

Qoboza, P.: 'The Press as I See It'. Paper presented at the conference on the Survival of the Media, Rhodes University, Grahamstown, 1979.

Rabkin, D.: '*Drum* Magazine (1951-1961) and the Work of Black South African Writers Associated with it'. Ph.D. thesis, University of Leeds, 1975.

Rees, M., and **Day**, C.: *Muldergate: The Story of the Info Scandal*. Johannesburg: Macmillan, 1980.

Rhodes, T. A. F.: 'Broadcasting Before the SABC Was Created'. Unpublished paper, SABC, Johannesburg.

Rogerson, C. M.: 'Corporate Strategy, State Power and Compromise: Television Manufacture in South Africa' in *South African Geopgraphical Journal* vol 60 no 2, 1978.

Roos, G.: 'Broadcasting in South Africa' in *Finance and Trade Review*, 1 July 1954.

Roos, G.: 'Die Uitsaaiwese in Diens van Ons Samelewing'. Unpublished paper, SABC, Johannesburg.

Rosenthal, E., and **Neame**, L. E.: *Today's News Today*. Johannesburg: Argus Printing and Publishing Company, 1956.

Rosenthal, E.: *You Have Been Listening: A History of the Early Days of Radio in South Africa*. Cape Town: Purnell, 1974.

Sampson, A.: *Drum: A Venture into the New Africa*. London: Collins, 1956.

Scannel, J. P. (Editor): *Keeromstraat 30*. Cape Town: Nasionale Boekhandel, 1968.

Seiler, R.: 'World Perspectives of South African Media' in *Communications in Africa* vol 1 no 5, 1972.

Shaw, G.: *Some Beginnings*. Cape Town: Oxford University Press, 1975.

South African Advertising Research Foundation: *All Media and Products Survey*. Johannesburg: Market Research Africa, various dates.

South African Broadcasting Corporation: *Annual Reports*. Johannesburg: SABC.

Steyn, M. T.: *Report of the Commission of Inquiry into Reporting of Security Matters Regarding the SADF and SAP*. RP 52/1980. Pretoria: Government Printer, 1980.

Steyn, M. T.: *Report of the Steyn Commission into the Mass Media*, RP 89/1981. Pretoria: Government Printer, 1981.

Stewart, G. M.: 'The Development of the *Rand Daily Mail* as an Intercultural Newspaper'. Honours thesis, Department of Communications, UNISA, Pretoria, 1980.

St Leger, F.: 'The African Press in South Africa' in *Communications in Africa* no number, no date, p 23.

St Leger, F.: 'The African Press in South Africa'. Ph.D. thesis, Rhodes University, Grahamstown, 1974.

St Leger, F.: 'The *World* Newspaper 1968-1976' in *Critical Arts* vol 2 no 2, pp 28 ff.

Strauss, S. A., **Strydom**, M. J., and van der Walt, J. C.: *Die Suid-Afrikaanse Persreg*. 3rd edition. Pretoria: Van Schaik, 1976.

Strydom, G. S.: *The Establishment and Expansion of the School Radio Service of Radio Bantu*, HSRC Report no 0-53. Pretoria: Human Sciences Research Council, 1976.

Stuart, K.: *The Newspaperman's Guide to the Law*, 3rd edition. Durban: Butterworth, 1982.

Switzer, L., and **Switzer**, D.: *The Black Press in South Africa and Lesotho: A Descriptive Bibliographical Guide*. Boston: G K Hall and Company, 1979.

Switzer, L.: *Politics and Communications in the Ciskei: An African Homeland in South Africa*, Occasional Paper no 23. Rhodes University: Grahamstown, 1979.

Switzer, L.: 'Steyn Commission I: The Press and Total Strategy' in *Critical Arts* vol 1 no 4, 1981, pp 41-45.

Tomaselli, K. G.: 'Six Days in Soweto: Can Propaganda Be Truth?' in *Ecquid Novi* vol 2 no 1, 1981, pp 49-57.

Tomaselli, K. G., and **Tomaselli**, R. E.:

'Ideology/Culture/Hegemony and Mass Media in South Africa: A Literature Survey' in *Critical Arts* vol 2 no 2, 1981, pp 1-26.

Tomaselli, K. G., and **Tomaselli**, R. E.: 'Steyn Commission II: How to Separate Out Truth From Fact' in *Reality*, May 1981.

Tomaselli, K. G., and **Tomaselli**, R. E., ' "How to Set Your House In Order", Read All About it in the Steyn Commission' in *Critical Arts* vol 2 no 3, 1982.

Van Vuuren, D. P.: *The Effect of Television on some Personality Dimensions of a Group of Afrikaans Speaking Standard Eight Pupils*, HSRC Report COMM-16. Pretoria: Human Sciences Research Council, 1980.

Van Zyl, J. A.: 'South African Television: What Kind of Service?' in *New Nation* vol 9 no 2, 1980.

Van Zyl, J. A.: 'Black Gold or White Elephant? Coordinated Marketing Conference on TV2/3' in *Critical Arts* vol 2 no 2, 1981, pp 84-87.

Varley, D. H.: *A Short History of the South African Press*. Cape Town: Nasionale Pers, 1952.

Work in Progress: 'The Press' in *Work in Progress*, April 1980, pp 30-33.

Work in Progress: 'The Press: A Response' in *Work in Progress*, July 1980, pp 62-64.